C000253690

Benedictines in Oxford

Benedictines
in Oxford

Edited by
HENRY WANSBROUGH
and
ANTHONY MARETT-CROSBY

Introduction by
CARDINAL BASIL HUME

DARTON · LONGMAN + TODD

First published in 1997 by
Darton, Longman and Todd Ltd
1 Spencer Court
140–142 Wandsworth High Street
London SW18 4JJ

ISBN 0–232–52176–X

A catalogue record for this book is available
from the British Library

Designed by Roger Lightfoot
Phototypeset by Intype London Ltd
Printed and bound in Great Britain by
Page Bros, Norwich

Contents

Preface

This volume has been produced to mark the centenary of the foundation of St Benet's Hall, now a Permanent Private Hall of the University of Oxford. But the focus of this collection is wider than the story of St Benet's alone. Writing in 1933 of the return of the Benedictines to Oxford, the Hall's first Master, Abbot Oswald Hunter-Blair, adopted the Latin motto *succisa virescit*, 'though cut down it grows green again'. This points to a clear awareness of a history of Benedictines in Oxford that stretches for many centuries before 1897, and much of this book is taken up with telling the story of that Benedictine history in Oxford. This is not simply a pre-history to St Benet's, but a history in its own right, and an integral part of that wider story of the fortunes of the university.

The relationship between the oldest of the religious orders and the oldest of the English universities has not always been a peaceful one, and was changed fundamentally by the experience of the Reformation. Part I of this book deals with pre-Reformation Oxford, and the contribution made to it by the monastic order. Particular attention is given to the three Benedictine colleges of Canterbury, Durham and Gloucester. After telling the stories of these colleges, and describing life within them, a series of more specific studies examines both particular aspects of the monastic experience at Oxford and certain individuals who studied there during these centuries. Attention is also given to the presence of Cistercians within the university, and to the role played by women religious in the environs of the city. Part I concludes by examining the fate of those monks who lived to see the end of medieval Oxford.

But though the monastic colleges ceased to exist after 1540, the story of the Benedictine involvement with the university carried on, albeit in very changed circumstances. In Part II two articles describe this complex and illicit relationship, examining both Oxford monks within the restored English Congregation and the hidden work of that Congregation in and around the university. By the eighteenth century, connections had become remote, but as the emancipation of Catholics became first a possibility and then a reality, the desire for a Catholic presence in Oxford grew. Part III of the book describes the development of this aspiration during the nineteenth century, and its expression in the foundation of a Benedictine House at Oxford. This house became St Benet's Hall, to which monks from a widening circle of houses came to study. The volume concludes with a series of portraits of three of its Masters and an epilogue, taking the story of St Benet's up to the present day.

The reader will find that this volume comprises individual contributions, each having its own perspective and approach. Some articles are annotated with extensive notes, and these will be found at the end of the book. Other articles conclude with a list of further reading, where that has been felt useful. Where this has not been included, the reader is referred to other articles covering the same period.

The work of editing a volume of this nature has inevitably involved many people at many different stages. The editors are indebted in the first instance to the contributors, whose generosity of time and expertise has been overwhelming. Their contributions were then handed over to the staff of Sycamore Office Services, where the entire volume was prepared for the publishers. We are most grateful to Kirsten Phipps and her staff for their constant willingness to put up with requests. Their speed and accuracy have made the task of editing very much easier.

During the search for illustrations, assistance was given by a number of libraries and institutions. We would like to acknowledge the help of Dr Bruce Barker-Benfield of the Bodleian Library, and of the staff of the Print Room of the Ashmolean Museum. We are especially glad to acknowledge Mr Richard Sharp of the Hope Collection, Ashmolean Museum, for his generosity in making available from his private collection the Loggan print of Gloucester. It was only through the enthusiasm of Dr Alan Coates that we became aware of the St Benedict window at Trinity College, and we are indebted to the governing body of Trinity for their permission to publish the illustration.

It seems appropriate to record specially our thanks to Cardinal Basil Hume for his contribution of an introduction. At a time when he had much else to do, his willingness and interest was greatly appreciated.

Finally, we would like to thank all those at St Benet's who have provided their encouragement during the work of editing, especially Rupert McHardy, whose knowledge and interest have been a constant support.

If this volume has a dedication, it is to all members of St Benet's, past, present and future, who are part of the ongoing tradition of Benedictines in Oxford. *Succisa virescit.*

Henry Wansbrough and Anthony Marett-Crosby
St Benet's Hall, July 1996

Contributors

Benedicta Ward is a Sister of the Society of the Love of God and Fellow in Theology at Harris Manchester College, Oxford. Her publications include *Miracles and the Medieval Mind* (1982) and *The Venerable Bede* (1990).

Henry Mayr-Harting is Fellow in Modern History at St Peter's College, Oxford, and the author of *The Coming of Christianity to Anglo-Saxon England* (1977) and *Ottoman Book Illustration* (2 vols., 1991).

Alban Léotaud is a monk of Prinknash Abbey.

Rupert McHardy graduated in Modern History from St Benet's Hall in 1996.

Professor James Campbell is Fellow in Modern History at Worcester College, Oxford, and editor of *The Anglo-Saxons* (1982). In 1996 he delivered the Ford Lectures at Oxford.

Joan Greatrex is former Professor of Medieval History at Carleton University, Ottowa and Visiting Fellow of Robinson College, Cambridge. Her *Biographical Register of English Cathedral Priories of the Province of Canterbury* will be published during 1997.

Barrie Dobson is Professor of Medieval History at Christ's College, Cambridge. He is the author of *Durham Priory 1400–1450* (1973) and has contributed the chapter on the religious orders to *The History of the University of Oxford*.

Alan Coates has written widely in the area of library history, and his *Origin, Growth and Dispersal of the Book Collection of Reading Abbey* is to be published shortly. He currently works at the Bodleian Library.

Lesley Smith is Fellow and Bursar of Harris Manchester College, Oxford. Her publications include *Medieval Commentaries on the Book of Ruth* (1996), and *Codices Boethianae* (1995) and she is an editor of *Women and the Book* (1995).

Jeremy Catto is Fellow in Modern History at Oriel College, Oxford. He is the editor of the first two volumes of *The History of the University of Oxford*.

David Hugh Farmer has taught for many years at Reading University, and has written widely on hagiography. His publications include *The Oxford Dictionary of Saints* (1979) and *Benedict's Disciples* (1980).

Anthony Marett-Crosby is a monk of Ampleforth Abbey. He graduated in Modern History from University College, Oxford, in 1990 and is now studying at St Benet's Hall.

Peter Cunich is Professor of History at Hong Kong University. He is editor of *The History of Magdalene College, Cambridge* (1994) and is currently engaged on compiling a register of ex-religious in England and Wales, 1530–1603.

Philip Jebb is Prior of Downside Abbey and former headmaster of Downside School. He is the Archivist of the English Benedictine Congregation.

Geoffrey Scott is a monk of Douai Abbey and former headmaster of Douai School. He is currently chaplain at Stanbrook Abbey and is the author of *Gothic Rage Undone: English Monks in the Age of Enlightenment* (1992).

Anselm Cramer is Sub-prior of Ampleforth Abbey, monastic librarian and Archivist.

Patrick Barry is Abbot of Ampleforth and author of *St Benedict and Christianity in England* (1995).

Henry Wansbrough is Master of St Benet's Hall and lecturer in theology at Worcester College, Oxford. He edited *The New Jerusalem Bible* (1985) and is a member of the Pontifical Biblical Commission.

Abbreviations

AASS	*Acta Sanctorum*
AJ	*Ampleforth Journal*
BJRL	Bulletin of the John Rylands Library
BRUO 1	A. B. Emden, *A Biographical Register of the University of Oxford to 1500* (3 vols., Oxford, 1957)
BRUO 2	A. B. Emden, *A Biographical Register of the University of Oxford 1501–1540* (Oxford, 1974)
CCR	*Calendar of Close Rolls*
CLP	*Calendar of Letters Patent*
CRS	*Catholic Records Society*
DHGE	*Dictionnaire d'Histoire et de Géographie Ecclésiastique*, ed. R. Aubert
DNB	*Dictionary of National Biography*
EETS	*Early English Texts Society*
EHR	*English Historical Review*
HUO i	*History of the University of Oxford, vol. i: The Early Oxford Schools*, ed. J. I. Catto (Oxford, 1984)
HUO ii	*History of the University of Oxford, vol. ii: Late Medieval Oxford*, ed. J. I. Catto and R. Evans (1992)
HUO iii	*History of the University of Oxford, vol. iii: The Collegiate University*, ed. J. K. McConica (Oxford, 1986)
HUO v	*History of the University of Oxford, vol. v: The Eighteenth Century*, ed. L. S. Sutherland and L. G. Mitchell (Oxford, 1986)
JEH	*Journal of Ecclesiastical History*
Knowles, *RO* i–iii	D. Knowles, *The Religious Orders* (Cambridge, 1948–59)
Pantin, *Canterbury* i–iv	W. A. Pantin, *Canterbury College* (OHS (n.s.), vols. 6, 7, 8, 30)
Pantin, *Chapters* i–iii	W. A. Pantin, *Documents illustrating the activities of the general and provincial chapters of the*

	Black Monks, 1215–1240 (3 vols., Camden Society, London, 1931–37)
OHS (o.s.)/ (n.s.)	*Oxford Historical Society* (old series/new series)
PRO	*Public Record Office*
Monasticon	W. Dugdale, *Monasticon Anglicanum* (6 vols., London, 1817–30)
P&P	*Past and Present*
RB	*Rule of St Benedict*, tr. J. McCann (London, 1952)
SMon	*Studia Monastica*
TRHS	*Transactions of the Royal Historical Society*
VCH (Oxon)	*The Victoria County History of the County of Oxford*, ed. L. F. Salzman (London, 1907–)
YAJ	*Yorkshire Archaeological Journal*

Illustrations

Introduction

CARDINAL BASIL HUME osb

Benedict was a young man when he arrived in Rome to pursue his studies. His biographer, Pope Gregory the Great, recounts how Benedict 'found many of the students there abandoning themselves to vice . . .'[1] So, Gregory tells us, Benedict turned his back on further study, left Rome and eventually sought solitude and silence in a cave some thirty-five miles from Rome at a place called Subiaco. He left Rome *scienter nescius et sapienter indoctus* – knowingly unknowing and wisely untaught. This might suggest that Benedict was less than well educated, and possibly even against academic pursuits. We do not know. It is unlikely that he would despise any of God's gifts, especially one of the noblest of them, our intellects.

There is, however, another knowledge and wisdom that are the fruit of prayer and of the prayerful study of the Word of God. It is a knowledge such as a lover may have of the beloved; it is a wisdom that sees, and clearly so, what is the origin and cause of all else. *Animae videnti Creatorem, angusta est omnis creatura* – 'to the soul seeing the Creator, all creation becomes small', wrote Gregory, commenting on Benedict's vision when he saw 'the whole world as if gathered in one sunbeam'.[2] Search for God and much else will be understood.

The followers of St Benedict's Rule became involved in academic pursuits early on in history. They copied manuscripts, clearly of vital importance in itself, but presumably also an appropriate occupation for monks. Copying led to the study of texts, and that study to commenting upon them.

St Bede is the typical monk-scholar. He said of himself:
'While I observed the regular discipline and sung the Choir
offices daily in Church, my chief delight has always been in
study, teaching, and writing.'

Not all monks are able to live as Bede lived. There are
different gifts and a variety of personalities among St
Benedict's followers. The Rule of St Benedict admits of different ways of being Benedictines. Schools are one such.
Schools need trained minds and an understanding and
appreciation of all that concerns the intellect. The universities make this possible. For a long time Catholics could not
attend Oxford or Cambridge, then in 1895 permission was
given to do so. The Ampleforth Community opened a house
in Oxford in 1897. It is right that tribute should be paid to
Prior Anselm Burge for doing so. He was a great monk,
gifted, a man of vision. Ampleforth owes much to him. Its
school could never have achieved high academic standards
without the advantages of study at Oxford. We would not
have been able to educate so many of our laity to make a
significant contribution to the society in which we live.

Oxford has given much to our monks, and we are grateful
for that. I like to think that our monastic presence in the
university has made some contribution to it. Prayer and
study go hand in hand at St Benet's Hall, each supporting
and inspiring the other. That is St Benet's' special contribution.

PART I

Monks, Nuns and the
Medieval University

St Frideswide of Oxford

BENEDICTA WARD SLG

In 1933 Canon Jenkins gave the shortest sermon on record on the feast of St Frideswide in the church which claims to have her relics. 'Saint Frideswide,' he said, 'never existed.' Before dismissing the patron saint of both the university and the city of Oxford entirely, it is perhaps as well to note what was meant. As a most able historian, Canon Jenkins was making the statement that any historian must make about Frideswide: that is, that we know of no historical evidence which would support the stories that have accumulated round the name of 'Frideswide'. And that is indeed the case. But that is all he was saying; and it is permissible to think that there may be more to say about both the legend and the cult of St Frideswide in Oxford than is suggested by his 'sermon'.

The oldest form of the life of St Frideswide is no earlier than the twelfth century; it is claimed there that she lived about four hundred years earlier. Significantly, her name does not appear at all in the detailed account of Anglo-Saxon monasticism for that period given by the Venerable Bede, the main source for knowledge of early English monasticism. The name of Frideswide and her connection with Oxford, however, was known in the early eleventh century; it is noted in the *Liber Vitae* of Hyde Abbey, where her name is entered between Cuthburh of Wimborne and St Cuthmann of Steyning: 'St Frideswide rests at Oxford'.[1] The name of Frideswide in connection with Oxford next occurs in a charter of Aethelred for 7 December 1004, which contains some revealing information about the position of the monastery in the town of Oxford and how it was seen by those living there:

> In the year of the Incarnation of our Lord 1004 the second indiction, in the twenty fifth year of my reign, by the ordering of God's providence, I Ethelred, governing the monarchy of all Albion, have made secure within the liberty of a privilege by the royal authority a certain monastery situated in the town that is called Oxford where the body of the blessed Frideswide rests, for the love of the all-accomplishing God. And I have restored the territories that belong to that monastery of Christ within the renewal of a new title-deed and I will relate in a few words to all who look upon this document for what reason it was done. For it is fully agreed that to all dwelling in this country it will be well known that a decree was sent out by me with the agreement of all my leading men to the effect that all the Danes who had sprung up in this island, sprouting like cockle among the wheat, were to be destroyed by a most just extermination, to be put into effect even so far as death . . . those Danes who dwelt in the aforementioned town, striving to escape death, entered this sanctuary of Christ having broken by force the doors and bolts, and resolved to make a refuge and defence for themselves therein against the people of the town and suburbs; but when all the people in pursuit strove, forced by necessity, to drive them out and could not, they set fire to the planks and burnt as it seems this church with its ornaments and books. Afterwards with God's aid it was renewed by me and my subjects, and as I have said above strengthened in Christ's name with the honour of a fresh privilege, along with the territories belonging to it and endowed with every liberty, regarding royal exaction as well as ecclesiastical dues.[2]

A list of the possessions of the monastery follows. The monastic church seems to have been regarded as a place of sanctuary, however misleadingly in this case. It also seems to have been a wooden building, easily burnt, but of sufficient interest to the Crown for it to be restored.

The name Frideswide also appears in the Domesday Book in 1086, where the entries for Oxford include the possessions of the canons of St Frideswide, which were at Cutteslow, Kirklington, Cadwell and Milton under Wychwood.[3] In each case, a good deal of property was associated with a monastery at Oxford under the name of Frideswide. The name survived, and in connection with Oxford and a religious house. Perhaps there was a real woman behind the myths; what is clear is that round her name lies the history of the most central monastic house in Oxford.

The stories later told about Frideswide were deliberately set in the seventh and eighth centuries, the golden age of Anglo-Saxon monasticism. They reflect the centrality of the royal monasteries of the time, and the leadership of abbesses. It may well be that a local prince founded a monastery in Oxford for his daughter. If the dates for 'Frideswide' are provisionally fixed between 680 and 735, she would have lived at a time when English monasticism was renowned for learning with the names not only of Bede, the foremost scholar of his day, but also Aldhelm, Boniface, Theodore, Hilda, Leoba and the nuns of Barking. If at these dates 'Frideswide' lived where the legends place her, near Oxford, this place, hardly more than a village, lay in the kingdom of Mercia, the last part of the septarchy to be converted, and still subject to warring kings and sub-kings. Ecclesiastically, Oxford formed part of the vast diocese of Lichfield; from both the ecclesiastical and the political point of view, the situation was highly unstable. Oxford does not seem to have been a place of any significance, except for its location on the Thames, but it may have been in the control of a local prince whose daughter wanted to become a nun.

In 1125, the Latin historian William of Malmesbury wrote his account of the bishoprics and monasteries of England, the *Gesta Pontificum Anglorum*. It included the earliest account of the legend of St Frideswide:

There was of old in the city of Oxford a monastery of nuns, in which rests the most holy virgin Frideswide. The daughter of a king, she spurned the marriage-bed of a king, dedicating her entire person to the Lord Christ. But when he had applied himself vigorously to wooing the virgin, having spent his prayers and blandishments in vain, he planned to carry her off by force. When Frideswide heard of this, she decided to flee into the woods. But this hiding place was not hidden from her lover and her coldness of heart did not deter him, so she who fled was pursued. When the young man's madness became plain, the virgin went further on through secret paths, protected by God, and she entered Oxford by night. But by morning her persistent lover had hurried there too, and the girl began to despair of escape; too tired to go any further, she prayed to God to protect her and punish her persecutor. When he and his companions entered the city by the gate, a blow from heaven struck him and he became blind. Realising the sinfulness of his persistence, he sent messengers to beg Frideswide to pray and with the same suddenness with which he had lost his sight he received it again. (Hence the kings of England have been afraid to enter that town and stay there because they think it is unfavourable to them and they have all shrunk from putting this to the test.) So there the woman, secure in the victory of virginity, founded a monastery and ended her days there obedient to her Bridegroom's call.[4]

Later accounts, one by the Prior Robert of St Frideswide's, embroidered these comments, giving details such as the names of Frideswide's parents and that of her suitor.[5]

William's story reveals several things. First, it is clear that by the beginning of the eleventh century Frideswide's relics began to attract attention to her monastic church in Oxford. William of Malmesbury had thought it worthwhile to visit it, inspect its archives and consult its inmates, who at that time were canons. Secondly, writing at a time when monastic idealism looked back to the golden age of Anglo-Saxon Christianity, and when he in particular had read and re-read the sources for those times, it is not surprising that he should place Frideswide in a royal convent. He is the only source for the statement that Frideswide was a princess and founded a convent for nuns; if the tradition he reflects is at all credible, then a convent there in the seventh century was more likely to be for nuns with priests and laymen attached. It may have begun as such a joint establishment, and later became a community for the men only, perhaps after the attacks of the Danes. Secular canons were established there in 1002 and regular canons replaced them in 1122. It was probably a house for thirteen canons, which later increased to eighteen after 1160. Master Wimund (1122–39), the first prior, had previously been chaplain to Henry I; he was followed by Robert of Cricklade, a former Canon of Cirencester, who was succeeded by Prior Philip until 1191; Prior Simon was next, until 1228.

Thirdly, another aspect of the story told by William of Malmesbury is the sense it conveys of the ethos not of the seventh but of the eleventh and twelfth centuries. There are no accounts of a personal tension between monastic and married life in the early days of Anglo-Saxon monasticism, nor of royal ladies fleeing from amorous suitors. It is the reforms of the twelfth century above all that reflect such a situation.[6] The exaltation of virginity in the tone of this story shows the concerns of William himself in particular, which were so clearly demonstrated in his account of the *Miracles of the Blessed Virgin Mary*.

The next mention of the monastery of St Frideswide occurred in 1180, when on 12 February a great number of illustrious people met there to witness the formal translation of her relics to a new shrine. An account of the miracles which ensued there was compiled by Prior Philip.[7] The miracles give glimpses of the life of the canons in the late twelfth century in Oxford. The previous prior, Robert of Cricklade, had been the subject of a miraculous healing, when, having hurt his foot on a walking tour, he was cured at the shrine of St Thomas at Canterbury. Later, when one of the canons of St Frideswide's was ill, he was cured by being given water from the Canterbury shrine to drink, an event which caused Robert to insist on a public acknowledgement by other canons of the power of the saints. Such a contact with Canterbury and its miracles may have turned the brothers' attention to the possibilities of the saint of their own house. Robert rewrote the life of St Frideswide and his successor, Philip, organised the translation of the relics with all possible splendour. He says that present were 'Robert Archbishop of Canterbury, Lord Richard of Winchester; Geoffrey of Ely; John of Norwich, Peter of St David's; and bishops and a multitude of clerics as well as lords and their men from all parts of England'. The Archbishop conveyed the bones to their new shrine amid the singing of the whole community. After his account of the ceremony, Philip then described various visions of Frideswide which had preceded the translation, mostly to local Oxford people, one of whom was a close relation of Philip and a servant in the priory. There follow accounts of 110 miraculous cures recorded at the shrine over the next month. Pilgrims came, mostly from nearby, many from the town itself, eager to seek cures either for themselves or their children. While the canons sang their office by day and night or celebrated Mass, crowds of people entered the church, a noisy and at times unruly crowd. The sick could lie on or under the shrine all night, or for several nights; they might be offered water to drink in which the bones of the saint had been washed. Innumerable ailments were cured, including the ultimate miracle of the raising of the dead. It was not a quiet and controlled situation: the sick might vomit in the church during the process of their cure, the mad caused endless disturbance with groans and shouts and manic behaviour. Not all were cured, but where even one in a hundred was healed, the cure called forth a clamour of excitement, which at times caused the canons to come and see what was happening. It was a cult deeply embedded in the life of the priory itself: twice at least children who were nephews of one or another canon had access to the shrine, and Philip devoted the longest section of his book to a description of how he was himself cured of a fever by appeal to the care of St Frideswide. Philip's account shows the canons as personally involved with the pilgrims, and indeed in contact with the townsfolk and their families before and after the miracles. One woman at least sought out the prior in order to confess her sins before approaching the shrine. Some of those cured became inmates of the priory, either as servants or as canons. Of course, the influx of offerings was by no means unwelcome and enabled the building of a more ornate shrine, to which St Frideswide's bones were moved.

The shrine of St Frideswide continued as the focus, devotional and financial, of the priory until the Reformation, when the few remaining canons were dispersed to make room for both Cardinal College (later known as Christ Church) and the seat of the newly created bishopric of Oxford. The problems which faced the reformers on such occasions are well illustrated by the actions of James Calfhill, a Calvinist Canon of Christ Church. In 1552 Catherine

Dammart, an ex-nun who had been the wife of Peter Martyr Wermigli, Canon of Christ Church and Regius Professor of Divinity from 1548, died and was buried near the former shrine of St Frideswide. In 1556, the commissioners of Queen Mary directed that Catherine's body should be exhumed and thrown on a dunghill; in the course of this, two silk bags were also disinterred, which the clergy of the old school claimed as the bones of St Frideswide. In 1561, the commissioners of Queen Elizabeth ordered the reburial of Catherine, and James Calfhill was charged with the arrangements. Discovering the bags which it was said contained the bones of St Frideswide, Calfhill was revolted by such evidence of continuing devotion from 'crazy old men and people deluded by popish auguries' but determined not to 'let anything unseemly or insulting be done with them'. So, he wrote later,

'I hit upon a scheme by which the bones could be dealt with decently, while at the same time all foolish superstition should be suppressed. After a sermon telling the people the reasons for my choice, they were buried, mingled and confused with the bones of Peter Martyr's wife in the upper part of the church towards the east, in the same monument, much honoured and frequented by men, on Jan 11th 1561.'[8]

In this Calfhill was acting according to a solid tradition, combining the putting down of idolatry with respect for the Christian dead; however bizarre his actions seem, he showed more sensitivity than others elsewhere. For him, the respect accorded to all the Christian dead included St Frideswide, but the fear of superstition made him ensure that her bones did not become a focus again for idolatry.

The grave of Catherine and Frideswide is now marked by a plain stone with the name of Frideswide engraved on it. Fragments from the shrine have been uncovered and are preserved in the cathedral. At Binsey, the holy well also has been restored as a centre for pilgrimage. Excavations in Christ Church have added to the sparse information of legend about a possible early convent there. However Frideswide is regarded, her name is a link with the earliest records of monastic life in England and the continuing tradition of religious life in Oxford. The name itself, meaning 'peace' and 'strength', surely makes her an excellent patron of both city and university.

2

The Role of Benedictine Abbeys in the Development of Oxford as a Centre of Legal Learning

HENRY MAYR-HARTING

In the early history of Oxford University the monks were nothing like as important as the friars, but they had a lot to gain from it; and men who profited also gave, because they stimulated intellectual activity and growth in general. Merton College was founded in 1264 so that Walter de Merton's scholars, having completed their arts courses, could sit at the feet of the friars to study theology.[1] There is evidence, not all of it yet well known, that the Benedictines were also quick to perceive the value of the friars' teaching in various ways. Alan Coates has recently shown how unexpectedly well versed in the theological and Aristotelian learning purveyed by the Oxford friars were the thirteenth-century monks of Reading Abbey, for instance.[2] Moreover, in a brilliant paper over thirty years ago, the late Eric Stone suggested that the phase of profit and loss accounting in the late thirteenth-century Benedictine cathedral priory of Norwich, which he preferred to view as an episode in intellectual rather than in economic history, was due to a group of Oxford-educated monks familiar with the methods of experimental science which we associate with the Oxford Franciscan friar Roger Bacon.[3]

All this, however, is thirteenth-century history, and my present purpose is to suggest how, at the very beginnings of the university's history in the twelfth century, before the age of the friars, the needs of Benedictine and other monasteries in the locality may have given a vital extra push to its development. I refer to their need of its legal scholars and legal expertise. As the reader will shortly see, this is really a point of Sir Richard Southern; I was merely in a position to exemplify his point and to date its context more precisely than he was. As to date, he would see the development of Oxford as a centre of legal learning (i.e. one of the branches of higher education) in the late 1180s and early 1190s; I, perhaps imprudently, would incline to see the 1170s as the decade when this occurred.

The belief that they, and they alone, have discovered the true origins of Oxford University is one that must have afflicted many vainglorious dons, and so it is with some diffidence that I declare myself to be of their number. I refer to the twelfth century, the best part of a century before colleges were thought of, and before there was even any known faculty organisation, when Masters were entrepreneurs and their students found what accommodation they could.[4] Where did I make my discovery? As might be expected of a period with gaping *lacunae* in the evidence, and of an institution with no formal or constitutional beginning and thus no formal record-keeping, it was in a most unexpected place, the cartulary of the Augustinian canons of Guisborough Priory, North Yorkshire; that is, the book in which the medieval canons copied out their title deeds and other documents relevant to their rights and properties, a book which was owned by Sir Robert Cotton in the seventeenth century and which is now in the British Library.

Some time between 1174 and 1180, John, Bishop of Chichester, Adam, Abbot of Evesham, and Baldwin, Abbot of Ford (Devon), acted as papal judges-delegate to settle a lawsuit which had been raging between Roger, Archbishop of York (a great hater of Thomas Becket) and the canons of Guisborough about rights over Kirklevington church and its dependent chapel of Eston. The settlement was made, as the text of the document itself informs us, at Oxford, by the advice of many men learned in the law (*plurimorum jurisperitorum*):[5]

Master John of Cornwall
Thomas, archdeacon of Wells
Jocelin, archdeacon of Chichester
Geoffrey, precentor of Salisbury
Master Gilbert of Northampton
Master Godfrey of Lanthony
Geoffrey *de Lardaria*
Richard, prior of Newburgh
Master Osbert of Arundel
and others (not named in the copy, alas!)

The second, third and fourth persons were probably at Oxford in the entourage of the judges, and the Prior of Newburgh in Yorkshire must have been present to support his fellow Augustinians in that shire, but for the rest we are probably looking at the earliest surviving list of Oxford dons. The document, which bears no date, is datable to the years 1174–80 because that was Bishop John's term as Bishop of Chichester; and in fact Archbishop Roger of York died in 1181.

When I first encountered this document I was not looking for evidence of Oxford learning and had no idea of its importance for the early history of our university; I was preparing my doctoral thesis on the bishops of Chichester in the twelfth century. It was only some years later that an oral account of a paper on the origins of Oxford University given by Sir Richard Southern (as he is now), was retailed to me. This paper formed the basis of what would become his masterly contribution to the *History of the University of Oxford.* His argument was that while Oxford was a promising centre of intellectual activity in the early 1130s when Robert Pullen taught here, after his departure in 1133 circumstances were not favourable to academic growth; that the period from 1135 to 1185 is 'an exasperating blank'; and that it was only around 1190 or just before that masters really began to congregate in Oxford, at first very much as teachers of law. Only from then could one speak of a continuous history of teaching and higher learning at Oxford.[6]

On hearing of this, I wrote to Southern with my evidence of the 1170s. He made generous acknowledgement of this case, but persisted in his scepticism about the 1170s in the

History of the University of Oxford,[7] presumably on the grounds
that one swallow does not make a summer. Granted, but one
has a pretty shrewd idea what season it must be if one sees a
swallow. Likewise, my document would seem to imply that
Oxford was already a reasonably significant centre of legal
learning. Why else should such distant judges and parties
gather here? The document implies that they gathered in
Oxford for the sake of the many learned lawyers whose
advice was to be had there. Southern also refers to the single
student mentioned in the record of miracles performed at
the tomb of St Frideswide in 1180, a clerk called Stephen,
from York, who was staying in Oxford at that time to study, as
a one-off case.[8] But this too would seem to imply a larger
context. Why should someone be drawn from York, if
Oxford was just like any other local school, of which England
by then had very many?

In reply to my letter, I received a delightful and fascinating
letter from Southern, dated 4 May 1973. After mentioning
that (at that time) he did not know the case which I cited
and which took the sequence of such cases back another ten
years, Southern went on to make a brilliant point about my
document which had not occurred to me. With his permission I quote:

> I said in my talk that we don't know whether it was the geo-
> graphical convenience of Oxford which drew cases here, and
> which in turn encouraged masters to set up teaching Law in
> the town, or whether the existence of masters encouraged the
> hearing of cases here, or a mixture of the two. I am inclined to
> think in fact that it was a mixture of the two and the present
> example would seem rather to support this view. In the first
> place, Oxford is ideally situated between the areas of the liti-
> gants and of the judges delegate. But it also seems very likely
> that John of Cornwall was teaching Law and/or Theology in
> Oxford after his return from Paris in about 1160 . . . Your
> charter, apart from anything else, provides evidence of an
> earlier association of John of Cornwall with Oxford than any
> previously known, and is therefore of substantial importance
> in filling the gap which you remark on.[9]

Before this correspondence, which advanced my knowledge
of the interesting Master John of Cornwall, I had already

come across this Master in connection with his Oxford teaching in the writing of two distinguished scholars (Stephan Kuttner and Eleanor Rathbone), who had turned up a canon law manuscript in the library of Caius College, Cambridge. It referred to a rather poignant Oxford disputation on marital law in which he had been involved at some date probably around 1190.

> A certain fornicator on his death bed, not wishing to renounce his fornication, took his concubine to wife notwithstanding his knowledge that he could never thereafter have sexual intercourse with her [most medieval canon lawyers considered consummation a vital part of a validly contracted marriage]. Was this a marriage? John of Cornwall says that it is a marriage (and brings in past intercourse, not to legitimate it, but as indicating consent). John of Tynemouth says that won't do, etc.[10]

Here, in a marginal note, we catch a small echo of Master John of Cornwall at his work in Oxford. One may think that we are getting remote from monastic concerns here, but as heads of religious houses were already in the later twelfth century acting as papal judges-delegate in all kinds of legal suits,[11] they needed to know about matters of this kind. Moreover, litigation concerning property, in which the Benedictines played a very full part in twelfth-century England, often turned on an issue of matrimonial legitimacy.[12]

John of Cornwall is one of four men in our list to be styled 'Master'. This style was like our 'doctor', virtually never used when it had not been earned, but sometimes dropped when it had been earned. In the twelfth century a person designated *magister* must have completed a long and gruelling arts course (if an Englishman, probably in France) in order to obtain the *jus ubique docendi*, the right to teach anywhere. Of the masters in our Oxford list, I cannot shed any further light on Masters Gilbert of Northampton and Godfrey of Lanthony, nor in one sense on Osbert of Arundel, except to say that it is as certain as such a matter can be that he was at Oxford as an Oxford Master and not in the entourage of the Bishop of Chichester, notwithstanding that he was presumably a Sussex man. For it is scarcely conceivable that someone of his education and importance should have sunk without trace in the Chichester records of the time, had he had a professional association with the bishop.[13] John of Cornwall, then, was clearly a teacher in the Oxford schools; the others, as Southern says, were probably both teachers and practising lawyers.

One might be tempted to say, 'So you have argued that the continuous history of Oxford as a centre of learning began at latest in the 1170s rather than in the 1180s, but what's in a mere decade?' The answer is, as between the 1180s and the 1170s, actually rather a lot. The 1170s was one of the great decades in the history of English law. After Thomas Becket was martyred in 1170, the system of jurisdictional appeal to Rome and the appointment of papal judges-delegate to hear and determine cases in England took a new leap forward. At the same time, this was the decade of vital development in the procedures which formed the basis of English Common Law, backed up by regular and comprehensive judicial eyres, and with even something like a court of appeal being introduced in 1178.[14] An Oxford of legal learning in the 1170s, therefore, looks much more like a stimulus to the current preoccupations of the ruling élite, and much less like a mere reflector of them, than would have been the case if our earliest evidence came from the late 1180s. Oxford, and more particularly the hunting-lodge of nearby Woodstock,[15] was an important place on King Henry II's royal progress. Oxford, even from its beginnings, has never been quite the academic ivory tower that some people suppose.

In his letter of 1973, Southern continued with another point, to which I alluded at the beginning of this paper, and which he took up again in the *History of the University* – the point that neighbouring monasteries could use the legal expertise of Oxford legal Masters. These are his words:

> It is quite clear that the existence of Oseney, St Frideswide (both houses of Augustinian canons) and Eynsham (Benedictine) meant that there would be a lot of legal business in Oxford – quite enough I guess to keep two or three masters busy.

None of the Masters in my witness-list of 1174–80 can appar-

ently be traced in the records of St Frideswide, Eynsham or
Abingdon, another important nearby Benedictine monastery (and the very full cartulary of Godstow nunnery still
awaits research),[16] but that does not necessarily signify. If
there is evidence that a clerk witnesses several documents of
a religious house, that is a positive sign that he is probably
working for it, but the reverse by no means holds. Then
again, it is clear from the witness-list of 1174–80 that there
were probably other names mentioned in the original document, with which the scribe of the Guisborough Cartulary
dispensed when he made the copy.[17] If we knew these other
names, they might be identifiable in the records of local
monasteries. The principle of Southern's remarks must
surely be right, even if it were impossible to exemplify it with
a single instance. One may cite various examples elsewhere
of secular clerks who worked for monasteries in the way
suggested, as drafters of documents perhaps and certainly
on occasion as legal representatives. Master Ralph of Ford,
for instance (who would become Official of St Hugh of
Lincoln and the Chief Clerk to Bishop Seffrid II of
Chichester) witnessed several documents for St Augustine's,
Canterbury,[18] in the early to mid-1180s and later; in the
1230s, Walter de Merton (though not a Master) did so for
Merton Priory in Surrey.[19]

There is, however, one exceptionally interesting example
to back up Southern's remarks. It is Geoffrey *de Lardaria*,
one of the names in the Oxford witness-list of 1174–80. He
surfaces very interestingly in other twelfth-century records.
In the Public Records Office are twenty-four folio volumes
into which have been stuck original documents of the
twelfth and thirteenth centuries, which no doubt originally
came into the royal exchequer at the time of the dissolution
of the monasteries in the 1530s, since most of them have to
do with monasteries. When I was a research student in the
late 1950s few people had gone through these volumes, and
the very last person who was in my mind when I made my
own searches was Geoffrey *de Lardaria*. But there he was, in
several witness-lists of documents relating to Bruern Abbey,
some of whose twelfth-century archive seems to have been
stuck into those volumes, and in each case he is now styled

Master Geoffrey *de Lardaria.* Bruern was a Cistercian (and hence of course Benedictine) abbey in Oxfordshire near Witney, and Geoffrey must have been retained to do legal work for them. He thus illustrates the shrewdness of Sir Richard Southern's observation that some Oxford Masters could have drawn an income from the legal business generated by local monasteries, though in Geoffrey's case from a monastery other than those mentioned by name in Southern's letter to me. I have noted him in eight witness-lists of documents (late twelfth century or *c.* 1200), issued in the names of eight different laymen making grants of land to the abbey, and in five of the eight he is listed as the first witness.[20]

By the 1180s, if not earlier, English Benedictine monasteries were beginning to perceive that *magistri,* or highly educated men, who were attached to them could be valuable in keeping them afloat during an age of increasing litigiousness. Not that all such Masters had originally studied law, but nothing strikes one so forcefully as the apparent twelfth-century view that men who had studied the arts and perhaps theology as well had the right kind of mental training to turn effortlessly to law. Gilbert Foliot was a learned theologian, but by the 1150s, as Bishop of Hereford, he was one of the most frequent legal assessors of Archbishop Theobald.[21] Roger of Worcester and Bartholomew of Exeter had both studied theology, but by the 1170s they had become the most often used papal judges-delegate in England.[22] Of the value attaching to *magistri* for legal purposes, Bury St Edmund is a case in point. When their Abbot Hugh died in 1180, two monks of the house, Master Samson (who had studied at Paris and succeeded to the abbacy) and Master R. Ruffus, went to the king to secure a suitable arrangement for the property and revenues of the house during the vacancy. Early in 1182, when a delegation of twelve monks was sent to treat with the king concerning the abbatial election, five of the twelve had the title *Master,* and one of these, Master Hermer, was still only a novice, which shows the keenness to press such educated men into service. Later, when a new prior had to be chosen at Bury, some wanted Master Hermer, by then sub-prior, saying 'trust the experienced Master' (*experto crede magistro*); others replied that he was hot-tempered and quarrelsome; but the fear of Master Hermer's party was that educated clerics might in future disdain the religious habit if a 'speechless figurehead' or a 'block of wood' were given preference.[23]

In 1176, when Odo, Abbot of Battle, was locked in a dispute with Godfrey de Lucy over Wye church, he wished he could draw on legal expertise within his monastery. All the expensive lawyers he approached refused his brief for fear of offending the king or Godfrey's father, the Chief Justiciar Richard de Lucy. Whereupon one of Odo's kinsmen (a monk, it seems) said to the wretched abbot, 'My lord, if you had only spent enough on me and your other relatives so that we could have attended the schools, we would long since have been knowledgeable in the law and the decretals, and could have been your defence in this and in other necessities.' To which the abbot was said to have replied, 'It is judgement on me for not having studied the law myself.'[24]

Oxford in the twelfth century was an exceptionally densely monasticised town and region, and it can be shown that the monasteries were not backward in litigation. Whether the easy pickings of legal expertise in Oxford made them less anxious to recruit it for themselves than Bury St Edmund were or than Battle should have been, we probably shall never know, for we lack sources such as the Chronicle of Jocelin of Brakelond (Bury) or the Battle Chronicle for any of them in the same period. But in their need for lawyers they are an obvious factor in the development of Oxford as a centre of legal learning.

3

The Benedictines at Oxford, 1283–1539[1]

ALBAN LÉOTAUD osb with
revisions by RUPERT G. M. McHARDY

In the thirteenth century Oxford was still in the fields. One
hundred years later there were only five small colleges,
accommodating in all a little less than eighty undergraduates, while about 3000 other boys between thirteen
and eighteen years of age lodged in private halls or lodgings.
There were few large buildings; most of the domes and
towers came with the Tudors and the Renaissance. But there
were fields all around of corn, rye, and barley; and in the
midst were a church, a cluster of buildings, a few religious
houses, some scattered manors in the suburbs, and the river
passing calmly through.[2] The boys added a touch of colour
and life to the surroundings by their gowns of green, blue,
and blood-red, and their unruly ways. The friars were established there fairly early; the Cistercians were at Rewley in
1280; and the Canons Regular at Oseney and St Frideswide's
more than a century earlier, but at first simply as inmates of
monastic houses independent of the university.[3] The first
mention of a Benedictine house at Oxford occurs in the
statutes of the General Chapter held at Reading in 1277,
when the Presidents imposed a tax of 2d. in the mark upon
all the monasteries of the southern province, for the
purpose of maintaining a house of studies at the university.[4]
This was repeated at the next chapter held at Abingdon two
years later. But these resolutions remained unfulfilled for
some time, owing perhaps to the passing of the Statute of
Mortmain,[5] which put a stop for the moment to any acqui-

sition of land for the purpose. There was a rejuvenation of study in the monasteries at this time. The Cistercians were sending monks to Paris, and the abbey of Fleury followed their lead. The Dominicans and Franciscans were by this stage already well known in all the universities of the world.[6] At the Council of Vienne, Clement V had directed the monasteries to provide for the instruction of their monks in the elementary sciences. The French Pope Benedict XII confirmed this and provided some practical means for its fulfilment, namely that out of every twenty monks in each house, one (or, in other words, five per cent of the whole number) was to be sent to the university to study theology or law.[7]

The next document which refers to monastic students at Oxford is in the form of a letter of Godfrey Giffard, Bishop of Worcester,[8] to the Chancellor and University of Oxford in April 1283. He writes to inform them that 'the supreme vicar of Christ thought that the study of theology ought to be increased, so that it may make its ropes longer by enlargement of the place of its tent'; and we are told of the praiseworthy and God-inspired devotion of the brethren of St Peter's Abbey, Gloucester, who 'now wish to depose Ignorance the mother of Error, and to walk in the light of truth, that they may become proficient in learning'. After this highflown introduction, the Bishop goes on to say that he is most desirous to help the Gloucester monks, and begs the masters of the university to give them a 'doctor of the divine page' (a DD), that the way of learning may lie open to those thirsting for wisdom, and so at least they themselves becoming learned, may be able to instruct the people to the honour of God and the Church.[9]

In the same year 1283, the annalist of Gloucester Abbey recorded (in the curtest language, as annalists do) that 'our house at Oxford was founded by the noble Sir John Giffard,[10] a monastic community being solemnly inducted there by the venerable Father Dom Reginald, Abbot of Gloucester: Sir John himself being there and agreeing to the same.'[11] This was the birth of the first and most important college of the Benedictines at the university.[12]

The new foundation was endowed for fifteen monks from

the community of Gloucester exclusively, and the church of Chipping Norton was appropriated for that purpose. The annals of Worcester are, however, a little more informative than those of the neighbouring abbey. They record that 'a certain nobleman named John Giffard founded a place at Oxford outside the walls, and gave possessions to maintain thirteen [*sic*] monks, whom he chose from the *conventus* of Gloucester, wishing that his soul and the soul of his late wife Maud (de Longespée) should receive perpetual benediction from the sons of St Benedict.'[13]

The presidents of the chapter of the southern province saw in this new college the germ of a more ambitious house of studies to be thrown open to the students of all the monasteries of the south. At the provincial chapter, therefore, held at Salisbury in 1291, on the day after the funeral of Queen Eleanor, a petition was made to that effect and five instruments were produced. By the first instrument the Abbot of Gloucester was enabled to renounce his jurisdiction over the college, to recall the students, and to release the prior of the college from all subjection to Gloucester Abbey. The second was a licence in Mortmain to Giffard, to grant four messuages and a toft to the residents of the new foundation. By the third instrument the property was conveyed from the abbot and chapter of Gloucester to the whole province 'to receive all monks from the monasteries of the Province of Canterbury, there sent or to be sent to study, in pure and perpetual alms'. Warranty of title was given on condition that the prior elect should always be presented to Giffard and his heirs. The last instrument declared that the house was immediately subject to the presidents of the chapter, and that the resident students had the sole election of the prior, though bound to present him to the presidents for approval.[14]

In this way Gloucester College became the common house of studies for the young monks of the south. The building which Giffard gave was originally the mansion of Gilbert de Clare, Earl of Gloucester,[15] for whom it had the advantage of being close to the Palace of Beaumont. His arms were still there in Anthony à Wood's time, 'fairely depicted in the window of the hall'.[16] But besides the mansion, there was a parcel of land given for the site of additional buildings. Each monastery was invited to build accommodation for its own students at its own expense, and a plot of land was allotted to those who wished to do so. The appeal was well received, and building soon started. Among those who sent students there were the monks of Glastonbury, Tavistock, Chertsey, Coventry, Evesham, Bury St Edmunds, Rochester, Burton, Malmesbury, Worcester, Eynsham, Muchelney, St Albans, Westminster, Winchecombe, and Pershore. Those who did not build houses of their own put their students as paying guests in the houses of others. The priories of Stokes and St Neots, which were to have contributed, refused to do so on the ground that they were subject to the abbey of Bec in Normandy.[17] The Cluniacs sent some of their students to Oxford, but they must have lived in scattered lodgings, for they had no college of their own.

Some of the houses built by the various monasteries at the college may still be seen to this day, incorporated within the modern buildings of Worcester College. They are small cottage-like houses, proudly called *mansiones*, built in a row, not apart like Carthusian cells but closely packed. Their roofs were contiguous, but each cottage had its own front door and its own staircase, and over the lintel of the door were carved the arms of the owners or the rebus of the ruling abbot.[18] Strictly speaking, this colony of small monastic houses was neither a college, nor a cell, nor even an independent priory. It was hardly a corporate body at all, but simply a collection of *camerae* each of which belonged to a different monastery.[19] John Giffard caused much greater confusion in 1298 by transferring the ownership of the college to the monks of Malmesbury, where he was spending his last years, and reserving certain powers over it to the presidents of the General Chapters. The connection with Gloucester was severed, but it continued to be called Gloucester College until the end. The monks of Malmesbury who controlled the site, and the General Chapters which framed its rules, exercised a divided control which must have made things unnecessarily complicated.[20] When Benedict XII united the northern and southern provinces into one chapter, by the constitutions of 1336, monks from the north were freely admitted into the common house of studies. All the students kept common hall and chapel.[21]

The first monk to take his degree at the college was Dom William de Brock of Gloucester Abbey. All the southern Benedictines united to fête the new graduate, and many came in person to celebrate the occasion. The annalist of Gloucester in 1298 recorded the event as a red-letter day for the abbey. He tells us that the Abbot of Gloucester made the journey to Oxford accompanied by his monks, priors, obedientiaries, claustrals, clerics, squires, and noblemen – the whole retinue numbering 100 horses in all. He also records that the Abbots of Westminster, Reading, Abingdon, Evesham, and Malmesbury were present, with many priors and other monks, who all brought gifts and *exennia* to the new bachelor: and indeed nearly all the prelates of the south who were absent sent various presents by their representatives.[22]

We have seen that the provincial chapter was entrusted with the government of the Oxford college. Among the capitular statutes of the fourteenth and fifteenth centuries, there are several items relating to the regulation of the house, either by the framing of constitutions, or the correction of faults and abuses. In 1363, Thomas de la Mare, the great Abbot of St Albans,[23] who was sole president of the chapter for that year, published several statutes intimately concerning the management of the common house of studies. There was to be a prior elected by the whole body of the students themselves, and he was to have jurisdiction over all the resident monks of the college. The students were to hold disputations constantly in term-time, two a week, one in philosophy and one in theology. They were to be carefully trained to preach, both in Latin and in the vulgar tongue. Superiors of houses were admonished to obey the decrees of Benedict XII with regard to sending their quota of students to the universities, and if they neglected to do so they were to be heavily fined. In their choice of subjects to be sent to the universities, superiors were to consider that youthful monks take more easily to the study of philosophy than old men: 'Although wisdom blossoms in old people and old age is venerable, nevertheless their minds are less alert than the minds of the young and less attuned to philosophical study . . . Therefore we decree that in future old men and those advanced in years should not be sent to the studium to study philosophy.' Then there follows a curious clause: if there were several from the same monastery residing at the college, one of their number was to be appointed to take charge of them to see that they applied themselves to their studies and their religious duties, and that none of them went to confession to any priest of another house, or received communion from any priest of another house, unless their own priests were unable to administer the sacraments at the time. But for some lawful cause, any student could go to confession to the prior.[24] The final clause forbids any student to incept under anyone but a Doctor of Divinity of their own order. It is thought that this was aimed against Henry Wodehulle, a monk of Abingdon, who caused a stir in Oxford three years before by trying to incept under a secular against the will of his abbot and of the university.[25] In 1343, twenty years before Abbot de la Mare's statutes, the presidents of the chapter had decreed that there was to be a chair of theology set up in the college, and occupied by a Black Monk. He was to receive a salary of £10 a year out of the common fund, which provided also for the expenses of their exercises and degrees with regard to fees and entertainments. The statutes of that year bound the students to attend office and Mass in the college chapel on all feast-days: if anyone failed to do so, he was to be fined by the prior.[26]

From a fragment of the acts of a provincial chapter (reckoned to be that of 1393), we learn that some of the superiors of the southern province were taken to task for not sending the required number of monks to the Oxford house of studies.[27] The Abbots of Muchelney and Faversham were reprimanded for not sending a scholar for three years; the Abbots of Evesham and Eynsham for not sending one for one year; the Abbots of Burton and Battle, for not sending scholars for one term; and one or two others. At the chapter of 1423, the Prior of Oxford attended in person and delivered a long report about the affairs of the college to the assembled abbots and priors. He thanked those abbots who had given money towards the building of the new chapel there; then he severely reproved certain others for not

sending students to study at the college. The Abbot of
Abbotsbury had withdrawn a scholar for seven years; the
Abbot of Chester had not sent one for twelve years, for which
he ought to be severely punished; the Abbot of Hyde had
refused to pay for the commons of one student for two separate years; the Abbot of Malmesbury had withdrawn one of
his subjects for two years, and this was not the first time; and
so on. After dinner the next day all the accused were fined,
but as they all made good excuses, and moreover as all of
them submitted graciously and humbly and promised to
amend, their fines were cancelled by the presidents, acting
with their usual fatherly kindness.[28] Some anti-monastic
writers, always ready to accuse rather than to excuse, have
used these lists of delinquents in their endeavour to show
up the intellectual apathy which they claim to have been
prevalent in the monastic houses at certain times. But the
lists might also be used to show, on the contrary, that delinquents were exceptional, and that they were often excusable.
Their excuses are not recorded in the minutes of the chapters, but as their fines were repealed by the presidents, we
may be sure that they had made out good causes for themselves. It may very likely have been a question of expense.
Not every monastery could have afforded an exhibition to
two scholars every year, for although they owned large
estates, their revenues were often unable to balance their
annual expenditure. Or again, the remorseless Black Death
sometimes swept away numbers of their communities, and so
with a depleted staff and many empty stalls in choir, they
would have found it difficult to spare two clever young men
for the university. Allowances ought to be made.

In the compotus rolls of the obedientiaries of Worcester,
there are many items which illustrate the life of a monastic
undergraduate of the later Middle Ages.[29] In these accounts
we are able to reckon that the allowances made to the
students of Worcester were greater than the best endowed of
the secular scholars at the other colleges in Oxford. From
1376 onwards there were invariably two scholars from Worcester at the university. The cellarers sent them regularly £6
each every year through the rent collector of the manor of
Blackwell. The chamberlain and the kitchener also sent

them £3 a year each, and the sacrist 4s. for 'green wax'. The cellarer's contribution was apparently for bread and ale and other necessities such as firewood, the chamberlain's for commons, and the kitchener's for meat. This last was paid by the Abbot of Oseney out of a pension he owed to Worcester for appropriating the church of Bibury.[30] In the lists of accounts are several items relating to the expenses of the students' books, allowances for blood-letting, travelling expenses, etc. In the summer of 1291, 3s. is given to 'two monks on their way from Oxford' (coming home no doubt for the long vacation); but for their journey back they receive 20s. The cellarer in 1336 hires a horse for one of the scholars going up. The next year he does not forget to send them their customary pittance for the cellarer's *O* in Advent, nor their 'minutiones'.[31]

Brother Stephen Tetbury went up for the first time in 1346; the precentor rode with him, and the cellarer bought him a new habit for the occasion. In 1392 Dom Dudley had to be fetched from Oxford in some kind of vehicle called the 'long cart' (*longe carecte*), at the cost of 5s.4d. Presumably he was ill, for all the others went to and fro with hired horses. In the cellarer's rolls for 1407, there occurs this interesting item: 'In expenses of Brothers Dudley and Fordham[32] riding to Gloucester to confer with the Lord King and the Lord Archbishop, and their expenses to Oxford to destroy the opinions of various heretics erring in the faith – £4.12s.9d.' They were both Oxford students. A few years later, the guestmaster contributed 1s. to new chambers for Worcester scholars at the university. The sacrist went there in 1423 when one of the undergraduates took his degree of DD, and he gave him a present of £2. Soon after, the cellarer had to pay 23s.6d. for the expenses of taking Dom John with his books and bedding to Oxford, and bringing back Dom Hugh to Worcester with *his* bedding and *his* books.[33]

The History of the Abbots of St Albans, compiled by Thomas of Walsingham, contains many references to the common house of studies at Oxford, and shows that the abbots of that famous monastery were among the most generous of its benefactors. Abbot de la Mare (1349–96) gave £40 and more for reparations of the houses and furniture of the monastic college. He also established an exhibition of one scholar-monk beyond the usual number, and sent other boys to study at Oxford. The historian records the celebrity of the Abbot's scholars, and incidentally the international atmosphere of Oxford at this time, 'where there was the greatest gathering of all nations at the time'.[34] Abbot de la Mare's successor spent £138.3s.2d. on the building of the new house at the university and gave a small donation towards the college chapel fund. In 1401, Abbot Heyworth completed the building begun by his predecessor, more lavishly than was fitting. The most generous of them all was Abbot Whethamsted, who had been prior of the college before his election as superior of St Albans. In 1420, he contributed lavishly to the building of the chapel. He also built a library on the south side of the chapel, its five windows giving on to Stockwell Street. He not only built the library but he gave many books of his own collection and his own writing, and also attracted the patronage of Humphrey, Duke of Gloucester, who also gave them books and other things.[35]

Since many, though not by any means the majority, of the monastic students came from monasteries exempt from episcopal jurisdiction, the situation became very delicate when Archbishop Courtenay informed the superiors of the college in 1379 of his intention to hold a visitation in his own person: 'He firmly decided to make a visitation of the College of Black Monks at Oxford, where the *Prior studentium* resides with many students both exempt and non-exempt, so that by such an event the diocesan ordinary may have a precedent for visiting them each year.'

The superiors of the college were most anxious lest the Archbishop should create a precedent, and so find an excuse for visiting them in future years. But Abbot de la Mare wrote the Archbishop a diplomatic letter, explaining that a visitation in term would disturb the peace and quiet of the scholars to the detriment of their studies. Courtenay did not insist, but when he went to Oxford he called the students together[36] and told them that his intentions had never been to molest them, but on the contrary to give them always his encouragement. After these kind words, which were greatly appreciated by all, the Archbishop (in the historian's opinion) 'miraculously dismissed them'.[37]

Among the muniments of the Dean and Chapter of Norwich, there are some rolls of the obedientiaries of the cathedral priory which mention payments made towards the building of their *mansio* at the common college. There is much more variety in the Westminster rolls, of which an abundance has come down to us. We know from them, for example, that a Westminster exhibition at Gloucester College was £10 a year for each scholar from about 1362 to 1435, when it was changed to ten marks or £6.13s.4d. There was no definite period for holding these scholarships. One held it for four years; another, who had to go on business to Avignon, interrupted his course during the journey, and had a further year at Oxford on his return; another held the scholarship for twelve years; a future Bishop of Carlisle held it for two, and needed an additional gift of £10 at the beginning of his study of the *Sentences*.[38] It may be gathered from the rolls of the sacrist that the Oxford scholars were called upon to preach the sermons at Westminster on Palm Sunday and Good Friday, the two great days for sermons in Benedictine houses. Dom Millyng, the future Bishop of Hereford,[39] came up at least five times for this, and there was frequent coming and going among the other students, always on horseback.[40] Among the muniments at Westminster is a schedule which gives the details and distribution of a deceased abbot's belongings; they included armour, bows and arrows, and catapults, and among the payments were 48s. for two Oxford scholars, and a sum of money for the building of the chapel there. In 1522 there were five students from the royal foundation up at the university, and on their patronal feast they took a day's rest from their studies and went into the country. A note in a manuscript is preserved at Westminster, showing how the students spent their holiday: 'This byll testyfyeth that we five scholars, with five others with us of the brethren of Glosset college, hath expended in the observance of holy St Edwards our patron's service, kept at Islip in his chapel, and the dirge and masses kept there – for the sowlys of the parents of our most worshipfull father in God ye Abbot of Westm. the summe of

10s., the yere of our lord a mcccccxxii the xv day next after mykylmas. By me rudely writen Dan Thomas Barton, Mk of Westm.'[41]

The Benedictine monks of the northern province were represented at Oxford by Durham College.[42] Richard de Hoton, who was elected Prior of Durham in 1289,[43] began the erection of the college. It was endowed in 1381 for eight monastic students and the same number of secular boys by the will of Thomas de Hatfield, by whose ordinance the former were placed in a position of what would in our days have been called fellows or full members of the society. The secular boys studying arts and grammar, who held their scholarships for seven years, waited upon the monk-scholars and took their meals at a second table in the hall.[44] So the northern foundation differed from Gloucester College by taking in mixed students, monastic and secular.[45] The Elizabethan *Rites of Durham*, speaking of the novices of the cathedral priory, says that 'if the master did see that any of them were apt to learning, and did apply his book, and had a pregnant wit withall, then the master did let the prior have intelligence. Then straightway after, he was sent to Oxford to school, and there did learn to study divinity; and the residue of the aforesaid novices was kept at their books till they could understand their service and the Scriptures; then at the year's end they did sing their first messe.'[46]

The monks of Christ Church, Canterbury, with characteristic singularity, had their own Oxford house of studies in Canterbury College,[47] which served them for two centuries until it was swallowed up by Wolsey's huge foundation. Canterbury College makes its first appearance as an exclusively Benedictine house in 1331, when a document of that year describes a *familia* of three Canterbury monks living in the parish of St Peter, under the charge of the senior of the three acting as superior.[48] The house was hired for six marks a year, and the scholars depended for their maintenance on the manor of Newington near Henley, the nearest estate belonging to the monks of Christ Church. This hired lodging quickly disappears from the records of the monastery, and we find instead a set of rooms in Gloucester College purchased for the scholars. In 1361 Archbishop Simon Islip[49]

founded a college in Oxford for the training of young
secular clerks destined to replace the clergy who had died
in such numbers during the great plague. The buildings
mentioned in the schedule were a group of eleven tenements on a site near the priory of St Frideswide, and six
tofts. These messuages, adapted to suit their requirements,
no doubt formed the home of the first set of boys until, at
the end of the fourteenth century, they were destroyed to
make room for a handsome new building, which was soon
put into the hands of the monks of Canterbury for their
own use.[50] Simon Islip had given the monks the right of
nominating from among their own numbers candidates for
the office of warden of the new college, but at the end of
his life the seculars who surrounded him persuaded him
to replace the monastic warden for a secular one.[51] Islip's
successor, Simon Langham,[52] took the side of the monks
and tried to reinstate the monastic warden. The seculars
appealed to Rome: Urban V appointed a cardinal to judge
the case: the cardinal decided in favour of the monks, who
were finally reinstated and held the college uninterruptedly
till the coming of Wolsey two centuries later.[53] The statutes of
Simon Islip are still in existence. The foundation was to be
called Canterbury Hall and there were to be eleven fellows
(*Socii*); the fellows were to elect the warden, or rather submit
three names to the choice of the Archbishop of Canterbury.
None was to be given a fellowship who was not honest,
humble, peaceful; nor, moreover, anyone who had a notable
facial disfigurement. The college was exempt from episcopal
jurisdiction and placed immediately under the eye of the
Primate.[54] In 1383 Archbishop Courtenay amended these
statutes and added some of his own, among which he legis-
lated for the endowment of five poor boys to be kept at the
college and educated.[55] The warden was to assign them
rooms and give them 10d. a week for their commons; their
course was to extend over seven continual years and no
longer. There were to be disputations in hall twice a week
after supper by candle-light, at the end of which the anti-
phon and collect of St Thomas were said. After this the
fellows were allowed a little drink and recommended to
retire to their studies immediately after, without any further

delay 'so that stories and such like vanities which might give rise of quarrelling, may be avoided'. The warden and fellows were strictly forbidden to alienate or pawn any books or plate, under pain of excommunication; if they infringed this rule they were to be recalled to their monastery without any hope of ever returning. Special Masses were to be said for the King and Queen, Islip, Cardinal Langham, and several others, and the boys were given certain prayers to say. As far as can be discovered, these statutes remained in force as long as the college existed, and the fellows continued to be selected from among the monks of Christ Church. On 4 June 1363 William de Islip[56] gave his manor of Woodford, with all its lands, meadows, rents, feudal rights, ponds, warrens, mills, gardens, dove-cots, and all its other appurtenances to the warden and the fellows and their successors for ever.[57] There is another document among the Canterbury papers in which the monks of Christ Church convey their *mansio* in Gloucester College to the abbot and monks of Westminster, since they now had no further use for it. The document states that the conveyance was made in the chapter house at Canterbury with the unanimous consent of the chapter fathers, and describes exactly the site of the cottage – 'adjoining the lower gate situated between the house of the abbot and conventus of A[bingdon?], and that of the conventus of Gloucester; and also a certain path leading to the meadow of the Abbot of Malmesbury . . .' There are also some chatty letters which passed between the officials at Canterbury and the students at Oxford.

Here is one in English from one of the scholars who had been hastily recalled to Canterbury to be sub-cellarer, and did not have time to pack up his things:

> To his friend Thomas Tystede, student at Canterbury College in Oxford
>
> [Ihesus Maria]
>
> Most trusty, I salute you, putting you to knowledge that I am full determined and fixed not to return to Oxford, and have an office in the monastery, which is subcellarer: wherefore I pray you truss up my stuff safe and send it by Buccke with all speed: and because the great coffer is cumbersome to carry,

truss them in my bed, laying my clothes in the middle of my stuff and my books thereupon and a great mantle ye shall receive for P. Iohnsons: and as for my two coffers, you shall let these remain for Peter Langlaye,[58] who is a chosen scholar and shall come to you shortly with Dom I. Crosse: but truss such stuff as I have in the coffers, and take a silken girdle that T. Frensche gave me, the boys know it: I pray you make good search therefore: and here is the key of the coffer wherein by P. Iohnson's books with other stuff. Sir David has Saint Jerome's epistles of mine: require it. If you have or can make money with my tables and trestles with the posts of my bed, do: if not, put them in safe guard: and among all other things I desire you heartily to cause my table of Saint Dorothy to be safe conveyed without hurt: and send me word what the contributions be and how much P. Iohnson is in the manciple's book, and in Pery's book, and I will send it to him by Crosse. You shall receive with this letter 1 noble for to discharge my stuff both in Oxford and also to the ship. And herein you shall desire Buccke in my name to take so much pain as to deliver it to a ship of Faversham, whereof he shall not fail weakly: you taking the pains to write on parchment, and surely sewn upon each truss, that they be delivered to Faversham, and from thence to our monastery, expressing my name. The bottles I trust you have not forgotten. Send word when the children shall be at Gravesend, and if you have made sale of any of my stuff, send me six pairs of gloves, buttoned in cheverell. For lack of time, vale. *Cantuarie*, the day of annunciation.

[Benedictus nomine.]

Nicholas Bennett[59]

In substance this letter might have been written by a twentieth century undergraduate, though in detail it is archaic. Another student writes from the college to his prior asking his permission to read law: 'I have had, thank your Fatherhood, a long prose in Arts, and the season is in a manner but lost . . . if it shall please you that I go rather to Law, then such small crumbs as I have gathered in Arts may somewhat feed me in Law.'[60]

The whole course of studies required of a medieval undergraduate was far lengthier than that of his modern equivalent. The curriculum for graduation in theology at

Oxford in the later Middle Ages covered a relatively long period of years, even for a BD. For their 'opponency', MA candidates were given a course of four or five years of study, including three years *auditio* of the Bible; for other candidates eight years in the study of arts were required before they proceeded to their theological course. A BD needed two more years; and for a doctorate the candidate had two years of further study, and was required to have lectured on one book of the Bible and on the *Sentences*, to have delivered an examinatory sermon at St Mary's, to have made eight responsions to non-graduate opponents, and to have disputed with every divinity regent. There were, however, certain concessions made to religious attending the university.[61] A regular was only required to spend one year studying theology at the schools in Oxford before his opponency. The rest of the period to be devoted to arts and theology could be spent elsewhere, so long as his studies were under the direction of a Master. In the fifteenth century an additional sermon was added to the course; sometimes a candidate would supplicate to preach in English at St Peter's-in-the-East instead of in Latin at St Mary's.[62] A scholar's private *camera*, if indeed he was allowed such a luxury, could be made as cosy a place as possible. The clay or tiled floors could be strewn with hay, and wooden shutters put up at the windows; a truckle-bed, an oak table piled with copies of the *Summa* or Duns Scotus, an iron candlestick, a chest or coffer in one corner, a 'presse' for books, and perhaps a lute if he were musical. The supposition that a student would have a fire in his study hangs upon the slender evidence of a fifteenth-century inventory of Durham College, which contains allusions to andirons.[63] Windows with glass in them were a luxury. When the price of candles was 2d. per pound, poorly pensioned monks could hardly afford to read for any length of time in the winter evenings, so that they were frequently employed during this time in public disputations and repetitions, at which a single candle might suffice for the whole company. An unworldly monk would require not much more than Chaucer's poor 'clerk of Oxenforde':

> For him was lever have at his beddes heed
> Twenty bokes, clad in blak or reed,
> Or Aristotle and his philosophye,
> Than robes riche, or fithele, or gay sautrye.[64]

Cardinal Gasquet made a study of the official registers of the university for the whole century preceding the Reformation, and showed that a good percentage of Benedictines took their degrees every year.[65] During the period 1449–59 there were forty Benedictines who graduated at Oxford; from 1500–39 there were 200; 'even with their cloisters falling on all sides round about them, in the last hour of their corporate existence, that is in the year 1538–9, some fourteen Benedictines took their degrees at Oxford.'[66] At this hour, however, Oxford had become a dangerous place for a studious young monk. Some of them were infected with the 'new learning' of Luther and Tyndale which was raging like an epidemic all over the university.[67] In 1528 Wolsey was informed that among the monastic scholars who had caught it were two from Edmundsbury and one from Glastonbury.[68] Some years later another student, Dom Thomas Coventry, a monk of Evesham, wrote to Cromwell begging that if his monastery was to be suppressed, his exhibition might be continued. 'I study Greek, Latin and Hebrew,' he writes, 'and refute papistical sophistry.'[69] In 1535 one or two of Cromwell's men passed through Oxford on their official visitations, during which Dr Layton wrote to his master: 'We have sett Dunce (Duns Scotus) in Bocardo, and have utterly banished him from Oxforde for ever with all his blind glosses . . . The second time we came to New College, we found the gret quadrant court full of the leaves of Dunce, the wind blowing them into every corner.'[70] After this suppression of scholastic philosophy typified in the works of Scotus, the end could not be far off. It came at the same time as the dissolution of the monasteries themselves, for since the colleges were dependent on them, they were naturally involved in their destruction. The students had to be recalled and pensioned off, and many of the buildings, left derelict, were soon reduced to ruin. Whethamsted's chapel and library at Gloucester College fell to pieces: his books were either lost or purchased, or else passed on to the libraries of other colleges, where they were seen by an eye-witness still bearing their donor's name.

4

Gloucester College

JAMES CAMPBELL

Gloucester College[1] was founded in 1283 and perished with the dissolution of the monasteries in 1539. The College was the centre of study in Oxford for Benedictine monks, until 1338 for those from the province of Canterbury, thereafter for those from the province of York also.

In the thirteenth century the confidence of the great medieval monasteries of England had begun to be shaken. There was an uneasiness that the world was passing the Black Monks by. Two threats converged. First: the rise of the universities, and in England in particular, the rise of Oxford, ensured that Benedictine monasteries were no longer what some of them had been for centuries – the principal centres of intellectual life. Second: in the 1220s the Dominican and Franciscan friars came to England and soon flourished greatly there. Their way of life presented a contrast to that of the Black Monks and implied criticism of it. Their popularity among all ranks of society was a galling challenge, greater even than that of the Cistercians in the previous century, to the great houses which had for so long been central to the life and piety of England. What is more, the friars soon became deeply and very influentially involved in the universities. No longer did an intending benefactor, or a bright young man, think first of a Benedictine house when it came to seeking a home for money or for intellect.

Something had to be done to establish a closer link between the monasteries and the university. Fortunately, from 1215 the Black Monks had the means of concerted

action. Until that year they were not organised in an order
as, for example, the Cistercians were. Every house acted
independently. But in the Fourth Lateran Council it was laid
down that there should be an annual chapter of the
superiors of the Benedictine houses of each province to take
counsel and to legislate for reform. It was at a meeting of the
chapter of the province of Canterbury in 1277 that a crucial
decision was taken: to found a house of studies at Oxford for
Black Monk students, the project to be financed by a levy of
2d. (later 1d.) in the mark (13s.4d.) on the income of each
house.

For some years the project hung fire. No student of the
affairs of the Benedictine chapter could be surprised at this.
An assembly of the heads of independent institutions, all of
whom were deeply suspicious of any threat to that independence and quick to take an obstructive point or to feel a
slight, was not easy to move to effective action. (Oxford poli-
ticians can think of it as like an extreme version of the
Conference of Colleges.) Some abbeys were co-operative:
Norwich regularly paid its levy. Others were not: Christ
Church Canterbury usually boycotted all the chapter's proceedings. However, in 1283 came a hopeful step forward. Sir
John Giffard brought from the Hospitallers a site in Oxford
and gave it to St Peter's, Gloucester. Either then, or soon
after, he intended this to provide the Benedictines with the
base they needed in the university. Some very complicated
choppings and changings followed; at one stage the benefactor seems to have been on the verge of losing his temper
and claiming his property back. Some monk students seem
to have been in residence in the early 1290s but the legal
position did not get fully sorted out until 1298.

In that year Giffard decided that not Gloucester but Malmesbury, the abbey in which he was spending his declining
years, should be the owner of the site. On it were to be
erected buildings for the general use of the students, to
be built at the common expense of the abbeys of the province of Canterbury. Students' rooms were to be built by each
abbey for its own men. From then on Gloucester College
(the name was retained, though Malmesbury College would
now have been more appropriate) was a going concern,

though it still had many difficulties to face; not least the reluctance of many houses to pay their contribution to the building costs.

In 1320 or 1321 came a major stroke of luck; an opportunity to extend the site. The origins of this chance lay in the battle of Bannockburn, 24 June 1314. Edward II was in imminent danger of capture by the Scots, and vowed to found a house of Carmelite friars if he escaped. After his escape he was about as good as his word. He gave the Oxford Carmelites the royal house there (which later antiquaries called Beaumont Palace). Up to this time the Carmelites had been the next-door neighbours of Gloucester College. The site which Giffard had given the college probably comprised most of that which is now occupied by the eighteenth-century buildings in the front of the present Worcester College and by its front quad. The Carmelites were immediately to the south, occupying the site of Pump Quad, and a large area beyond. The 'Beaumont Palace' site stretched to the east of the present college on the other side of the road, occupying most of the space now occupied by Worcester Cottage, the west end of Beaumont Street and part of the area between Beaumont Street and Gloucester Green. The first inclination of the Carmelites was to hold on to both sites, and in 1318 they obtained a licence for a tunnel to join them. (A tunnel is still required at that point, and still not built.) However, in 1320 they decided to put their old site on the market. This was too good an opportunity to miss and the two presidents of the Benedictine chapter, acting on their own responsibility, snapped the old Carmelite site up for the large sum of 800 marks.

A further step forward came with the legislation from Pope Benedict XII in 1336 and 1338. The crucial thing about this was that it made it compulsory for Benedictine houses to have a proportion of their monks studying at a university: one in twenty. Hitherto it had been up to each monastery as to whether it sent monks to Gloucester College or not; now it was not so. Though the legislation was not universally observed, it had a considerable effect. By the middle of the fourteenth century Gloucester College's constitution was settled much as it was to remain until the

dissolution. It was complex. This was not a college in
the sense of being legally an entity of the same kind that all
colleges are now and some were then. It was not a corporate
body with any powers of owning property. The site was
owned by the abbey of Malmesbury, who appointed an
officer whose functions are not clear. The most important
officer, responsible to the abbots president of the Benedictine chapter, was the *prior studentium.* He was appointed by
the Abbot of Abingdon. Individual abbeys had accommodation within the college, acquiring licences to build
from Malmesbury.

Who came to study at Gloucester College and what did
they study there? The requirement that all Black Monk
houses should have at least one in twenty of their monks at
the university at any given time was not universally observed,
and in any case not all monk students came to Gloucester
College; some went to the Oxford colleges owned by Christ
Church Canterbury and Durham, some to Cambridge.
Nevertheless, many monasteries did send students; at least
thirty-eight, and probably more, did so at one time or
another. Some houses were more strongly and continuously
represented than were others. Westminster sent considerably more monks that it was bound to do. The only date for
which we have a list of the monks present is 1537, when
there were thirty from thirteen or more different monasteries. Almost certainly there were more at earlier periods.
In theory there should have been over a hundred; and the
college could have held so many. It is likely that in practice
the number present was generally somewhat lower.

A full university course leading to a Doctorate in Divinity
took seventeen years: eight years for arts (principally logic
and philosophy) and nine years for theology. Some monks
did spend so long a period. Exemption from part or all the
arts course was granted to those who could attest that they
had pursued equivalent studies at their monastery, and most
did so. Of these, many did not proceed beyond a bachelor-
ship in theology. A high proportion did not take a degree at
all, but simply came for a few years, perhaps above all to
learn how to preach.

How old were the students? Our best information comes

from Westminster (though this may not have been typical). A majority came within six or seven years of entering the monastery, that is to say they would be in their early or mid-twenties. Quite a number were younger; some were much older. In some cases when there was a little group from a monastery an older monk would be sent to keep an eye on the younger ones. There may sometimes have been something of a random element in who was sent – it may on occasion have been a question of who could best be spared to keep up the quota, or whose company could his confrères best do without.

When they left the college very nearly all went back to their monasteries. A few of these went on to grander careers outside the cloister and a handful became bishops. The most remarkable career was that of Adam Easton. A monk of Norwich, born in about 1325, he was at Gloucester College, though not continuously, from 1355 until 1366 when he became *prior studentium* there. In 1369 he went to Rome. In 1376 he became proctor for the English Benedictines at the *curia*. At about this time he wrote an enormous book, the *Defensorium ecclesiasticae potestatis*, remarkable in many ways, not least because in order to make best use of the Old Testament he learned Hebrew, one of the very few scholars of his day to do so. In 1381 he was made a cardinal by Urban VI (he of the two popes produced by schism of 1378 whom the English supported). Urban VI was, to say the least, difficult, and deeply mistrustful of many of his own supporters. In 1385 he deprived Easton of his benefices, and had him imprisoned and tortured. In 1389 he was reinstated and he died in 1397. His tomb still stands in his titular church of St Cecilia in Trastevere.

Such grandeur was anything but characteristic of the careers of Gloucester College men. The overwhelming majority led quiet lives in their monasteries when they went down. As men more highly educated than their confrères, they provided a considerable proportion of those who were elected to become heads of their houses or who held administrative offices within them. How considerable a proportion has not been determined. At Westminster only half the abbots between 1350 and the dissolution had been to

Gloucester College. None of the monks who had been to the college wrote a book such as to demand even brief notice in a substantial history of medieval thought, Easton apart, though a considerable number wrote books of one kind and another. But the collective influence of the men who had been to Gloucester College on the Benedictine monasteries of England was pervasive and great.

Gloucester College was a very agreeable place in which to be. Its environs were infinitely more pleasant than they are now. The college stood somewhat outside the city walls (which curved towards the castle rather to the south of the present line of George Street). Between the college and the river stretched marshes drained by dykes. To the north stretched open countryside. Opposite the east front of the college stood the buildings of the Carmelites: almost nothing is known of these but they were probably very grand. Anthony Wood says they included a 'steeple with bell': probably they did. It was one of eight monasteries and houses which were scattered round the outside of the western half of the oval city of Oxford: all, except St Frideswide's, totally lost apart from mere fragments. Opposite Gloucester College on the west, just on the other side of the river stood the Cistercian abbey of Rewley; beyond that lay the Augustinians at Oseney (approximately on the site of the cemetery familiar to the traveller by train). Four hundred yards south-east of Gloucester College lay the Franciscan friary; two hundred yards beyond, the Dominican; three hundred yards beyond that the Augustinians of St Frideswide's, whose church is now Christ Church cathedral. All these monasteries had buildings of some, or great, splendour. One of the most abiding memories from Gloucester College must have been that of living within sight or sound of the most astonishing aggregation of monasteries anywhere in England.

We have a good idea of the nature of the buildings of Gloucester College as they were in its last years, partly from documents, but more particularly from the excellent engraving made by Loggan in 1675 (see plate 1). Though one must bear in mind that not only had demolitions taken place since the dissolution but there had certainly also been alterations and possibly additions. In considering the Loggan print there is no difficulty in seeing where one is. It is not hard to identify most of the common buildings of the late medieval college. The hall runs north-south from the north side of Pump Quad. It was, says Hearne (writing when it was still standing), 'a noble room', sixty-three feet by thirty-three. This would have been a noble room indeed; the present Hall is sixty feet by thirty. The Loggan print, if accurately proportioned, suggests that it was more like fifty feet long (including the gallery at the north end), but probably Hearne is more trustworthy. The chapel, which stood partly on the site of the present chapel, was about forty feet by twenty, had been built in or shortly before 1424, and was completely in ruins by 1675. The new kitchen built in 1423 was the little wing which still runs on the garden side of Staircase 11 parallel to the cottages, and its great chimney is still there. (The tradition of having the kitchen at a decent cooling distance from the Hall has been piously preserved.) Most of the other buildings were the quarters belonging to individual monasteries. However one reckons them up, there do not seem to have been more than twenty such units, and far more monasteries than that sent monks to Gloucester College. Those which did not have a set of rooms of their own hired from or shared with those who had. But in any case there were a whole series of separate dwellings, as can still readily be seen by looking at the cottages.

The identification of the ownership of particular – I will call them houses – is sometimes easy, sometimes difficult or impossible. (And it is important to remember that they sometimes changed hands from one monastery to another.) The most westerly of the cottages on the south side of the quadrangle undoubtedly in the last years of Gloucester College, and perhaps earlier, belonged to Pershore. Its arms stand to the right of the niche above the door, the rebus (a comb and a tun) and initial of its penultimate abbot, William Compton, stands to the left. The griffin over Staircase 12 indicates that here we have the Malmesbury house. The cross over Staircase 11 is that of St Augustine's Canterbury. Over Staircase 10 is the splendid cross and virgin of Glastonbury, but it does not belong here, having been moved from

Pump Quad where the Glastonbury property was. The ownership of a number of others can be identified at one stage
or another. The L-shaped house towards the west end on the
north side belonged to St Alban's. The second house from
the east in the north range (whose truncated east end,
housing the Senior Common Room, remains unnoticed by
most visitors to the college) seems to have belonged first to
Bury St Edmund's and later to Hyde.

The Bury building is of special interest because a memorandum survives describing its rooms. The building was much
more extensive than the surviving fragment. It is that which
can be seen running along the front of the college in the
Loggan print with nine uniform two-light windows, only its
eastern wall still being standing at the north end in 1675. It
did not all belong to Bury, for a library for the common use
was constructed at the same time as part of the same
building. The Bury rooms were, first, a *camera*, 'under the
library and next to the chapel', twenty-two feet or more long
by eighteen feet or more wide, and next to it another room
under the library, twenty-four feet or more long by eighteen
feet wide. (Thus we can see that the library was on the first
floor and was about forty-six feet long and eighteen feet
wide. Its east windows must have been those standing shat-
tered in the Loggan print.) Then came an *aula*, a hall, thirty
feet long and eighteen feet wide and on the ground floor.
There was a *camera* above the *aula* and of the same dimensions, then came two *camerae*, one above the other, each
twenty-one feet by eighteen.

What was the interior accommodation like at the end of
the Middle Ages? More could be done than has been done
to work this out. I can only offer some suggestions. The Bury
block built *c.* 1424 (not necessarily typical because so large)
had an *aula* on the ground floor; this was presumably used as
a kind of sitting room or common room. It must have been
heated, and one can indeed see its big chimney on the
Loggan print, to the right of the third window of the Bury
range (though there is another possibly relevant chimney on
the west side). It is likely that each of the houses now called
the cottages had such a room as its ground floor; the present
staircase doors entered straight into these rooms (though

there could have been a lobby). The actual staircases are relatively modern. Ascent to the first storey in medieval times would probably have been by a much narrower winding stair or by a ladder; the very small windows beside the doors of Staircases 8 and 10 may have been intended to light the stairs. Perhaps the upper floors were divided into a couple of rooms, perhaps there was just one big room.

One last aspect of the physical nature of the college may be noticed: the way in. It will readily be seen that there was no entrance corresponding to the present Worcester College lodge. What one did was to enter by the doorway, which still survives, at the extreme north of the medieval buildings, one then went along a lane bounded by a wall on the north and the present Senior Common Room block on the south. After about thirty yards one turned sharp left through a gap between two of the houses (it can just be seen on Loggan). It is the nature of this entry which explains the siting of the Malmesbury arms, the red griffin *segreant* which is still the brightest feature of the front quad. The Malmesbury family were, as is shown above, the owners of the site. So they kept for themselves what was, if one thinks of Gloucester College from the inside, the central situation; and ensured that what you saw as you entered the front quad, was their arms, larger than anyone else's arms, straight ahead of you.

There is a question as to whether, if you entered the front quadrangle in *c.* 1500 and looked up to your left, you would have seen a clock. Anthony Wood refers to the building to the north of the Gloucester Hall as 'the clock house', and on Loggan one can indeed see a gable which could well have been for a clock. But was it a Gloucester College or a Gloucester Hall clock? More probably the former.

The medieval buildings as they survive are, in the main, wrecked shells. Much of the pleasure and beauty of the buildings lay in their decoration and furnishing. The chapel had stained glass windows showing a Crucifixion, the Virgin and John the Baptist. Hearne says (he is writing of one of the cottages): 'and in the same windows here as in many other places about the College, several rebuses, mottoes, and allusions as also portraitures of saints, bishops, and monks, with inscriptions under them were (either by the childishness of students not long since inhabiting therein, or by the iniquity of envious times) for the most part blemished and obliterated.' The plate and chapel furniture were taken away in early 1539.

The present college has only one thing, stone and mortar apart, which belonged to Gloucester College. This is a manuscript: a collection of tracts directed against Lollardy, well written, and illuminated, taken away at the dissolution and generously restored by Merton College in 1938. It was given to Gloucester College by John Whethamstede, Abbot of St Alban's 1420–41 and 1465. Whethamstede was a conspicuous figure; learned, a kind of proto-humanist, the reformer of the finances of St Alban's; a great builder and organiser. He did much for Gloucester College, rebuilding the St Alban's house, and building the new chapel. The book is one of those he gave to the college library. It is mentioned (with a sister-volume, now in the British Library) in a very long list made at St Alban's of *Expensae Abbatis Johannis Whethamstede Notabiles*. It is in as good order as it was when his donatory verse was written in it.

Perhaps this manuscript, not strikingly beautiful, but decently elegant, and thoroughly well made from the best materials, tells one something about the ethos of Gloucester College. The abbots who were responsible for its building and furnishing were virtually to a man the sons of minor gentlemen or yeoman farmers; all had serious administrative experience, and knew how to get value for money; their nature and that of the institutions they served was such as to lead them to think of future generations and to prize durability. They did not seek great magnificence in their Oxford establishment; many had magnificence and to spare in their abbey buildings at home. Nor did they wish to provide luxurious accommodation for monk-students. They did seek a degree of solid comfort for men who were intended to live disciplined, but not sparse, lives at the university, and who, as monks of ancient and often rich abbeys, were men of some consequence. (The annual allowance of the Westminster monks at Gloucester College was £10 or £6.13s.4d a year – a man could be counted a gentleman in the fifteenth century on £5 a year.) And they wanted the college to be well and agreeably built and to be worthy of the great institutions which it served. The north front of the cottages is, in a sense, of a piece with the manuscript; so well built of very good Burford stone that it has never needed refacing, while nearly all the stone of the eighteenth-century buildings opposite has required renewal at great expense.

The cottages say something else about the spirit of the Benedictines. Their very nature is an expression of the particularism of the monasteries. This appears even in the roofline: one roof up a little, another down a little. Yet the range marries together extremely well. Gloucester College was an extraordinary architectural phenomenon in its combination of unity and diversity. Everywhere it revealed its composite nature; yet there was a real, if strange, pattern and order to it. As it stood in its last, its finest, days it revealed the ultimate good sense, and the very good taste, of the Black Monks.

5

From Cathedral Cloister to Gloucester College

JOAN GREATREX

INTRODUCTION[1]

The English Benedictine monk in the later Middle Ages was subject to several periods of study at different stages of his monastic life. Immediately after his admission and clothing in the monastic habit he began his initial training, what today is often described as his religious formation; this included a detailed exposition of the Rule which, along with the psalter and parts of the divine office, he was expected to learn by heart. After he had performed this feat of memory and had become familiar with the discipline and customs of the house, he was examined by a board of senior monks. Instruction in grammar, logic and philosophy occupied the young novice's attention during these first few years, and, for the select few, this served in part as preparation for more advanced studies at the university. These are the general outlines based on references drawn from the relevant manuscript sources of the cathedral priories whose plentiful records provide many an informative detail. Monks from two of these cathedral priories, Canterbury and Durham, were sent to their own respective colleges at Oxford and are discussed elsewhere in this volume; the monks of Ely Cathedral Priory were found only at the 'other place', mainly, no doubt, because of its proximity; monk students of the remaining six cathedral priories – those of Bath, Coventry,

Norwich, Rochester, Winchester and Worcester – will be the subject of this chapter.

In common with other major Benedictine establishments, these cathedral monasteries played a prominent role in supporting their common house of study, the foundation of which in the late thirteenth century has been described in another chapter. The Norwich and Worcester monks shouldered their responsibilities in sending both financial contributions and students from the earliest days and, even before the papal regulation of 1336 requiring one monk in every twenty to attend the university, they appear to have been maintaining and exceeding that quota.

SOME GENERAL STATISTICS

Counting medieval monastic, in contrast to secular or lay, heads is potentially more rewarding if one is content to accept the limitations. Numbers are recorded from time to time – of those present at an episcopal visitation, or receiving items of clothing or pittances – but the degree of accuracy is often undermined by other contradictory evidence. Hence, statistics are based on approximation, but are none the less sufficiently reliable to reveal general trends and fluctuations. The previously mentioned one-in-twenty ratio prompts an inquiry into the size of the cathedral communities under consideration. Three of them – Bath, Coventry and Rochester – were relatively small, despite the significance of their status as cathedral chapters: numbers at Bath and Coventry ranged between a high of thirty and a low of about twenty during the two and a half centuries before the dissolution of the monasteries. Rochester, only slightly larger, had about thirty-five monks before the Black Death (1349) and just over twenty in the early sixteenth century. Norwich Cathedral Priory, with its six dependent cells (or outlying priories), contained a total of about sixty-five monks in the mid-fourteenth century and probably over fifty in the opening years of the sixteenth. St Swithun's Winchester was also a large house before the Black Death, with sixty-four brethren in 1325; however, numbers slowly declined in later years to fluctuate between thirty-five and forty. In the early fourteenth century Worcester numbered just below fifty; two centuries later, in 1534, the total was forty-one.

As previously noted, Worcester monks were residing in Gloucester Hall as early as 1292/3; in that year both John de Arundel and William de Grymeley received about 20s. for their commons from the monk cellarer at Worcester, and to this would have been added contributions towards their expenses from some of the other monastic office holders or obedientiaries.[2] In this same year there were unnamed monk students from Norwich at Gloucester College who received at least 50s., according to obedientary contributions entered in surviving accounts, along with additional sums paid to the prior of the Oxford house: 40s. for the monk students' commons and 15s.3d. towards the completion of the building complex (*ad studium Oxon' erigend*). In 1295/6 one of these Norwich students was Geoffrey de Totyngton, and two years later Hervey de Swafham is first mentioned.

None of the Bath and Coventry records that might have proved informative for the early generations of monk students has survived; all we know is that the Black Monks' meeting at their triennial chapter in Northampton in 1343 listed Bath Cathedral Priory among the defaulters who had no students at Oxford. Before the middle of the fourteenth century and the drastic fall in the monastic population caused by the Black Death, we might expect to find at least one monk from each of Bath, Coventry and Rochester priories registered at Gloucester College, three from Norwich and Winchester and at least two from Worcester. In fact, on the few occasions when precise figures were recorded these estimates are close to the facts: Rochester had two monk students in the 1320s, although probably not simultaneously; Worcester had three in the 1330s and Norwich had four in 1336/7 and 1345/6. The earliest known monk student from Winchester was Philip de Lusteshall who was at Oxford in 1306; in the 1340s two deliveries of cheese were made by the reeve of the manor of Woolstone to the St Swithun's monk student(s) at Oxford, no doubt a welcome supplement to college fare, home produced on one of the priory estates.[3] However, the Black Monk Chapter in 1343 reprimanded the prior because none of his monks were currently students according to the college records.[4]

DEPARTURES AND ARRIVALS

Prolonged absence from the monastery in which the monk had made his vow of *stabilitas* was recognised as potentially harmful to his and to the community's well-being. The continuation of a monastic routine within Gloucester College, though adapted to a scholar's daily timetable, was intended to reduce this danger and to preserve the monk student from at least some of the unsettling influences that held sway among students and masters in the heady atmosphere of academic debate and the more general exuberance of youthful encounter and argument. Nevertheless, the university milieu tended to foster a spirit of individualism and a degree of independence that could prove disruptive of community life on the student's return to his monastery. With these problems in mind, how soon after a young monk's profession, which generally took place no more than a year after his admission, was it considered advisable for the chosen few to leave the cloister and embark on their university experience? The answer seems to lie, on average, between four and six years after profession, often before ordination to the priesthood and sometimes while still in subdeacon's orders. John de Ealding, who was one of two Rochester monks to receive licences for study at Oxford in October 1387, was not yet a deacon, an order which he received from the hands of Archbishop Thomas Arundel in London the following May. However, John Holyngbourne, another Rochester monk, who went up to Oxford in October 1382, was at the time only an acolyte and received the next two orders while a student from the Bishop of Winchester in his episcopal chapels at Highclere and Esher in February and May 1383. These arrangements with the Archbishop and Bishop William Wykeham were patently more convenient than a long journey back to Rochester. It is uncertain how long Ealding and Holyngbourne had been members of the cathedral community, possibly for slightly under four years. The general pattern seems to be similar at Winchester and Norwich as far as we can tell, although John Pynchebeke of St Swithun's may have been sent off to Oxford in 1476/7 with a bare two or three years of monastic life behind him. A few more variations have also been found at Worcester, possibly because of the fortunate survival of a large quantity of medieval records, most of them still *in situ.* Ralph Fylkes, for example, who was professed in 1393 went up to Oxford less than three years later; again, William Alston and William Barndesley were both ordained acolytes after their arrival in Oxford, at St Frideswide's Priory in September 1497. Since they both received deacons' orders the following March, at Oseney Abbey, they were presumably about nineteen years of age, but their first ordination is for both of them the earliest record of their inclusion as members of the Worcester chapter.[5]

The question of age arises here, as it must have played some part in the assessment of the prospective university candidates by the prior and his senior monk advisers. For admission to a Benedictine house the minimum age requirement was eighteen and for profession nineteen. The order of subdeacon, according to papal regulations, could not be conferred under the age of seventeen, while for the diaconate and priestly orders the applicant had to be at least nineteen and twenty-four years of age respectively. How frequently dispensations were given to relax these minimum age requirements is unknown, but there is sufficient evidence to make it plain that admission, profession and ordination sometimes occurred under these limits, although not generally more than a year or two below. With this proviso it is safe to presume that the average age of the monk students on arrival at Gloucester College would have ranged between seventeen and twenty-three.

For a Benedictine, university training and a university degree could never be seen as ends in themselves, although learning was encouraged and intellectual endeavour highly regarded. Impressive and wide-ranging collections of books were available to the monk in his own cloister and claustral lectures were regular features in the cathedral priories. Nevertheless, a period of residence in a monastic college at

Oxford brought the monk into direct contact with the centre of learning where the best minds of the day expounded and exchanged ideas. To be caught up in this stream of debate and to participate with other religious, notably the friars, provided him with a first-class theological education which he might later put to practical use.

SURVIVAL AND PROGRESS

By the time that the Black Monk Chapter ruled, *c.* 1363, that nothing less than £15 exclusive of travel allowances was sufficient to maintain one monk student for a year, there must have been a number of serious complaints on the part of students in debt and of monasteries with shrinking financial resources. In the 1330s, for example, the three Worcester students were surviving on 16d. each per week supplied by their cellarer, and fifty years later the amount had risen only to £6 a year. There were additional contributions by other monk officials: money for clothing from the chamberlain, for lighting in the form of wax candles from the sacrist and for travel from the precentor; but these sums would not have added up to much more than half of the £15 minimum. Money for the cost of purchasing stationery supplies and books is rarely mentioned, apart from an occasional gift from a prior. Thomas Hosyntre had run up a debt of 23s.4d. to the butler of Gloucester College and owed sums to two Oxford tradesmen in 1444/5, the year he died; it took the cellarer nine years to pay off all the debts accumulated by Hosyntre and two other contemporary monk students.

The plight of Norwich monks at Oxford is depressingly similar but little is known of their consequent individual financial difficulties. All the Norwich obedientiaries made regular contributions of varying amounts to make up the total pension provided for each university monk; as at Worcester this seems to have come to little more than half the prescribed sum.

The length of a monk's stay at Gloucester College was determined by his monastic superiors who assessed his progress and decided on a course of study that served the best interests of the house. The acquiring of skills in the art of preaching well grounded in a knowledge of Scripture and theology was one of the chief priorities, and the Black Monk Chapters stressed that preachers were to be competent both in Latin and the vernacular. Monks who were members of cathedral chapters were especially liable for public preaching to large congregations on important festivals and for diocesan gatherings of secular clergy and layfolk. On such occasions it was considered important for the Benedictines to demonstrate their expertise in their own pulpits and thus replace and challenge the mendicant orders in this public arena. At the university the monk students were instructed in the approved form of sermon construction with its elaborate arrangement of texts, exegesis and *exempla.* They were also recalled to preach on their home ground on major holy days and feasts when an opportunity for evaluating their progress would enable their superiors to decide on the future course and duration of their studies. Thus in 1405 John Wodeward returned to Worcester to give the Christmas Eve sermon in the cathedral and he rode back again to preach on Good Friday 1406. Another Worcester monk, John Lawerne, was summoned from Oxford to give the sermon on the eve of the Assumption in 1437, and the precentor was charged with his travelling expenses of 8s.7d. However, when Adam Easton, the noted Norwich monk-scholar and preacher, was ordered home in the 1350s in the middle of his university studies in order to preach 'true doctrine and confound the friars', he may have remained in Norwich for up to five or six years before being allowed to return to Oxford to complete his doctorate.[6]

RESIDENCE, STUDIES AND GRADUATION

The proportion of monk students who were permitted to reside long enough to take a first degree was, not surprisingly, small; in the case of Norwich there were only twenty-nine out of a total of eighty-one monks who are known to have spent time at university;[7] a few more stayed long enough to graduate but there is no evidence that they did so. Of the sixty to sixty-five Worcester monks who attended university, twenty obtained degrees. For both priories this amounts to about one-third. For the other cathedral priories under consideration here much less information has been preserved. Only six monks of Bath are known by name to have been students and three of them were probably resident at Canterbury College rather than Gloucester College. The names of only seven Coventry monk students have been recorded, but a statement issued in 1426 by the Black Monk Chapter stated that the priory usually sent one of their number to Oxford; on the basis of this report many Coventry names have been lost. Two are known to have had rooms at Canterbury College and another went from Oxford to lecture on Hebrew at Louvain in 1520. There were also Rochester and Winchester chambers at Canterbury College in the fifteenth and sixteenth centuries; Thomas Wybarn, one of the twelve Rochester monks known to have studied at Oxford, may have occupied the former in the 1460s, and three out of the thirty Winchester monk students made use of the latter. There seems to be no obvious reason for some cathedral priors on occasion to prefer to hire rooms for their monks in Canterbury College unless Gloucester College was short of space. But as the latter was probably capable of accommodating about a hundred, this seems unlikely. Two fifteenth-century leases that have been preserved in a Worcester cathedral register describe in detail the size and location of the chambers within Gloucester College allocated for the use of the Worcester students; they lay between the Tewkesbury and Winchcombe chambers and contained several good-sized rooms on two levels.

It had been laid down by statute that the two fields of study open to Benedictines at Oxford were theology and canon law. Most monks chose the former or, more probably, had it chosen for them; in fact, no Worcester or Coventry monks are on record as having become canonists. By custom gradually acquired and later conceded by statute, the monks were exempted from the initial arts programme which was the normal prerequisite for theological studies. This privilege was based on the assumption that when the monk student

arrived at the university he had been sufficiently well
grounded, during his years of preparatory study within the
cloister, in grammar, logic, and philosophy. However, since
some of the monks came from small houses with limited
resources and there were inevitable variations in the standard of competence among the instructors provided, it is
not surprising that for some monks at least a certain amount
of supplementary tutoring was required. This may partially
explain why even a first degree in theology might take as
long as six to ten years. It is a rare occurrence to come across
the exact date of commencement of a particular monk's
university career, and, unless he completed a degree that can
be traced in surviving records, there can be no certainty
about the length of the period of study he was allowed by his
superiors. John de Ealding is one of the exceptions; he was
at Oxford for a total of fifteen years between 1387 and 1402
and had obtained a bachelor's degree sometime before the
latter date, when he was recalled to Rochester to take
the office of precentor, which would have included responsibility for the library.[8] Hervey de Swafham, the earliest known
Norwich monk to have taken a degree, was at Oxford, probably residing at Gloucester College, by 1297/8 and remained
almost continuously until 1320, although he had incepted as
doctor in theology in 1314, a total of some sixteen years
for both degrees. The length of time required between the
bachelor's degree and inception as doctor also varied for
reasons that remain unclear. Ralph de Basyng probably went
up to Oxford from Winchester in 1361, the year of his ordination as subdeacon, and he obtained his doctorate in
canon law after thirteen years of study; he must have known
the Norwich monk, Thomas Brinton, another canonist (and
later Bishop of Rochester) who completed his doctorate in
1364. Theological studies were reputedly somewhat more
demanding, as Swafham's lengthy sojourn at Gloucester
College suggests; but the academic career of Thomas
Ledbury, a Worcester monk, was stretched over a period of
some eighteen years, from 1405/6 to 1423/4 and possibly
even a year or two more. In his case, however, we must allow
for an interruption of uncertain length when he
accompanied his prior, John Fordham, to the Council of

Constance. Despite the scarcity of evidence, it is probable that some monks pursued their studies on a part-time basis, with residence limited to less than full term, though there were at least a few who obtained permission to remain to study throughout the vacation.

Where the university registers survive, more precise details are available in the record of the supplications presented and graces granted. John Avynton of St Swithun's stated that he had studied logic, philosophy and theology for thirteen years, for which he was admitted to the status of bachelor in 1514, and within only five years he was allowed to proceed to inception. Richard Petersfeld, also a Winchester monk, made a similar supplication for a first degree after a mere eight years and was admitted in 1522, and Humphrey Webley of Worcester was granted his B.Th. in 1529, after nine years. However, Richard Barnacle of Coventry, who tried to get away with only six years behind him when he supplicated to oppose in theology, was kept waiting for another three years, during which time he presumably continued his studies in order to fulfil the requirements.

On admission to oppose, the bachelor was expected to deliver a series of lectures in the form of a commentary on the *Sentences* of Peter Lombard, a twelfth-century theologian whose work was the standard textbook in the medieval universities. Among the few cathedral priory references to this stage in the monk's progress there is one in the form of a letter from the Norwich prior to John de Mari at Oxford written *c.* 1321 concerning de Mari's request for permission to commence lecturing; the other is in the notebook of a Worcester monk who began his lectures in October 1445, after thirteen years of university study, but, surprisingly, only three years before he was admitted to the doctorate.

The heavy financial burden that had to be carried by the monk student's monastery at the time of his inception sometimes discouraged or, at least, delayed the completion of a second degree. There is one instance of a clever young Worcester monk, John Dudley, who, being reluctant to ask his prior's permission to incept because of the expense it entailed, turned to Thomas of Woodstock, the Duke of Gloucester, for advice. The Duke and his wife both wrote letters of recommendation to the prior on Dudley's behalf, but there is no indication that their words were supported by a tangible donation. It was the Black Monk Chapter which provided the necessary funds for his inception in 1392/3, to add to what the Worcester chapter was able to raise. The amount given was not stated but was probably £20, in accordance with a statute of the Black Monk Chapter published in 1343.

COLLEGE OFFICIALS

The *prior studentium* was the equivalent of the Warden of Canterbury and Durham Colleges. His appointment lay with the presidents of the Black Monk Chapter to whom he was held responsible, and he was normally chosen from among the members of the college, often before or just after they had obtained their doctorates. Five monk students from three of the cathedral priories which concern us here are known by name, among whom were Adam Easton of Norwich (*c.* 1366), William Wroughton, a Winchester monk (1446), and three monks of Worcester, John Fordham (1401–7), Thomas Ledbury (1417–23) and Humphrey Webley (in 1531/2). The Black Monk Chapter also maintained a regent doctor of theology, a member of their order who was normally located at Gloucester College and was frequently chosen to serve in this capacity for the year following his inception. Hervey de Swafham, the Norwich monk mentioned above, is the earliest known; he stayed on at the college as regent master from *c.* 1314 to *c.* 1316. John de Mari, another Norwich monk, did the same in the 1340s and was probably followed by another Norwich monk, John de Stukle, who was himself the author of a commentary on the *Sentences.* Although others are not named, it is probable that many, if not most, of the monk students who, like John Dudley and John Fordham of Worcester, stayed on after their inception, had been appointed to this post.

The Witness of Student Notebooks

The preceding paragraphs are ample proof of the difficulties that confront any attempt to give an accurate description of the typical monk's progress through his university course. There is, unfortunately, no evidence in the form of a monastic diary, but there are a few extant notebooks and some correspondence which shed a little light on the monks' activities.[9] Among the notebooks, four that belonged to Worcester monk students are still in their original home in the cathedral library, where they continue to be of great interest to scholars. The earliest includes treatises on logic and works of Aristotle annotated by John de Aston who was at Oxford in the 1290s; two others are early fourteenth-century lecture notes, reports and sermons written and copied at Oxford, and the fourth is a fifteenth-century manuscript containing notes on logic in the hand of John Broghton who died in 1448 before completing his degree. In that same year John Lawerne, another Worcester monk, recorded his inception in his personal notebook, in which is found a miscellaneous compilation of theological lectures, disputations, sermons and letters; some of the correspondence concerns Gloucester College and university affairs, but there are many personal letters addressed to his brethren in Worcester expressing warmth and friendship.

Not only did Lawerne and other monk students take volumes from the monastic library with them to Gloucester College,[10] they also purchased books in Oxford, which eventually found their place in the claustral library to the benefit of the whole community at home. Here again we must resort to evidence from Worcester, whose monks tended to insert explicit entries on the fly-leaves. John de Preston, for example, put his *procuravit* and the date, 1348, in two volumes, and John Grene in one volume of a four-volume biblical commentary, noting that he obtained them in 1386 '*ad communem utilitatem claustralium*'.

CONCLUSION

The only surviving list of monks registered at Gloucester College is dated 1537 and records a mere thirty names, none of whom were from the cathedral priories.[11] By the late fifteenth century most of the Norwich monks were making the much easier journey to Cambridge, although two were studying at Oxford in the late 1520s and early 1530s. A complaint emanating from a disgruntled and possibly envious monk of this house against the two younger brethren at Oxford amounted to nothing more than a drawing of attention to man's fallen nature, his own included. Moreover, by accusing them of causing dissension within the community by their snobbish behaviour he was exposing his own intolerance and lack of charity.[12] Coventry was supporting as many as four students at Oxford, which it could probably ill afford, and three Worcester monks were at the college during 1531/2, one of them in the position of *prior studentium*; the two Winchester monks who were then at Canterbury College would have been under his jurisdiction.

The remarkable continuity of the medieval Benedictine commitment to university studies through two and a half centuries is significant. It was brought to an abrupt end by two acts of Parliament which dissolved all the religious houses, and, in so doing, drastically reduced the universities' theological faculties and their students. It is surely an irony of history that in the 1530s there appears to have been a noticeable increase in the number of those seeking admission to the monastic life and a corresponding increase in the number of monk students at Oxford and Cambridge. The significance, however, bears no relation to the impact of the enduring Benedictine presence at Oxford, for that was slight in terms of visible intellectual achievement. It is the influence of Oxford on the Benedictine order which, though outwardly imperceptible, was profoundly felt in the cloister through the transmission of the learning acquired by the university-educated monks to their brethren in teaching and in the general exchange of new ideas and insights. In the sharing of the fruits of the intellect the fruits of the spirit were also nourished.

6

The Black Monks of Durham and Canterbury Colleges: Comparisons and Contrasts

R. BARRIE DOBSON

Within the long and complex history of the University of Oxford, an educational institution which has undergone innumerable minor but very few major misfortunes, the abrupt and unexpected suppression of its ten medieval religious houses at the hands of Henry VIII and Thomas Cromwell must now seem the greatest misfortune of them all. It is therefore all the more surprising that the educational, religious and architectural disasters which laid waste so much of Oxford during the late 1530s have still received comparatively little attention, even from the most critical historians of the English Reformation. Obviously enough, the Anglican clergy who came to dominate Oxford university and collegiate life from the sixteenth to the nineteenth centuries had a vested interest in ignoring or denigrating the activities of their monastic or mendicant predecessors. But even in more recent times the task of defending Oxford's monastic colleges from the well-known indictment that they 'possess very little importance in the history either of learning or of education' can hardly be said to be complete.[1] For there is perhaps yet another explanation for posterity's failure to appreciate quite how 'important' these medieval monastic colleges and friaries actually were: it has been, for several centuries, more or less impossible to find them. On the very eve of the Reformation itself, the physical appearance of Oxford – and especially of its northern and western environs – was dominated by religious houses whose remains are now rarely apparent except to the most persistent of local historians or archaeologists.[2] Of the once major abbeys of Oseney and Rewley, of Oxford's four once-celebrated mendicant convents and of its fifteenth-century collegiate foundations for Cistercian monks and Augustinian canons (St Mary's), the modern visitor is usually left completely unaware. Only perhaps by contemplating the Benedictine *studia* which now constitute the south range of the main quad of Worcester (once Gloucester) College, or by worshipping within Oxford cathedral (once the monastic church of the Augustinian priory of St Frideswide), it is still possible to gain a visual impression of how considerable and diverse the monastic contribution to medieval Oxford undoubtedly was.[3]

The historian of the two small but not at all insignificant medieval Benedictine collegiate establishments which form the subject of this chapter, Canterbury College and Durham College, is much less fortunate. A few years after its surrender to the Crown on 10 April 1540, Canterbury College and its adjacent properties were absorbed into Henry VIII's new foundation of the Cathedral Church of Christ; but of the buildings of that college, demolished in the 1770s to make way for James Wyatt's small but monumental Canterbury Quad in the north-eastern angle of Christ Church, there are now no existing remains at all (see plates 4 and 6).[4] Nor has the medieval fabric of Durham College, which formed the original nucleus of Trinity College when the latter was founded by Sir Thomas Pope in 1555, been much more successful in surviving the ravages of time. The Durham university monks' greatest architectural memorials, their Hall and Chapel, were both completely destroyed, at the beginning and close of the seventeenth century respectively, to be replaced by new structures erected in accordance with later architectural taste. Only the east range of Trinity College's much altered Durham Quad, first built by the monks of St Cuthbert *c.* 1417–21 to house their library, preserves something of the atmosphere of the original Durham College.[5]

Those who wish to recapture the rhythms of academic and religious life among the Black Monks of Canterbury and Durham Colleges in medieval Oxford must accordingly rely not on architectural but on documentary evidence. In that respect, however, they are able to count upon some very considerable blessings indeed. Precisely because these two Benedictine colleges were cells or dependencies of their great mother houses at Christ Church, Canterbury, and Durham respectively, the foundation, title and other deeds relating to their endowments were zealously preserved in the archives of those two cathedrals. More valuable still are the long series of college accounts which were once regularly dispatched to Canterbury and Durham, where many of them still survive, by the wardens of their two academic daughter houses. The Canterbury College account rolls and inventories, together with copies of some of the once extensive correspondence which regularly passed between the priors of the cathedral and the wardens of their Oxford cell, have now been published in more or less complete form by the late Mr W. A. Pantin. By contrast, and despite a preliminary survey of these sources by the late Revd H. E. D. Blakiston a century ago, the Durham College records at Durham still urgently await a similarly full-scale edition.[6]

Thanks to the survival of so many of their original sources, the two small Benedictine *studia* of Canterbury and Durham Colleges may well be the best documented monastic educational establishments of medieval Christendom. Such a comparative wealth of documentation, remarkable though it is, does not of course make it possible to appreciate all or indeed most of the problems faced by the Black Monks at the two colleges during the later Middle Ages. In the first place, as readers of college accounts in any age are well aware, such records tend to place most emphasis on financial issues – most obviously, the sources of income needed to sustain the academic community – which tend to interest the religious or educational historian least. More unfortunately still, the documents relating to both Canterbury and Durham Colleges tend to be much more voluminous and informative after rather than before the late fourteenth century, precisely when both establishments at last overcame the long and sometimes intense crises and uncertainties of their early years. Throughout many of the decades between the 1280s and 1380s it is by no means easy to assess whether the two cathedral communities of Canterbury and Durham ever seriously expected to be able to maintain a formal college at Oxford in perpetuity. If the early history of these two Benedictine communities has any one general moral to impart, it must undoubtedly be that it could be extremely difficult to establish an Oxford academic college – especially perhaps a monastic college – on a secure constitutional and financial basis. The foundation and (even more) the survival of Canterbury and Durham Colleges proved a triumph of persistence and resilience on the part of their mother houses, supported by a few of their archbishops and bishops, against some very formidable odds indeed.

Not that there could ever have been much doubt that if any two religious houses in medieval England possessed the resources and influence to create and sustain their own academic colleges, those two monasteries were likely to be the cathedral priories of Christ Church, Canterbury, and of Durham. In the first place, it seems absolutely clear that throughout the fourteenth and fifteenth centuries (and probably in the late thirteenth century too) the Black Monk communities of Canterbury and Durham cathedrals were much the largest monasteries in the English kingdom. Each of these two monastic colossi were able to sustain a complement of approximately seventy to eighty monks when they began to contemplate sending some of their more talented younger brethren to study at a university in the late thirteenth century. Nor was recruitment to their ranks seriously affected by the onslaught of plague from 1348 onwards. Between 1400 and the 1520s the Christ Church community usually oscillated at around eighty monks: during the same period the numbers at Durham cathedral similarly remained remarkably stable at about seventy, of whom however twenty or more were at any one time obliged to serve its nine daughter houses.[7] Needless to say, Canterbury and Durham Cathedral Priories (with gross annual incomes of £2900 and £1600 respectively according to the *Valor Ecclesiasticus* of 1536) were among the twelve or so wealthiest corporations in late medieval England. Of even more significance to the Benedictine communities of St Thomas Becket and St Cuthbert was their position as the custodians of the shrines of the greatest thaumaturges, the most illustrious English saints, that late medieval England had to offer.

As the most visited as well as the most prestigious Black Monk monasteries in the country, the religious communities of Christ Church, Canterbury, and of Durham could therefore hardly fail to react – sooner or later – to the new educational opportunities and challenges presented by the University of Oxford, as that still largely informal federation of masters and scholars expanded at a bewildering rate during the course of the thirteenth century. Above all, the monks of Canterbury and Durham cathedrals became gradually aware that they had to find a means of establishing some form of distinctive institutional base at Oxford without compromising what they saw as their inalienable immunities and prestige. In other words, as they made extremely clear, they had to discover a way of avoiding co-operation with the common higher educational initiatives of the General Chapters. Those initiatives led, remarkably rapidly, to the foundation in 1283 of the English Benedictines' joint *studium* at Oxford, that curiously hybrid federal institution which was soon to be known, however inaccurately, as Gloucester College.[8] Somewhat ironically, Durham and Canterbury Colleges were therefore created, and deliberately created, to emancipate the monks of St Thomas Becket and of St Cuthbert from the need to join forces with their fellow English Black Monks. As Prior John Wessington of Durham (1416–46) made quite explicit over a century later in his so-called *Responsiones Contra Priorem Studentium* of 1422, neither he nor his predecessors ever conceded for a moment that the co-operative Benedictine *studium* on Stockwell Street might possess any academic, let alone jurisdictional authority over their own Oxford daughter house. In the case of the Benedictine monks of Canterbury cathedral, their independent stance on this issue is clearer still. It was only after 1379, when the monks there had at last obtained complete legal immunity from intervention by the chapters, that they felt confident enough to inaugurate a fully articulated

Oxford college constitutionally responsible only to themselves and to their archbishops.[9]

Not of course that all the most academically qualified Benedictine monks of Canterbury and Durham cathedrals had to wait until the formal creation of their Oxford colleges to experience the pleasures and benefits of university education. As the internal administrative records of the largest English Benedictine houses, even those of Canterbury and Durham, rarely survive in quantity before the 1270s and 1280s, the exact extent of monastic participation in the formative years of Oxford University will always remain highly mysterious. However, it is likely to have been much more considerable than most historians, understandably impressed by the achievements of the early mendicant orders at Paris and Oxford, have usually assumed. Thus, according to Matthew Paris, John de Cella, Abbot of St Alban's Abbey as early as 1195 (he died in 1214), was a highly trained Master of the University of Paris. The distinction of being the first recorded Benedictine master at Oxford must probably go to his contemporary, Thomas de Marleberge, who arrived at Evesham soon after 1190 with an extensive collection of books 'covering all departments of higher learning in addition to civil and canon law'.[10] It was in fact by no means difficult for individual Benedictine monks to find satisfactory accommodation in thirteenth-century universities; and it seems evident, for example, that some priors of Christ Church, Canterbury, like the formidable Henry Eastry (1286–1331), usually preferred to send their most talented young monks to study at Paris rather than at Oxford. Members of the Benedictine fraternity at Christ Church are recorded to have been studying at Paris in 1288 and 1304–6 and then again in 1307–9.[11] Partly because of the ready accessibility of this alternative university and partly because of the Canterbury Chapter's determination not to jeopardise its claims to complete independence from the English Black Monk Chapters, there is no clear evidence that Christ Church scholar monks took up residence in Oxford itself until as late as 1331.[12]

The Prior and Chapter of St Cuthbert at Durham, without much doubt always the most energetic advocates of university education for Black Monks in medieval England, felt under no obligation to wait for anything like so long to establish their own academic colony at Oxford. Small groups of monk-scholars from Durham had indeed already found their way to the university by at least 1278, five years before the foundation of the joint Benedictine *studium* on Stockwell Street. However, according to the chronicle written more than a generation later by Robert de Graystanes, himself a Durham university monk of the 1320s, the decision to send 'monks to study at Oxford' on a regular basis was the by-product of a bitter personal feud between two senior Durham monks, Hugh de Darlington and Richard de Claxton. When the former was elected Prior of Durham for the second time in January 1286, he exiled the sub-prior, Richard Hoton, to the convent's cell at Lytham in Lancashire and began sending some of his convent's junior monks to the university, presumably in an attempt to persuade Hoton's partisans of his own benevolence. But when Hoton, in his turn, succeeded Darlington as prior in March 1290, he decided to go one better and proceeded to found and build a Durham study centre at Oxford ('*locum Oxoniae comparavit et aedificare fecit*').[13] Graystanes' account of the foundation of Durham's cell in Oxford is undoubtedly too brief and probably too tendentious to carry complete conviction. As early as 1286 the prior and chapter had already secured from the Abbess of Godstow a suitable site for what was to be their new 'manse', namely some five acres of arable land 250 feet north of Canditch or Broad Street. Quite how, when and where Prior Hoton and his brethren secured the financial resources to acquire and then build upon this site still remain very obscure questions indeed. Nevertheless much of this admittedly small Durham *mansio* north of the city walls of Oxford must have been constructed at great speed. One of the accusations subsequently brought against the unpopular Geoffrey de Burdon, an early resident of the Oxford cell (and later a Prior of Durham between 1313 and 1321), was that he had admitted a woman to the common dormitory there. A more gratifying testimony to the early academic success of Durham's new daughter house at Oxford occurred in 1311 when Geoffrey de Haxby became the first Durham monk ever to incept in theology. As Bishop Richard Kellaw was quick to point out on hearing this welcome news, 'it has hitherto been unknown for any member of the church of Durham to become sufficiently proficient in Holy Scripture to deserve the degree of Doctor of Divinity.'[14]

Although the cathedral priories of Durham and, much later, Canterbury were the only religious houses in medieval England ever able to finance residential university colleges under their own direct and more or less exclusive control, such an arrangement had the obvious merit of providing the monk-scholars in question with the best possible prospect of reconciling the sometimes contradictory claims of their religious and their academic lives. The attractions of founding a daughter house at a university had indeed not been lost on several of the great French Benedictine houses of the thirteenth century. As early as 1247, Abbot John of Saint Benoît-sur-Loire (Fleury) had begun to contemplate providing his community with a permanent residential base at Paris; and by 1258 this first of all regular Benedictine *studia* in a northern European university was firmly established. Within a few years monks from the abbeys of Cluny (Collège de Cluny), Saint-Denis (Collège de Saint-Denis) and Marmoutier (Collège de St Martin) were occupying similar academic establishments at the University of Paris.[15] Even for such celebrated French monasteries, however, the financial burdens entailed in maintaining their university colleges placed a very considerable strain on their resources. It is therefore hardly surprising that for many decades the Durham cell at Oxford remained small and comparatively impoverished, apparently dependent for its very survival on large financial contributions from the obedientiaries of Durham Cathedral Priory itself. Admittedly, the transitory groups of Durham university monks who studied at Oxford in the fourteenth century were not devoid of genuine academic distinction. As early as 1333, the community of St Cuthbert included three doctors and one bachelor of theology among its members. More impressive if less anticipated was the emergence of one Durham monk, the celebrated Uthred of Boldon, as the most gifted Benedictine theologian of late fourteenth-century Oxford. For twenty years (1347–67) Uthred was more or less permanently resident at Oxford as a practising teacher and controversialist; 'never was there a monk of Durham College more learned than he.'[16] Although Uthred of Boldon founded no distinctive school of theology either at Oxford or in his mother house at Durham, his own intellectual fame probably helped to persuade the elderly Bishop Thomas Hatfield of Durham to take the critical step of converting his monks' little manse at Oxford into a properly endowed and constituted college. Appropriately enough, Uthred's own last recorded visits to Oxford and to London were devoted to the promotion of this new Durham College, formally created by a quinquepartite covenant or 'ordinance' of 1 March 1381.[17]

Only three years later, in January 1384, Archbishop William Courtenay finally produced the lengthy statutes which provided Canterbury College too with all the appurtenances of collegiate status. For a variety of reasons, the struggle of the fourteenth-century priors and chapter of Christ Church to achieve this triumphant outcome to a long and strenuous campaign had proved to be much more contentious and controversial than had been the case at Durham. Although a small group of Canterbury scholar monks first began to occupy a hall near the church of St Peter in the east during the early 1330s, this promising start was succeeded by a period of great unease at Christ Church itself about both the cost of university education and the availability of suitable accommodation in Oxford. While still fighting their ultimately successful *cause célèbre* for independence from the authority of the Black Monk Chapters, the Canterbury community soon became even more apprehensive about the unpredictable and often wayward responses of their archbishops to their plans to found a duly constituted monastic college at Oxford. By 1361 Archbishop Simon Islip's ambitious if curiously muddled plan to create a mixed Oxford establishment of twelve monks and secular clerks, to be known as Canterbury Hall, finally seemed to offer them the opportunity of a permanent *studium* at the university. However, a few months before his death in April 1366, Islip suddenly decided to eject all the Christ Church monk-fellows from his new foundation; and he then appointed Master John Wycliffe as warden of what was now to be an exclusively secular college. Paradoxically enough, the most illustrious of all superiors of Canterbury Hall or College was before long to become the most formidable of all late medieval critics of Benedictine monasticism.[18]

Fortunately for the Prior and Chapter of Canterbury, if not for Wycliffe, their next archbishop was Simon Langham (1366–68). Langham, as a *quondam* Westminster Abbey monk-scholar himself, was eager to restore his predecessor's Oxford college to its original mixed status. After yet further delays, and a protracted and closely contested lawsuit at the Curia, it was finally determined by a papal sentence of July 1369 that the monks of Christ Church were to enjoy sole use of Canterbury College thereafter. Although a small group of Christ Church monks began to settle in the college two years later, it was only after Thomas Chillenden, later prior of the cathedral (1391–1411), went to Rome in 1378–9 to procure papal confirmation of the appropriation of the Sussex church of Pagham to this new monastic college that its financial survival was properly assured.[19] Once Archbishop Courtenay's detailed statutes for Canterbury College had been promulgated five years later, the legal position of Christ Church's daughter house at Oxford was at last impregnable.

As in the case of Durham College earlier in the decade, the elevation of a small and irregular colony of monk-scholars to formal collegiate status was not without its ironies. Had it not been for the support of their titular abbots, the archbishops of Canterbury and the bishops of Durham, the communities of St Thomas Becket and of St Cuthbert would never have been able to establish proper monastic colleges in Oxford at all; but when those foundations had at last been achieved it was the cathedral chapters and not their prelates which took effective control of their educational and religious destinies.

From the 1380s onwards, as never before, the young Christ Church and Durham monks selected for study at Oxford could therefore be gradually assured of a reasonable degree of financial and institutional stability within their respective colleges. Admittedly, few medieval university foundations can have experienced a more testing and litigious infancy than Durham College. Although Bishop Hatfield's initial legacy of £3000 to his refounded college of 1381 was handsomely large, uncertainties about its most sensible investment as well as grave economic problems at the mother house itself soon forced the Durham monks into serious debt. In 1404, when the financial condition of Durham College was still extremely feeble, the chancellor and masters of the University of Oxford took the very unusual step of prosecuting the Prior of Durham in the church courts for his alleged failure to maintain the statutory number of eight monks and eight secular students at the college. However, once this highly humiliating crisis had been averted, the financial position of Durham College rapidly improved. In the long term the decision to utilise Bishop Hatfield's munificent legacy to buy the appropriations of four churches (Bossall, Ruddington, Fishlake and Frampton; to which Brantingham in Yorkshire was added in 1458) proved a highly satisfactory means of guaranteeing the future financial security of the college. By the 1430s it was receiving a fairly stable net annual revenue of some £175 from these four churches; and the net income was still valued at £115 at the time of the dissolution.[20] By contrast, the economic state of Canterbury College was a cause for more continuous concern. Its principal endowment, the appropriated rectory of Pagham, usually produced over £50 a year in the mid-fifteenth century; but this was a slender financial base from which to support the activities of an entire college. Small wonder perhaps that after a short period in the 1380s and 1390s when there were as many as seven Canterbury monk fellows at Oxford, for much of the fifteenth century the college's accounts rarely record more than three or four Christ Church monks resident in Canterbury College. For obvious reasons, and like their counterparts at Durham College, the Canterbury university monks were always eager to supplement their college's income by hiring rooms to paying lodgers, several of whom were monks from other Benedictine houses. Even more welcome were occasional benefactions, none more so than that of Archbishop Morton who in his will of 1500 created two additional monk fellowships at Canterbury College by a bequest of £6.13s.4d. to each of these for a period of twenty years.[21]

Neither Canterbury nor Durham College was therefore ever particularly well endowed. Despite the prevailing atmosphere of frugality within these small academic communities, a frugality which equally applied to the great majority of fifteenth-century Oxford and Cambridge colleges, the university monks of Canterbury and Durham were, however, surprisingly well provided with handsome and comparatively spacious collegiate buildings. In both colleges the half-century or so after their elevation to full collegiate status in the early 1380s witnessed an impressive series of building campaigns. At Canterbury College the task of transforming a heterogeneous collection of tenements and houses into a regular quadrangle was in fact already under way by the 1370s, the decade during which the hall and at least two *camerae* were also being constructed. By the early years of the fifteenth century the college chapel, gateway and most of the living accommodation was complete. Even before the north range of the quadrangle had been built by 1440, the college could house not only its own three or four monk-scholars and the five poor secular students on the foundation but also a wide variety of paying lodgers. As has been seen, the latter included a number of Benedictine university monks who preferred to reside there rather than at Gloucester College. Thus student monks from Rochester and Winchester Cathedral Priories lent the names of their mother houses to the 'Rochester Chamber' and 'Winchester Chamber' within Canterbury College; and Black Monks from Reading, Evesham, Bath, Coventry and Peterborough also hired rooms there at not infrequent intervals.[22]

A not dissimilar situation prevailed at Durham College, although there it was naturally university monks from Benedictine houses in the northern province, notably from the abbeys of Selby and St Mary's, York, who tended to look for accommodation in the company of St Cuthbert's monks. To judge from its surviving inventories and accounts, Durham College was considerably more spacious and well-appointed (it certainly had a much larger garden) than its Canterbury counterpart. Between 1405 and 1425 the Durham monks replaced the buildings of their previous Oxford *mansio* with a completely new and highly impressive collegiate complex. By 1407, the chapel (measuring sixty by twenty-six feet) had been constructed at a cost of over £135; and within the next few years the '*novum opus Oxonie*' or college quadrangle had been erected to the north of that chapel. This quadrangle, still clearly visible in Loggan's engraving of Trinity College in 1675 (see plate 1), incorporated the hall and more than sufficient residential accommodation for Durham College's full complement of eight monk fellows and eight secular students in grammar and theology. Its eastern range included a custom-built college library, constructed in 1417–18 at a cost of about £42 and adorned with panels of armorial stained glass.[23] By 1449 the monks of Canterbury College had also started to build what they called their 'new library'; and even before that date it is clear from surviving catalogues and book lists that the libraries of both colleges could stand comparison with all but the very oldest book-collections in medieval Oxford.[24]

Even more significant for the religious welfare of many Canterbury and Durham monk-scholars were the warden's apartments within the two daughter houses. Naturally enough, these were not only more lavishly appointed than any other *camerae* in the college but they also tended to serve as its central administrative office and 'as a kind of treasury'.[25] Although assisted by two monk bursars at Durham College (an office much less prominent at Canterbury College), the warden had in effect sole responsibility for the economic welfare of his daughter house. Directly accountable to his prior at Christ Church or Durham, he inevitably spent many weeks of the year travelling across the country to supervise his college's various sources of income. Nor can it have been at all easy, as many letters to and from their cathedral priors make clear, for the warden to protect his brethren and young secular students from the many non-academic distractions which Oxford had to offer. Even less well disciplined were many of the college's servants, of whom there were ten at Durham College in the 1530s. Potentially most troublesome of all the inmates of the two colleges were the lodgers living within their precincts, even when the latter were Benedictine monks themselves. In the 1480s one Warden of Canterbury College was particularly incensed because a group of his sojourners, from Peterborough Abbey, were not 'gydid as scolerys schuld be, for they be noo studentys'.[26]

In such circumstances it is not hard to appreciate why the priors and chapters of Canterbury and Durham took considerable pains to appoint as wardens of their respective colleges monks of considerable administrative experience as well as academic seniority. Yet another reason for promoting trustworthy university monks as college wardens was that they were *ex officio* expected to hold a position of considerable influence and prestige in the university at large. Thus Dr John Langdon, Warden of Canterbury College for twelve or so years after 1410, was a member of a committee appointed to investigate the survival of Wycliffite heresy in Oxford: he also served as the commissary of the Chancellor of the university. When Warden John Burnby held the same university office thirty years later (in 1447–50), the Chancellor's court usually met within the precincts of Durham College.[27] From the time that the relevant records begin to survive in the late fifteenth century the Benedictine Wardens of Canterbury and Durham Colleges also figure prominently in university processions and as university preachers. They continued to play a leading role in Oxford university administration until the very eve of the dissolution. Doctor Hugh Whitehede, the last Prior (1520–40) and first Dean (1541–50) of Durham cathedral, had been a Chancellor's Commissary in 1514; and the second last Warden of Canterbury College, Richard Thornden, served as pro-Vice Chancellor at Oxford a decade before he became the first Bishop of Dover in 1545.[28]

Like experienced heads of houses at all stages of the university's existence, the Benedictine Wardens of Canterbury and Durham Colleges were therefore more integral to the administrative processes of late medieval Oxford than has usually been assumed. On the other hand, as the talents of these wardens were equally in demand within their mother houses, they were never allowed to entrench themselves permanently in their colleges. All late medieval Canterbury and Durham College wardens had already spent several years at their colleges while young student monks in their twenties; but they only tended to return there, after a long interval at home in their cathedral priories, when they were in their early forties. Thereafter their terms of office as wardens at Oxford were rarely allowed to exceed five or six years before they were called back to senior administrative positions in their mother houses. Of the sixteen Wardens of Durham College between 1450 and 1540, only the last (Edward Hyndmarsh, 1525–41) held office for more than a decade. During the same ninety years, when there were similarly sixteen successive Wardens of Canterbury College, Richard Thornden was the only one to remain in office for as long as ten years.[29] For most ex-Wardens of Canterbury and Durham Colleges, a highly active and distinguished monastic career accordingly still awaited them after they had left Oxford for ever. Indeed, some Superiors of Canterbury College enjoyed such high reputations that they eventually left their original community altogether. Warden William Dover, at Oxford in the 1380s, became Prior of Dover in 1393; while Thomas Chaundler (warden in 1495–1501), that 'flower of St Benet's order' according to Cardinal Wolsey, died as Abbot of Eynsham.[30] Within the intensely loyal community of St Cuthbert at Durham such migrations from one's mother house were almost unknown, not least because there the rewards awaiting an ex-Warden of Durham College were the greatest the monastic *cursus honorum* had to offer. All the seven last Priors of Durham cathedral, the superiors of their convent for almost a century (1446–1540), had previously been wardens of the convent's college at Oxford.[31] But then no monastery in the English kingdom, Benedictine or non-Benedictine, was so completely under the control and influence of university monks as was the cathedral priory of Durham.

No doubt the ex-Wardens of Canterbury and Durham Colleges constituted an immediately recognisable élite within their communities. So too did all the monk graduates who had once been fellows of the two colleges. These university monks were not, of course, the only élite within their monasteries, but there is every indication that they were increasingly influential as the two Oxford colleges became ever more securely established in the university world. Of the value increasingly placed by the two Benedictine cathedral chapters themselves on a higher university degree there is certainly no doubt whatsoever. Despite the long years of study and the exorbitant cost of the graduation festivities, the acquisition of an Oxford bachelor's or doctor's degree in theology was an aspiration to be positively encouraged among the more intellectually qualified young monks in the community. The university monks of Canterbury were not debarred, like their counterparts at Durham College, from the study of canon law; but of the thirty-nine Christ Church brethren known to have attained a higher degree at Oxford between 1363 and 1540, all but seven graduated in theology. Of the fifty-eight monks of Canterbury Cathedral Priory on the eve of its suppression in 1540, three were then doctors and five were bachelors of theology; two were currently studying at Canterbury College; and yet another two were said to be residing 'at Parrys at stody'.[32] These are not unimpressive figures, even if – predictably enough – they were surpassed by the community of St Cuthbert in Durham. When the last sixty-six Durham monks surrendered their convent on New Year's Eve 1539, they included not only five doctors and nine bachelors of theology among their ranks but also Warden George Clyff and his seven young brethren still studying at Oxford. As these eight fellows or *bacularii* were still receiving commons at Durham College until at least 1542, they deserve to be remembered as the last of all Benedictine monks, if now alas monks without a monastery, in the history of medieval Oxford.[33]

Admittedly, and even within the prevailing academic atmosphere of Great Britain in the 1990s, it may be unwise to assess the value of any academic institution too exclusively in terms of the number of higher degrees it manages to produce. The late medieval Oxford colleges of Canterbury and Durham always found room for many monks from their respective mother houses whose academic ambitions were considerably more modest. For several late medieval Black Monks, as for so many students at Oxford in more recent times, a comparatively brief exposure to university influences could serve as a sort of finishing-school before they returned home to the cares and responsibilities of the duties awaiting them there. At this level too it is clear that the total number of Benedictines from Canterbury and Durham cathedrals at Oxford increased appreciably towards the close of the Middle Ages. Of the seventy-two monks who formed the community of St Cuthbert when Bishop Hatfield refounded Durham College in 1381, only eight are known to have studied at Oxford; by 1450 that proportion had increased to twenty out of seventy-five, and it was still as high as twenty-two out of sixty-six in December 1539.[34] Whatever the attractions of an alternative traditional and more introspective 'monastic culture' within the two greatest Benedictine monasteries in England, there is clearly little doubt that more rather than fewer of their monks wished to study at Oxford as they entered the last stages of their long history. At the very least it is not altogether easy to reconcile such an increasing appetite for the experience of university life and study with the 'spiritual rusticity' which some historians have diagnosed as the essential characteristic of English medieval monasticism during its final phase.[35]

All the available evidence accordingly confirms the impression conveyed by the author of the post-medieval 'Rites of Durham' that masters of the novices and their priors were in continuous search for young monks who were 'apte to lernyng, and dyd applie his booke, and had a pregnant wyt withall' – and was so suitable to be 'sent to Oxforde to schoole'.[36] It is clear that enthusiasm for scholastic learning on the part of the Black Monks of Canterbury and Durham was much applauded rather than criticised outside their own cloisters – by the Benedictine chapters, by the University of Oxford and by reforming bishops alike. Moreover, the purchases of printed books made by the last two generations of university monks from Canterbury and Durham suggest that it might be a mistake to underestimate either the range of their scholarly interests or their ability to embark upon radical intellectual change if such were needed. The fact is that the presence of Benedictine monks at the colleges of Canterbury and Durham in late medieval Oxford had always been something of an experiment, an unexpected variant upon the traditional patterns of both the religious and the learned life as advocated by the Rule of St Benedict itself. All the more unfortunate that this experiment was to be cut so abruptly short at exactly the time when it showed clear signs of becoming more interesting than ever before.

7

Benedictine Monks and their Books in Oxford

ALAN COATES

'A monastery without a library is like a castle without an
armoury.' So wrote an unnamed monk in *c.* 1170. This
comment clearly focuses on the great importance of books
to the medieval monk: indeed, they were essential to the
performance of his monastic duties, namely the *opus dei*, and
the *lectio divina*. This emphasis is further revealed by Pope
Benedict XII's bull *Summi Magistri* of 1336. By this, the
Pope required that each monastery should provide teaching
within its walls, preferably by a qualified member of the
community, but otherwise by an external teacher, either
from another religious order or a secular master; this person
was to teach the 'primitive sciences', that is to say grammar,
logic and philosophy. To supplement this, one in twenty of
the more able monks should be sent to a university, to study
theology or canon law, assuming that suitable candidates
could be found. Chapters 6 and 7 of *Summi Magistri* are
devoted to the arrangements for the teaching within the
monastery and to the choice of students to go to the university.[1] The following article concentrates chiefly on the way
later medieval monks obtained and used books in this university context.

THE PROVISION AND USE OF BOOKS

Benedictine monks studying at Oxford, and residing at Gloucester College, Durham College or Canterbury College, obtained their books from three principal sources. Some were provided by the mother house of the monk(s) concerned, and some were acquired by the monk himself at Oxford, either for his personal use there or to be taken or sent home. There is also considerable evidence for the transfer of books between monks studying at the university.

Books from the mother house were supplied in two ways. Durham College received consignments of books sent from Durham Priory for the use of all members of the Oxford house: three lists of such books survive dating from *c.* 1400, 1404 and 1409.[2] The items in the first of these lists are mainly glossed books of the Bible, those in the last list principally theological treatises. The volumes were clearly intended to supplement the biblical commentaries, patristic writings and other theological texts known from an earlier book list to have been in the college by the middle of the second decade of the fourteenth century;[3] by the end of the century, philosophical texts and works of logic had been added, along with a few medical texts, but hardly any works of canon law.[4] These lists are considered further below. More books were, apparently, sent in 1418 and 1419, whilst the new library was being built at Durham College, and a further consignment followed in 1435–6, after the new desks had been installed.[5]

The statutes of Canterbury College laid down by Archbishop Courtenay of Canterbury decreed that, on a monk from Christ Church being sent to the university for the first time, the Succentor of Christ Church (the deputy to the Precentor or Cantor, who was in charge of both the music and the books in a medieval Benedictine house) should send the Warden of Canterbury College a list of the books put aside for that new student's use; such collections were to be examined by the Warden and two senior fellows once or twice a year.[6] This was, therefore, following very closely the Constitutions of Benedict XII, with their stipulation on the provision of books for student monks by their mother house.[7]

Numerous examples are known of individual monks from Benedictine houses receiving allocations of books for use during their time at Oxford. Parkes has noted that John Wickham, a monk of Bury St Edmunds at Oxford during the fifteenth century, had the use of a twelfth-century copy of Anselm's works, apparently through an extension of the *electio* system (the arrangement by which monks were able to borrow books from the library of their mother house), and the manuscript bears an inscription detailing this arrangement.[8] Under the *electio* system, books were distributed, usually once a year, at a meeting in the chapter house, when the precentor read out the names of each of the monks and the book(s) they had borrowed, after which the monks would return the books and borrow for the next year. Two further examples are Thomas Wybarn, of Rochester Cathedral Priory, who was a scholar at Oxford in 1467–8, and whose name can be found in a dozen books from the cathedral, with three containing specific memoranda that Wybarn had them whilst at Oxford; and Thomas Ledbury, from Worcester Cathedral Priory, who was resident at Gloucester College between 1405/6 and 1413/14, where a copy of Kilwardby on the *Sentences* contains the note that it was 'in the custody of master Thomas Ledbury', which, it must be presumed, was written whilst he was studying at Oxford.[9]

Benedictine monks also acquired books, either for their own personal use or for that of their house (ultimately it amounted to the same, since they passed subsequently into the collections of the monastery) whilst they were in Oxford. For example, John Aston, of Worcester Cathedral Priory, was given 30s. by his house to buy books for his own use whilst at Oxford in 1294–5, and two other Worcester monks, Richard of Bromwich and Ranulph Calthorpe, obtained books while at the university.[10] Thomas of Westoe, a Durham monk, made a number of purchases for his house at Oxford, as did Robert Graystanes, another member of the same community; Thomas de Lund, a third Durham student in Oxford during the 1330s, obtained a manuscript, formerly used by the Oxford Dominican theologian, Thomas Sutton. Dobson has estimated that most of the new books which

entered the library of Durham Priory during the fifteenth
century were acquired by fellows or former fellows of
Durham College: indeed, under the foundation statutes
of Bishop Thomas Hatfield, the resident fellows of Durham
College were entitled to a regular book allowance from the
two college bursars.[11] Thomas Clare, from Bury St Edmunds,
bought a copy of Peter Auriol's *Compendium Sacrae Scripturae*
and a version of the *Tabula Septem Custodiarum*, the latter
having been copied by Frederich Naghel, of Utrecht, known
to have been working in Oxford during the first quarter of
the fifteenth century.[12] Clement Canterbury, a monk of St
Augustine's, Canterbury, who is known to have been a
student at Oxford in 1468–9 and 1473, purchased a Bible
from the Oxford stationer, Thomas Hunt.[13] Dom William
Edys, a monk of Burton-upon-Trent, who was up at Oxford
probably between 1510 and 1517, was to provide valuable
information for later historians by the inscriptions written in
the books he purchased, including those acquired whilst
at Oxford. In 1517, he bought a twelfth-century *Life of St
Modwenna*, who was the joint patron, with the Virgin Mary, of
his house at Burton. His other Oxford purchases in
theology, logic and philosophy, show that he bought recent
publications printed in Paris, Lyons, London and Cologne.
They included, in 1515, the acquisition of the edition of
the humanist Johannes Trithemius' important work *On the
Writers of the Church* (Paris, 1512).[14]

Some monks also had books bound for them in Oxford.
Richard of Reading, a monk of Reading Abbey, had a copy
of Justinian's *Digestum Vetus* bound during the fourteenth
century; Richard was probably the first Reading monk to
study law at Oxford.[15] Thomas Wybarn from Rochester had a
copy of Jerome's *Letters* dating from the twelfth century
bound in Catte Street in 1467.[16]

Although the great days of extensive monastic copying
were long since past, many Benedictines at Oxford clearly
continued to do their own copying. For example, Nicholas
Faux of Glastonbury copied various treatises in Oxford in
1389, including works by Richard FitzRalph, Holcot and
Wycliffe.[17] And a second Thomas Clare, from Bury St
Edmunds, copied commentaries on Aristotle's *De Anima*

whilst at the university in 1441.[18] More original writings of
some Benedictines at Oxford have also survived, including
drafts of lectures by Richard of Bromwich, academic exercises and disputations by John Lawerne of Worcester, and
the tables to the works of Aquinas begun by William
Sudbury, of Westminster Abbey, while a scholar at Gloucester
College in 1382.[19]

Another way in which monks acquired books for their
own use was by transfer from one monk-student to another.
Several examples of this type of transfer survive, involving
monks of Durham. William Ebchester, Warden of Durham
College from 1419 to 1428, transferred a copy of Bede's *Life
of Cuthbert* to William Elwick, a scholar at the college from
1454–57. Elwick later gave his copy of *Aquinas on the Fourth
Book of the Sentences* to John Auckland, scholar at the college
from 1454–65. John Munby, who was resident at Durham
College from 1471 to 1477, received a book from Richard
Billingham, scholar and Bursar of Durham College from
1446 to 1457.[20] Of course, books were also passed on to
monks who then did not in fact study at the university: Dom
Christopher Willey of Durham acquired a printed copy of
various monastic rules, probably whilst a scholar of Durham
College between 1506 and 1513, which he subsequently gave
to William Brantingham, another Durham monk, who does
not appear to have studied at Oxford.[21]

Transfers and loans also took place between monks from
different houses, although these probably happened mainly
within the loose federal structure of Gloucester College,
where monks from one house do seem to have been allowed
to borrow books belonging to one another. For example, in
1298, William Brock, a monk of Gloucester, is known to have
borrowed a Worcester book, a copy of Aristotle's commentary on the *Ethics.* Roger Swyneshead, of Glastonbury,
borrowed two Malmesbury books: these were returned by his
abbot to Malmesbury after Roger's death in 1365. Richard of
Bromwich pledged Hilary of Poitiers' *De Trinitate* to Philip de
Lusteshalle, a monk of Winchester, for the loan of *Distinc-
tions on the Psalms* and a table of Augustine's works.[22]

Some borrowing also took place from outside the Benedictine community. For example, John Beverley of Durham

pledged a copy of *Huguccio* with the Oxford Franciscans, to provide security for the loan of Joachim of Fiore's *Commentary on the Apocalypse.*[23]

Books in medieval Oxford as elsewhere were not only important for their contents, and therefore a necessity for student-monks, but were also items of intrinsic value in their own right. This is shown by the fact that they were frequently used in the medieval university context as pledges and cautions, not only for other books, as noted above, but also for sums of money. To obtain loans in Oxford, books were often lodged with one of the many university loan-chests in return for money, a system of supplying credit which had begun in the 1240s and had grown after the expulsion of the Jews in 1290. Several chests were established by university benefactors who were persuaded that this was a suitable form of charity, namely to support poor students. The chests themselves were kept first in St Frideswide's Priory, then in the University Congregation House, with each chest having a number of keepers – and a corresponding number of keys. The use of books as pledges and cautions was usually expressly forbidden by monastic authorities, as in Archbishop Courtenay's statutes for Canterbury College.[24] Such regulations were, however, if included in the statutes, clearly ignored with some frequency. Robert Graystanes of Durham pledged two books obtained whilst in Oxford to university chests: *Aquinas on Aristotle* to the Burnell Chest in 1306, 1323, and 1325, and *Grosseteste on the Posterior Analytics* to the Winton Chest in 1324 and 1325. A twelfth-century manuscript, of known Reading Abbey provenance, containing various works of Augustine, was pledged to the Robury Chest in 1325, 1326 and 1327, along with other goods, including a Bible, for the sum of two marks in each case, the pledge being in the name of William of Bucklebury. Nothing further is known about William, but it must be assumed that he was a Reading monk studying in Oxford (Bucklebury was a Reading manor).[25] On some occasions Benedictine monks pledged books in conjunction with others, both religious and secular: John Warder of St Albans joined John Consobryne (João Sobrinho), a Portuguese Carmelite, to pledge a copy of Pliny's *Natural History* in the Queens' Chest in

1453–4; and in 1482, John Benet, of Worcester Cathedral, pledged a Bible in conjunction with Mr T. Reve.[26]

Pledges need not always be made with official bodies, such as university chests. They were often made to other individuals: for example, William Haltwhistle of Durham pledged a copy of Innocent IV on the *Decretals* with Mr Nicholas Lusby of Balliol College in 1339, and with another master in 1341, and Thomas Wybarn of Rochester pledged a copy of Peter Comestor's *Historia Scholastica,* from Rochester, for the price of a copy of Duns Scotus on the *Sentences* in 1467, with William Goldwyn, possibly a Fellow of All Souls.[27]

CATALOGUING OF BOOKS

The surviving catalogues of the library at Canterbury College can all be found in inventories drawn up at the time of arrival or departure of a warden of the college.[28] They range from that in the inventory of Warden Robert Lynton on entering office in 1443, to that in Warden William Sandwich's inventory on entering office in 1534. There are also a number of lists of books surviving, which are personal lists of books granted by the Prior of Christ Church to a particular monk-fellow for his private use; these, like the college book lists, appear among larger inventories, in these cases of all the goods of the particular fellow.[29] Unlike Durham College, no lists survive of books transferred from Christ Church, Canterbury to the college in Oxford, and Pantin noted the difficulty in tracing such books through the surviving Christ Church catalogues.[30]

The Canterbury catalogues are divided roughly by location (e.g. chapel, library, warden's chamber, etc.), and approximately by subject – canon law, philosophy, etc. They reveal that the collection grew from ninety-six books in 1443 to over 300 in 1501, thereafter decreasing to something over 200 in 1510, the decrease reflecting, no doubt, the fact that books had either been returned to Canterbury or were out in the warden's or fellows' rooms, and therefore escaped detection. The later catalogues list the books rather more systematically than do the earlier ones,[31] although, as Ker has suggested with reference to the dispersal of Robert Holyng-bourne's books after his death in 1508, the inventories of common college property did not extend to books belonging (in whatever sense) to individual monks. There-fore some were returned to Canterbury, whilst the smaller volumes, according to the note of his successor, William Gil-lingham, were distributed within the college, and some volumes of what Ker describes as being of 'an intermediate kind', became common college property.[32]

As mentioned above, several lists of books survive from Durham College; one is included in an early inventory of the college, whilst three of the others are lists of books sent to Oxford from the college's mother house in Durham; the final item is a catalogue of the college's books, dating from the period *c.* 1390–1400.[33] The contents of the first of these, the list in the 1315 *Status Collegii*, the college inventory, are mainly theological, including biblical commentaries and the works of the Fathers, particularly Augustine, but also some scientific texts. The catalogue of *c.* 1390–1400 is undoubt-edly the most valuable of all the book lists, providing the most complete picture of the books which were in use in the college. It is an extensive list of some 109 volumes, divided into five sections, namely theology (45 books), philo-sophy (15), logic (22), medicine (3) and ending with a rather miscellaneous selection, including some theology, the Rule of St Benedict, and a life of St Cuthbert. The almost total absence of works of canon law may be explained by Bishop Thomas Hatfield's statutes for the college, in which he decreed that the monks of Durham were to study only theology and philosophy at their Oxford college.[34] Indeed, Dobson has noted that this type of balance in the holdings of the library, with its concentration on theology and philo-sophy rather than canon law, should be seen as representative of other similar monastic collections.[35] It is worth recording that two fifteenth-century lists of service books for use in college chapel also survive, in the college inventories for 1428 and 1456.[36]

The paucity of administrative documents, and the com-plete absence of any surviving library catalogues or book lists for Gloucester College, makes it extremely difficult to provide a picture of the development of the college's library and book collections. Indeed, not only do no catalogues survive, but there are only four extant fifteenth-century manuscripts (two of which were originally in one volume) from the communal college library; three of these were given to the college by John Whethamstede, Abbot of St Albans.[37]

LIBRARY BUILDINGS AND THE HOUSING OF BOOKS

From its foundation until the mid-fifteenth century, it is not known for certain where the monks of Canterbury College housed their books. The first of the fifteenth-century catalogues, Pantin's catalogue 'A', contained in the inventory of 1443 (the inventory taken when Warden Robert Lynton entered office) reveals that some standard theological works and canon law texts were kept in the chapel, along with duplicates and the (chained) works of reference, and, of course, the liturgical books. The books for study were all chained; the rest of the collection was kept in the warden's chamber and books from it were presumably issued as required.[38] The book list drawn up in 1459, as part of the inventory of Warden William Thornden when he left office, shows a similar arrangement.[39]

The first reference to the construction of a specifically designated library room occurs in the college accounts for 1448–9, when Merton College was paid 7s.2d. for stone and its carriage to the site.[40] The building work clearly took some time: £112.8s.6d. was spent during the year 1454–5.[41] By 1455–6, the new building, which contained the library, was obviously ready enough for the rooms below the library room to be let.[42] From this it is clear that the library, as was the usual practice, had been placed on the first floor, away from damp and vermin; the floor seems to have been paved with stones, which means that the chambers below must have been vaulted both to support the weight and to provide added safety in the event of fire.[43]

The exact position of the library cannot now be ascertained with certainty: it is known to have been on the west of the site, probably at right angles to the hall, and extending into the garden: indeed, Dom Henry Readinge, a monk of Reading Abbey, is named in the college accounts for 1498–9 and 1500–1 as paying 10s. for the 'little room in the garden, below the library', and he was almost certainly the unnamed Reading monk resident there in 1499–1500 and 1502–3. This would, no doubt, as Pantin observed, have given the library (and the residential rooms below) a pleasant view.[44] The windows of the library were glazed, as is known from the various references in the college accounts to repairs being carried out from 1459/60–1489/90,[45] and obvious but necessary measures were taken to ensure security and tidiness: the room was locked and brushes were provided.[46]

Books were not finally moved into the library until 1459/60, more than twenty years after the first reference to the purchase of stone to begin building;[47] as will be seen, it took the monks of Durham College a similarly long time to have their library completed. The new library was, of course, a chained one, and references survive in the college accounts to the purchase and fitting of chains during the period 1469/70–1489/90. As Pantin noted, this clearly shows that the library was intended to be a place for work, not merely a store-room.[48] Unfortunately, there is no evidence as to the exact nature of the furnishing of the library: although the 'stall system', with book cases extending out into the library room at right-angles to the wall and usually with desks attached, began to be adopted in Oxford college libraries in the early sixteenth century, the old 'lectern system', with its single row of chained books down the middle of the room may have been retained here, given the relatively small number of books involved.[49]

With the establishment of the library room, the majority of the college's books were duly housed there, although the various sixteenth-century catalogues note that some were kept in the chest in the warden's chamber and by fellows in their rooms. At first sight, this may give the impression that the college had, at some stage, established the system of *electio* by which books were loaned to fellows. However, Pantin suggests, on the evidence of the inventories of 1521 and 1524, that the books not in the library are listed there as being in chests in the warden's chamber and study, and in the senior fellow's chamber, and that they were not part of any *electio*, but were merely put in the chests as being secure places, so that the college was spared the need and expense of chaining them. These books presumably could be borrowed; the nearest thing to the *electio* in the college was probably the private collection of books which could be held by fellows with the permission of the Prior of Christ Church.[50]

Our knowledge of where books for study were housed during the early years of the history of Durham College is as incomplete as it is for Canterbury College.[51] Service books would, obviously, have been kept in the college chapel: perhaps other books were also kept there, as at Canterbury College. The first reference to a library building as such appears in the college *Compotus* (college accounts) for 1417, with the building work, costing £42, being financed by contributions from the mother house and from other Durham cells.[52] Although the bulk of the work was completed by 1418, the interior does not seem to have been fitted out with 'desks and tables and other necessary items', at a cost of £6.16s.8d., until 1431.[53] It appears that the library was furnished with two-sided lectern presses standing at right-angles to the wall, between the library windows, as was the arrangement at New College and at All Souls.[54] An entry in the *Compotus* for 1474 confirms that the library was chained, with, again, perhaps as at All Souls, each fellow having a key;[55] it is not clear whether or not there was a circulating library: on the basis of the situation at Canterbury College, it seems probable that there was not. Piper and Doyle have noted that several books from Durham College, which survive in the Cathedral Library, have numbers written at the top of fore-edge, and have suggested that these numbers may refer to the shelves on which they were kept whilst at Durham College.[56]

The dimensions of the library room (twenty-seven by eighteen feet), which still survives and remains in use as a library today as the Fellows' Library of Trinity College,[57] made it shorter than those at All Souls, New College and the mother house, but almost as wide.[58] Its original four-bay layout was very closely modelled on that of New College, with a similar width of bay (just over six feet as against eight feet), and with transomed windows six feet in height, those at New College being seven feet.[59] The present ceiling is flat: however, since this comes down below the level of the top of the south window, this clearly suggests that the original ceiling was either higher or barrel-shaped or both. The stonework in the south window is noteworthy, being of a style transitional between Early English and Decorated. It is in this window that there remains the only light of stained glass known to be contemporary with the construction of the library and in its original position: this is the coat of arms of Bishop Thomas Hatfield of Durham (1345–81).[60] The *Compotus* record of 1436 showing a glazing bill for 26s.8d. may have been for this window; panels in the other windows in the library, which include medieval glass, have been reset on several occasions.[61] The original furnishings were still in the library in 1541, but were certainly removed between that date and 1625, when the present bookcases were erected.[62]

The same paucity of administrative records from Gloucester College, as mentioned above in relation to the library catalogues, makes it difficult to offer a precise and detailed picture of the housing of the college's library. It would appear that construction of the library, which was to the south of the chapel, was begun in 1424 and probably completed in 1429, the cost being borne by Abbot John Whethamstede of St Albans; it was on the first floor, was about forty-six feet long and eighteen feet wide, and had a similar pattern of windows and bays to those of Durham College and New College.[63]

THE IMPACT OF PRINTING

By way of a postscript, it seems worth considering how much impact the advent of the printed book had on the Benedictine monks studying in Oxford at the end of the Middle Ages. The evidence for this lies both in the surviving catalogues and in surviving books.

The absence of late fifteenth/sixteenth-century catalogues for both Gloucester College and Durham College for the period from the beginning of printing is unfortunate. One printed book, with an *ex libris* inscription from Durham College is known to survive, and more than 100 others from the old Cathedral Library are known to be in existence. It is likely that some of these were obtained in Oxford by Durham monks studying there and then later returned to Durham, some ultimately to be dispersed further afield.[64]

Ker has suggested that the position at Durham College may have been similar to that at Canterbury College, where, as has already been noted, seven lists of books survive in inventories covering the period of the early years of printing. These various lists give the impression that the Canterbury College collection was being added to until after 1510, but that it 'became practically a closed collection after 1521, [and] to the last it seems to have been almost entirely a collection of manuscripts.'[65] In the 1501 inventory, there are five books listed as being printed, in that of 1521 twelve.[66]

That this is not the whole picture has been demonstrated by Ker, who noted that the various personal inventories of books surviving from Canterbury College contain a very much greater number of printed books, indeed that the monks of Canterbury had 'the use of them in abundance by the end of the first decade of the sixteenth century'. Dobson has seen this as 'the rapid triumph of the printed book from the 1480s onward'.[67] When Robert Holyngbourne, Warden of Canterbury College, died in Oxford in 1508, most of the books found in his chamber were probably printed, rather than manuscript.[68]

This picture would appear to be corroborated in the use of printed books by individual monks of Durham, when one looks at the surviving books. Ian Doyle has studied many of these, which are still at Durham, and has shown that their owners acquired them whilst they were studying at Oxford.[69] He records that one of the earliest imprints to be acquired by a Durham monk was a set of patristic sermons for the church year in two volumes, printed at Cologne in about 1475; its owner was William Law, Warden of Durham College from about 1475 until his death in 1481.[70] A copy of Alexander Carpenter's *Destructorium Viciorum*, printed in Cologne

in 1480, and bound by the Oxford 'Rood and Hunt Binder',
bears an inscription showing it to have been returned to
Durham Cathedral.[71] William Wylom spent 3s.8d. on a copy
of Lombard's *Sentences*, printed in Basel in 1516, in the year
he went up to Oxford, and also acquired other printed
books whilst there from another Durham monk, Peter Lee.[72]
The effect of this and other acquisitions noted by Doyle
would have been to reinforce the amount and spread of
typical materials for study at the university; the majority
of incunabula were printed in either Venice or Cologne,
hardly surprising given the well-established trade-routes
through Europe for books from these locations, whilst two-
thirds of the sixteenth-century items were printed in Paris.[73]

Evidence also exists for the acquisition of printed books by
monks of other houses than Durham and Christ Church,
Canterbury, whilst they were studying at Oxford. A copy of
Boethius's *Consolation of Philosophy*, printed at Lyons in about
1496, was almost certainly bought in Oxford by William God-
mersham, of St Augustine's Abbey, Canterbury, who
graduated B.Th. in 1505 and had presumably been at
Oxford for at least seven years before that.[74] Thomas Barton,
a monk of Westminster Abbey and a scholar and in 1512
Prior of Gloucester College, is the first known owner of a
copy of Holcot's *Quaestiones* on the four books of the *Sentences*, and one of Badius Ascensius' *Quaestio de imputabilitate
peccati*, etc., printed in Lyons by Johannes Trechsel in 1497;
the ownership inscription records that he was already a
B.Th., to which degree he was admitted in 1512, after which
he presumably remained in Oxford to supplicate for his
D.Th. in 1516. It was almost certainly between these dates
that he acquired the Holcot.[75] William Dersham, of Bury St
Edmunds, had obtained an Oxford B.Th. before 1496 (the
year in which he transferred to Cambridge): it seems likely,
nevertheless, that he purchased whilst studying in Oxford a
book containing Johannes Nider's *Consolatorium* (Paris,
1478), Petrus de Osma's *Commentary on the Athanasian Creed*
(Paris, 1478) and Rufinus' *Commentary on the Apostles' Creed*
(Oxford, 1478), all bound in one volume, the binding again
by the 'Rood and Hunt Binder'.[76]

The impact of printing on members of the Benedictine

community in Oxford was clearly, too, carried home by some of the departing graduates. In 1528, John Scolar, a printer, who had worked in Oxford, and produced seven known editions between December 1517 and June 1518, reappears after a ten-year gap, at Abingdon Abbey, where he printed a Breviary according to the Abingdon custom, which he completed on 12 September. The abbot at this time was Thomas Rowland, an Oxford graduate.[77]

This article has attempted to show the central role played by books, both manuscript and printed, in the lives of the medieval Benedictine monks, in this case those studying at Oxford. The two-fold importance of books to the medieval world is clear, namely their value not only for the texts they contained, but also, in monetary terms, as individual artefacts which could be used to obtain loans. Books were an expensive item for the monastic student, and one student, therefore, frequently borrowed from another. The fact that books were so valuable in both senses meant that they had to be looked after: they were catalogued, as were other similar properties of monastic houses, such as vestments and relics; and they were housed securely in purpose-built library rooms. The comments of the unnamed twelfth-century monk, which opened this article, were to remain just as appropriate in 1470 as they had been in 1170.

FURTHER READING

A. Coates, 'The Library of Durham College, Oxford', *Library History* 8/5 (1990), pp. 125–31.

R. B. Dobson, 'Canterbury in the later Middle Ages', *A History of Canterbury Cathedral*, ed. P. Collinson, N. Ramsay and M. Sparks (Oxford, 1995), esp. pp. 99–115.

A. I. Doyle, *The Printed Books of the Last Monks of Durham* (Durham Cathedral Lecture, 1974), revised as 'The Printed Books of the Last Monks of Durham' (Graham Pollard Memorial Lecture, 1987), published in *The Library* 6th ser., 10/3 (1988), pp. 203–19.

N. R. Ker, 'The Provision of Books', *The Collegiate University*, ed. J. McConica (*The History of the University of Oxford*, 3) (Oxford, 1986), pp. 464–5.

M. B. Parkes, 'The Provision of Books', *Late Medieval Oxford*, ed. J. I. Catto and T. A. R. Evans (*The History of the University of Oxford*, 2) (Oxford, 1992), esp. pp. 446–55.

A. J. Piper, 'The Libraries of the Monks of Durham', *Medieval Scribes, Manuscripts and Libraries: Essays Presented to N. R. Kerr*, ed. M. B. Parks and A. G. Watson (London, 1978), pp. 213–49.

8

Benedictine Women at Oxford: the Nuns of Godstow

LESLEY SMITH

In the year of the Great Fire of London, Anthony Wood, the unpleasant and irascible Oxford antiquary, stood by the Thames at Godstow and drew a plan of the abbey buildings (see plate 3). In fact, nothing of what he could see was original, for the abbey had been expanded and rebuilt since its foundation, had suffered badly in the Civil War, and had burnt down in May 1645.[1] Since the dissolution, it had been in private hands, being a gift from Henry VIII to his private physician, George Owen, from whom it had passed to the Duke of Marlborough and the Earl of Abingdon. Further, although Anthony Wood himself places and dates the plan 'Godstow Nunnery taken from the East 1666', we may well think he was mistaken. For his notes[2] for 1666 have no entries about Godstow, though they do mention outbreaks of plague in the dry, hot summer, the Great Fire, and Parliament's censuring of Mr Hobbes' work, *Leviathan*. Since Wood was fond of walking out of Oxford of an evening to drink his pint of ale at a village inn, often in Headington or Botley, he may have visited Godstow too many times to remark. Nevertheless, his diaries *do* tell us of a visit he made to the site in 1660, and the entry is suggestive enough for us to think he may have been mistaken in his dating of the drawing. For in early November 1660, Wood's notebook records being shown around the buildings which were 'once a pretty nunnery (well endowed) ... but now nothing but

ruins appear; such is the instability of earthly things.'[3] He
tells us he made 'of this nunnery a prospect of its ruins a
copie'. This 'copie' is now missing from Wood's notebook,
but it seems very probable that the plan of 1666, reproduced
here, is a later version of the original, if not the original
itself.[4] It is to be found pasted onto a front flyleaf of one of
the only three surviving manuscripts from Godstow, Oxford,
Bodleian Library, MS Rawl. B. 408 – in Wood's words, 'the
English Leiger Book of Godstow Nunnery'.[5] Wood is indeed
correct: the manuscript is an English translation of Godstow's register of charters, with an account of its foundation,
an 'ABC of devotion' and a liturgical calendar.[6]

According to the foundation narrative, Godstow was
founded by a wealthy widow, Ediva or Edith of Winchester.
After her husband's death, Edith was told in a vision to lodge
somewhere near Oxford until God made clear how she
should be of service. Accordingly, she went, it seems, to
Binsey, home of St Margaret's church and holy well, where
she was told by a heavenly voice to found a nunnery for
twenty-four sisters at the place where she would see a cele-
stial light falling. This place was what is now called Godstow,[7]
then an island in the Thames outside Oxford city proper, but
still within its jurisdiction. Edith did as she was bidden,
setting herself up as first abbess, with her daughter Emma
as first prioress (her second daughter, Avice, was later also
prioress). Edith must have used a good deal of her own
money to found the abbey, but she also pulled strings with
friends in high places. To begin with, she went to Henry I for
help. The nunnery was founded and dedicated to St Mary
and St John the Baptist on Easter eve. Since the Anglo-Saxon
Chronicle mentions a miraculous light from heaven
appearing in the sky near the area in January 1131, and
Henry I left England (and never returned) in August 1133,
we may assume that the nunnery was founded between these
dates. Moreover, Edith's influence appears to have secured a
particular privilege for the place, for only three of the
twelfth-century foundations of Benedictine nunneries were
abbacies rather than priories, and Godstow was one.[8]
Although the abbey itself was built on land provided by John
de St John (hence, undoubtedly, its dedication to the

Baptist), the nuns were always to elect their own abbess when a vacancy arose. This kind of independence was important, for it meant that Godstow was not subject to any other authority; it testifies to Edith's business sense, her secular importance, and her useful status as a widow, controlling her late husband's goods. Before the Conquest, when women had money and land of their own to use in foundations, they were more able to found independent abbacies. The alteration in women's legal position after 1066, when land-holding became closely tied to military service, made this much more unusual.[9]

Edith's abbey church was consecrated in 1138/9, and once again her social pull is in evidence, for the roll call of those present and making gifts reads like a *Who's Who* of twelfth-century England. Both King Stephen and Queen Matilda were at the service, together with their son, Eustace. Stephen and Eustace each gave 100s., and Matilda 10 marks (£6.13s.8d.). Stephen added to this the proceeds of three days of a fair held at St John Baptistide. One hundred shillings were also given by Theobald, Archbishop of Canterbury, and Alexander, Bishop of Lincoln, in whose diocese Godstow stood. The Bishops of Gloucester and Salisbury, and the Abbots of Westminster and Abingdon (Ingulphus, who was succeeded by Edith's son) each gave 40s. These were simply the major gifts. Many more local bigwigs gave smaller gifts in money or in kind. The house was also exempt from entertaining the Archdeacon of Oxford during his visitation, was to be given its blessed chrism and oils of unction free of charge, and was to have control over its own chaplains. Edith had made sure that her foundation had the best possible start in life.

Godstow does not seem to have had difficulty in finding twenty-four gentlewomen to join. The royal connection attracted numerous vocations and corrodians (women and men who surrendered their estates to the monastery in return for a life interest in the house – a sort of private pension scheme). The status of the house was confirmed and enhanced by its most (in)famous inmate, Rosamund Clifford, mistress of Henry II, who may have ended her life, and was certainly buried, in the nunnery around 1176. By

this time control of the abbey land had passed from John de
St John to his heirs the St Valery family. It was they who,
following on the link with Rosamund Clifford, gave Henry
the demesne and advowson of the nunnery, making it into a
royal abbey under his protection.[10]

These aristocratic and, indeed, royal connections lead one
inevitably to wonder who Abbess Edith was. We know that
she was the widow of one Sir William Lancelyne; but that
connection seems of less value in tracing her origins than
her own links with the city of Winchester. Winchester was, in
the words of a modern study, 'pre-eminently a royal city',[11]
and had been so since the early Anglo-Saxon period, having
a royal palace from about the mid-seventh century. As well as
the Minster, Winchester was home to a number of monastic
houses, including the abbey of St Mary, known as Nunnaminster. Although Winchester was omitted from the
Domesday Book, we are lucky enough to have two subsequent surveys of the town (the Winton surveys), made in *c.*
1110 and 1148, predominantly of the king's holdings. From
these we know that both the St John and St Valery families
held property in Winchester. John de St John, donor of the
land at Godstow to Edith, was brother to Thomas, who was
sheriff of Oxfordshire from *c.* 1110 to 1117. The St John
family seem to have been royal officials in Winchester and
elsewhere. Their property and that of the St Valeries was in
High Street, which was largely populated by important families enjoying royal favour. In the survey of 1100, we find a
tenement in High Street south held by an 'Edeva' (= Edith),
one of the few women listed, who 'was a burgess and performed the custom'. Part of her holding was on the king's
land and part on the abbot's. All was incorporated into the
king's house (i.e the royal palace).[12] A further entry for
Bucche Street (Busket Lane) reads, 'Alfred paid 8d. and
the custom TRE [*tempore regis Edwardi*]. Now Edeva owes the
same.'[13]

Obviously, it is impossible to prove, with the information
to hand, that this is our Edeva. However, it is clear from the
description of Godstow's foundation that Abbess Edith is a
woman of wealth and influence; she is described not simply
as the relict of Sir William Lancelyne, but as Edith of Win-

chester, clearly indicating that her former life in the city was important in itself. Even if the two Ediths are not the same, the holder of a city tenement in a fashionable part of town would certainly fit the bill as the *sort* of woman we should be thinking of as the Godstow founder. Moreover, the Winton survey of 1148 has two other suggestive entries. In High Street we read that 'Avice pays the king 6d. and receives 5s.'[14] In Busket Lane we see that 'the nuns of Godstow have that land in their seisin.'[15] Although, admittedly, there was not an enormous number of streets in medieval Winchester, nevertheless, the confluence of High Street and Busket Lane with names that we recognise in both periods is more than interesting, and it seems likely that we are on the right trail.

The constellation of names involved in setting up Godstow is also thought-provoking. Edith, Alfred, Emma and Havis are all Anglo-Saxon names; but William, St John and St Valery are Anglo-Norman. Was Edith part of a top Anglo-Saxon family who had married into the Norman invaders? Or was she part of a Norman family trying to make themselves part of their Saxon heritage? For the moment, we cannot know more than that she had Anglo-Norman links at the highest levels. This is surely confirmed by looking at the foundations of the only two other nunneries founded after the Conquest that were abbacies rather than priories – Elstow and Malling. Elstow was founded *c.* 1078 by William the Conqueror's niece, Judith, the wife of Waltheof Earl of Huntingdon and Northamptonshire. Malling, in Rochester diocese, had been an Anglo-Saxon nunnery. Duke William gave it to his half-brother, Odo of Bayeux; but it was retrieved by Lanfranc and returned to Gundulph, Bishop of Rochester, who refounded a nunnery there *c.* 1090.[16] Both the other abbacies, then, had connections at the summit of Norman society. Edith's foundation cannot have been any different. When her husband (the elusive Sir William Lancelyne) died, Edith, who had lived near, or knew, Nunnaminster in her native Winchester, thought to found a nunnery for herself and her daughters. It was to be an aristocratic foundation for gentlewomen. She needed land; and this was provided by her St John–St Valery connections who owned property in Oxfordshire, where Thomas of St John had been sheriff. An island close by a church dedicated to St Margaret, near the growing town of Oxford, which was within reasonable distance of Winchester and London, was ideal. Edith set up her sisterhood, and respectable women from the best families went, or were sent, to join her.

The Benedictine life attracted both men and women of piety. For women, as well as religious motives, there was the added attraction of avoiding marriage, or remarriage in the case of widows. Women's rights to property and self-determination declined substantially after the Conquest but, even before, women without husbands were social oddities. A widow with property, in Norman England, would find herself preyed upon by suitors and strongly pressed to marry again. Particularly for devout women, a nunnery was an attractive proposition – especially so if one could take up a position of power. For families with too many daughters for whom to find dowries, a respectable convent was a secure and, perhaps, pleasant life for those who could not be married. Of course, there were also less worthy motives – women who were forced by relatives to enter religious life, or a forgotten corner for politically dangerous women, half-wits, or the illegitimate. Nevertheless, such a life could prove attractive to a wide variety of candidates.[17]

Most research has focused on male religious life. Partly this is simply historians' bias; partly it is because there were fewer houses of religion for women than for men; and partly it is a result of the comparative poverty of women's houses, which has left us with few physical survivals of their clois-tered lives.[18] Very few women's houses could compare with men's foundations for wealth.[19] One or two of the most important nunneries could match the men's income, but, more importantly, the great run of women's houses were very much poor relations. Whereas the majority of monas-teries for men had incomes grouped at the middle of their overall income levels, the majority of women's houses were at the very poor end of the scale. Thus at the dissolution (when, admittedly, some houses were worth less than they had been at some other points in their lives – Godstow included), only two nunneries, Syon and Shaftesbury, had incomes of more than £1000 per year. A further five

(Barking, Wilton, Amesbury, Romsey, Dartford) were worth more than £500. Godstow figures in the next group – five houses with incomes of more than £300 (St Helen's Bishopsgate, The Minories and Haliwell, all in London, with Elstow and Godstow). Seventeen houses had incomes of between £100 and £300, but the final seventy-three women's communities were worth less than £100 per year.

Clearly, with such meagre resources, it is not surprising that few women's houses have left much evidence of their existence. For example, let us consider that staple of monastic (especially Benedictine) life – books. From about 144 post-Conquest, pre-dissolution nunneries only 161 attributable volumes – 144 manuscripts and 17 printed books – survive from forty-six houses.[20] A further nineteen houses have preserved miscellaneous records, such as the thirty-five surviving cartularies, of which two are from Godstow, one in Latin and one in English. It is hard to draw generalisations from these figures. Book survivals are entirely serendipitous: the wealthier the monastery, the more books tend to survive – perhaps, but not always, reflecting the size of their original holdings. Men's houses were luckier than women's, especially those monasteries whose churches were cathedrals, or were converted into cathedrals at the dissolution. Here the 'continuity of custodianship'[21] made survival much more likely.

David Bell, their most recent historian, believes that the general run of nuns were better read and better educated than we have commonly given them credit for.[22] At the end of the eleventh century, Margaret, learned and saintly Queen of Scotland, sent her two daughters, Matilda and Mary, to Romsey Abbey in Wessex. There they appear to have received an excellent education, for Matilda wrote to Archbishop Anselm in a scholarly Latin and quotes both the Roman classics and the Latin Fathers. Matilda corresponded with and patronised learned men all her life.[23] The English Godstow cartulary, in the Rawlinson manuscript, is prefaced by a translator's introduction. It reads:

> The wise man teaches his child to read books gladly and
> understand them well; for where there is no understanding

you will often get negligence, hurt, harm, and hindrance, as
experience shows in many places. And religious women have
been excused from a good understanding of Latin books,
since it is not their mother tongue . . . For this reason, a poor
brother, a well-wisher [offers this] to the good abbess of
Godstow, Dame Alice Henley, and to all her convent, who are,
for the most part, well-read in English books . . .[24]

Alice Henley died in 1470, giving us a date at which the
Godstow nuns were well read in English but not Latinate.
This would seem to accord with a general trend in the
country. The first movement was from Latin to French,
the language of the Norman élite. In 1310, the Bishop of
Winchester sent his list of injunctions to even the educated
nuns of Romsey in Latin with a French translation; Archbishop John Peckham sent his injunctions to Godstow in
Latin in 1279 but with added French in 1284. English,
however, was making fast progress. It was first used at the
opening of a session of the Westminster Parliament in
1363.[25] Few documents directed at nunneries were written
in French after 1400, making the Godstow English translation of *c.* 1470 comparatively late. If some of the nuns were
able to read Latin up to that point, they must have been
better educated than many of their contemporaries, male as
well as female.

It might seem possible that Godstow's proximity to the
burgeoning schools of Oxford would provide greater opportunities for learning. Of course, women themselves could
not attend the schools: that privilege was reserved to men
who had taken the tonsure.[26] But did they not benefit from
conversation with the scholars themselves? Godstow owned
land on which a Hall of the university was built.[27] Certainly,
the sources repeatedly mention congress with the scholars,
but the occasions were not ones to be encouraged. Although
the character of the first century or more of Godstow's existence seems to have been blameless, Peckham's 1279 and
1284 injunctions to the nuns, the first sent after a visit to
them, suggest that behaviour was not all it should have been.
Peckham emphasises the need for strict enclosure – a point
he similarly made in his injunctions to Barking Abbey
around the same time.[28] He lays down limits for who may

speak to a nun in private – no one but her mother, father, brothers and sisters. Even confession should be heard in full public view, in front of the abbey church altar, by an approved list of priests (preferably made up of two or four Dominicans and the same number of Franciscans). In particular, he says (in Latin), 'we order you to refuse to converse with the scholars of Oxford coming for that purpose; nor shall you desire to be united in any special tie of familiarity with them, for such affection often excites unclean thoughts.'[29] And in his 1284 letter (in French) he repeats, 'We also forbid this at God's place, that any nun speak to an Oxford scholar who is not her close relative, and even this only with the special permission of the abbess.'[30] Peckham also included prohibitions against missing services, coming late to office, and so forth: it would seem that some nuns were less interested in the religious life than previously. But this is not to suggest that wayward behaviour is one-sided: Peckham says that nuns travelling into Oxford or elsewhere should not lodge with male religious or clergy 'or in other suspected habitations'.

In the letter of 1284, Peckham wrote to Godstow's abbess, Mabel la Wafre, to record his disbelief in stories of imprudent behaviour he has heard told against the prioress. He sends more advice about avoiding the appearance of impropriety, especially with monks, friars, and Oxford scholars. Of course, since these were almost the only men that the nuns would regularly meet, it could be that he was simply stating the obvious. But the rumours, at least, continued for the next two centuries. The injunctions sent to Godstow by Bishops Alnwick and Gray in the fifteenth century give similar advice. Certainly, however interested the nuns were in their visitors, the visitors were clearly interested in the nuns – the convent gatekeeper is accused of smuggling gifts in to the nuns from Oxford scholars. And not only Godstow was a target. Dame Agnes Marcham of Littlemore told Bishop Alnwick that 'a certain monk of Rievaulx, who is a student at Oxford and is of the Cistercian order, has common and often access to the priory, eating and drinking with the prioress and spending the night therein, sometimes for three, sometimes for four days on end. Also she says that

Master John Herars, master in arts, a scholar of Oxford and a kinsman of the prioress, has access in like manner to the priory . . .'[31] At Studley, Alnwick heard the same story: 'it is not healthy that scholars of Oxford should have a reason for coming to the priory'.[32] Godstow, then, was no exception. Its abbess of the time, Elizabeth Felmersham (abbess *c.* 1435–*c.* 1450), reports that 'she cannot restrain students from Oxford from having common access . . . to the monastery and the claustral precincts. The nuns hold converse with the secular folk that come to visit the monastery, without asking any leave of the abbess.'[33] This follows on the injunction of Bishop Gray, fifteen years earlier (1432):

> That no nun receive any secular person for any recreation in the nuns' chambers under pain of excommunication. For the scholars of Oxford say that they can have all manner of recreation with the nuns, even as they will desire . . . Also that the recourse of scholars of Oxford to the monastery be altogether checked and restrained.[34]

Although scholars are once again high on the list of those complained about, other secular visitors were also sources of disturbance. Three separate bishops, in 1358, 1432–4, and 1445 attempted to forbid the nuns of Godstow from allowing corrodians and secular boarders. The nuns were in a quandary: they ought to obey their bishop, but they needed the revenue that secular boarders brought with them. They also had a duty to those outsiders who were genuinely in search of quiet and peace, away from the world.

Both at the time and subsequently, such incidents and reports were put down to the bad behaviour of the nuns. But the behaviour of their priests was a recurrent cause for concern. The nuns needed priests for their sacraments, but some priests could scarcely be trusted in the convent grounds. In 1358, Bishop Gynewell ordered that, 'for certain reasons . . . no friars of any order whatever be harboured by night within the doors of your house, nor by day save it be for great necessity and reasonable cause, and not habitually.'[35] And it was, of course, friars who had previously been specially recommended, by Archbishop Peckham, as confessors. Their reputation was rapidly falling. In 1392, one

John de Kirkeby, chaplain of Wolvercote, was forbidden to visit the abbey. In 1445, Dame Alice Longspey (whose thirteenth-century kinswoman, Ela, a benefactor of the university, had ended her life as a boarder in Godstow) was considered suspect, because she talked alone with an Oxford chaplain in the convent church. A week after the bishop had heard these rumours at Godstow, he discovered Alice had once previously run off with a monk, John Bengenworthe.

What were the nuns to do? Anthony Wood's drawing and his description of his Godstow visit give some clue. Wood was shown around by one Jeffryes, bailiff to David Walter of Wolvercote, who kept the keys to the ruins. He told Wood that the small chapel ('m' on the plan) (see plate 3) was dedicated to St Leonard. This would make sense: Leonard was increasingly popular in the twelfth century as patron of the sick, amongst others. He also showed Wood a smaller old chapel which he claimed was dedicated to St Thomas; but Wood noted the presence of keys and cockerels in the stonework, and concluded for himself that the more likely dedicatee was St Peter, and that the little building was a confessor's chapel. He describes it as part of 'a long range of buildings that reached from one side of the gatehouse or lodge, to the west end almost of the court'.[36] It seems to me likely that this is the structure on the far right of the plan, behind the main gate. The building has no reference in the key Wood provides, but some smudged writing is visible on the plan itself: certainly 'chap' is legible, and the three letters above ('pte', 'pts'?) may read 'priests', 'private', or 'peter's'. The building has not been noted before because in early engravings of the plan the long structure which seems to be a wall or cloister, culminating in the chapel, has been mis-rendered as a tower, complete with battlements.[37] This extra little chapel (the convent already had a main church as well as St Leonard's chapel) near the entrance to the monastery must have been conceived as a public place for confession, which obviated the need for clergy to enter the cloister proper.

Does this arrangement suggest that the nuns were not as black as they were painted? Godstow was dissolved in 1540, and the records we have of it for the twenty years previously all seem to testify to a blameless life. Not enough gentle-women were coming forward to fill the twenty-four original places (there were twenty sisters in 1535, with a net income of £258.10s.6½d.), but those who were there called forth only praise for their holy lives. It also seems that the abbey acted as a finishing school for gentry daughters: Thomas Cromwell's visitors reported in 1538 'that most of the young gentlewomen of the country were sent there to be bred, so that the gentry of the country desired the king would spare the house.'[38] When Dr London reported on the house to Cromwell, he asked for leniency: 'Many of the nuns be also aged, and as I perceive few of the other have any friends, wherfore I beseech your lordship to be good lord unto them.'[39] His appeal may have worked: when the monastery was finally surrendered to the Crown in 1540, the nuns were pensioned off well. The only possible sign that all might not be as it seemed comes from a note of 1528 in a Brasenose College manuscript, which speaks more than once of the Abbot of Osney, Godstow's monastic neighbours. It reads, 'false are the works wich this abbot writ in the abbie of Osney alias Godstow.' Since a note elsewhere leaves no doubt that the false works are of a sexual nature,[40] we may wonder whether the nuns were again being led astray by male callers.

It is hard to draw any firm conclusions about Godstow, simply because of the lack of surviving evidence. And yet Godstow was a comparatively wealthy house, with powerful friends; some women's houses have left even fewer extant traces – hardly more than their name and location. Apart from their probable aristocratic connections (indeed, a useful line of further research would be to trace the connections of the Godstow abbesses, of whom we have an extensive list), we can know little of the life of the women who made their home there. No doubt some were devout, others were less so; even those who ran away to marry, or who took lovers may not have been irreligious – rather, they had wanted a life for which the predominantly male hierarchical society of the time had no place. Certainly, it seems as though they bene-fited little from their proximity to Oxford and its schools. Nevertheless, for 400 years a continuous community of women lived the Benedictine life, as best it could, in the fields by the Thames. Like Anthony Wood in 1660, we who today make our way past the abbey remains (much less in evidence than in Wood's time) to the Trout Inn for an evening's recreation, might pause and consider the bright lives that once inhabited the ruins.

SUGGESTED FURTHER READING

L. Eckstein, *Woman under Monasticism* (Cambridge, 1896).

S. Elkins, *Holy Women of Twelfth-Century England* (Chapel Hill, NC, 1988).

E. Power, *Medieval English Nunneries* (Cambridge, 1922).

S. Shahar, *The Fourth Estate* (London, 1990).

S. Thompson, *Women Religious: the Founding of English Nunneries After the Norman Conquest* (Oxford, 1991).

9

The Cistercians in Oxford, 1280–1539

JEREMY CATTO

Among the religious orders, whose contribution to the University of Oxford is inestimable, the Cistercians have occupied one of the less prominent places. To some extent their obscurity is the result of their comparatively small numbers and consequent failure to develop an individual teaching tradition to rival that of the Franciscans, Dominicans and Black Monks. More to the point, the chance of survival, with the small number of literary works from Cistercian pens and in the absence of records of Rewley Abbey and (with a few exceptions) St Bernard's College, has allowed only a few glimpses of Cistercians at work in Oxford. The limited extant documentation does suggest, however, that the two and a half centuries of Cistercian Oxford witnessed much quiet achievement which has been underestimated. In Paris, they had not been slow to attend the university: a plan to found a Collège Saint-Bernard had been made as early as 1227 and was realised by the agency of an English Abbot of Clairvaux, Stephen of Lexington, in 1245. Cistercian masters at Paris included John of Limoges, Jacques Fournier (later Pope Benedict XII) and Peter Ceffons, a distinguished succession.[1] Though an occasional individual Cistercian may have attended the Oxford schools in the first half of the thirteenth century (for instance, possibly, the mathematician John Goddard, Abbot of Newenham, who had a university degree), any plan for an Oxford Cistercian *studium* had to await the munificence of Edward I's cousin, Edmund Earl of Cornwall, son of the founder of the Cistercian abbey of Hailes.

In 1280, Earl Edmund petitioned the General Chapter to be allowed to found a house of studies at Oxford, giving the manor of Yarnton in support. The result of their correspondence was the foundation *in regali loco*, or Rewley, of a *studium* and abbey, situated in North Osney, across from Gloucester College on one of the branches of the Thames. It was probably inaugurated at an unusual meeting of the English Cistercian abbots in Oxford at Michaelmas 1282. From the beginning it was both abbey and *studium*, unlike its Parisian counterpart, as the earl desired to make it a permanent community to commemorate his family.[2] The students were under the care of a regent master who carried the title of provisor. This arrangement was a source of friction from time to time within the abbey, especially since the Crown in 1300 assumed the patronal rights of its Cornwall cousins; a permanent community could not be expected to co-exist easily with a shifting population of monks from other abbeys. A further hindrance to the development of a Cistercian *studium* was the inability, or unwillingness, of English monasteries to conform to the decree of the General Chapter at Cîteaux that any house of more than twenty monks was bound to send one of them to Oxford with an annual allowance of 60 shillings; their marked reluctance roused the Abbot of Cîteaux, in 1292, to ask for the names of the defaulting abbots.[3]

But the positive achievement of the *studium* at Rewley in educating the Cistercians and developing in the British Isles a White Monks' version of the *moine universitaire* has probably been underestimated. Recent excavations on the site of Rewley have uncovered evidence of the abbey church and of a cloister on the north side which presumably contained the *studium*. The students' buildings within the precincts of the abbey had been 'constructed at the joint expense of certain abbeys of the order in England', it was recalled in 1381; they may have looked like the surviving monastic chambers of Gloucester College, though it is difficult to imagine that any Cistercian abbey could provide sufficient monks to house them together in one staircase as at Rewley's

Benedictine counterpart.[4] It is not possible at present to date the remains so far excavated, but some of the work is likely to go back to the foundation of Rewley, and much of the rest to the enlargement planned in 1354.[5] The letter book of the Abbot of Whalley allows a glimpse of one monk-student, Helias de Worsley, responding in the schools about 1304 before taking the degree of bachelor of theology. Worsley was doctor of theology by 1310, in which year he succeeded as Abbot of Whalley. A Worcester notebook of about 1299 contains brief notes of some twenty-one *quaestiones* disputed in the theology schools by a White Monk who appears to be Thomas Kirkeby; evidently a permanent monk of Rewley, he became abbot in 1310. His participation in the debates of those years made him a colleague of Scotus, William Ware and other luminaries, who together constituted perhaps the most brilliant generation of theologians in the long history of the faculty.[6] On a more mundane level, the *studium* turned out numerous leaders of the English Cistercians throughout the fourteenth century: Richard de Straddel, Abbot of Dore (died 1346); John Brid, Abbot of Combe and Bishop of Cloyne (died 1351); Adam de Stanlegh, Abbot of Rewley (died after 1368); William Rymington, Prior of Sawley and Chancellor of the university in 1372–3, who was one of Wycliffe's most formidable opponents (died after 1384); Geoffrey Pickering, Abbot of Byland and in his Oxford years a close follower of Wycliffe (died after 1400), and William Slade, Abbot of Buckfast (died after 1415). Besides a collection of sermons which is extant, and which may have circulated among the Cistercians, Straddel composed biblical commentaries probably compiled for and only preserved at the community at Dore, while Slade produced a number of philosophical tracts for the monks of Buckfast; neither tracts nor commentaries survive, but they are witness to the spreading educational influence of the *studium* throughout the English houses of the order.[7]

The enlargement of accommodation planned in 1354 must have been one consequence of success; the Cistercians' capacity to contribute vigorously to the religious orders' resistance to Wycliffe and his followers was another. Their stand was it seems not wholly unanimous, in the light of one monk's association with Wycliffe: 'Geffrye of Pikeringe, monk of Biland and a maistir of dyuynyte' was among those who 'taughten and wroten bisili this forseide lore of Wiclef'.[8] This was at most a youthful excess, soon abandoned, and it was more than made up for by the eloquence of the regent or former regent master of the *studium*, Henry Crumpe of Baltinglass Abbey in Co. Wicklow. His violent words against the Lollard masters in 1382 brought him under the censure of the university; thereafter, his invective against the mendicant orders in Ireland and back in Oxford ten years later led to his condemnation by the church authorities. He remained in Oxford until at least 1398, renting a room from University College.[9] By that time, however, the co-existence of the *studium* with the permanent community of Rewley Abbey had broken down irretrievably. It was probably at the insistence of the Abbot of Rewley that royal letters patent were obtained in 1381 to declare the joint property of the Cistercian abbots in the site forfeit for breach of the Statute of Mortmain, and to grant it to Rewley for its own purposes. The *studium* remained for the present, as is shown by the Crown's recognition of the spiritual jurisdiction of the Abbots of Rievaulx and Wardon over the students in 1383. By 1398, however, it is not clear whether any remained at Rewley. In that year the provincial chapter received a *querela* from the students at Oxford, whose tenor (the precise wording is not extant) was that buildings, books and furnishings were in a state that reduced them to misery. At least one monk in 1398–9 was living in University College, and another, perhaps more, at the same time in Trillock's Inn, an academic hall; in 1399 only five Cistercians turned out in procession to greet Henry IV, and their numbers must have been greatly reduced. The response of the English abbots was to try to bring Rewley to make a new accommodation, for which they proposed to tax the whole province; but nothing seems to have come of it.[10] From 1399 to 1412, and possibly to 1438, the monks rented a 'dormitory' or staircase at Trillock's Inn, where there seems to have been a chapel for their use, and maintained the title of provisor for their master; they were referred to in 1433 as 'St Bernard's College' and John Blonton, monk of Jervaulx, was their provisor.[11] Not all of them lived under the one roof of Trillock's Inn, but 'lived separately, dispersed in various halls and places', it was said in 1437, 'and are unable to perform the proper offices or follow the laudable observances and customs of the order'.[12]

It was obvious that this arrangement was far from satisfactory. The General Chapter held in 1411 at Cîteaux had appointed the Abbots of Rewley and Dore to visit and reform the *studium,* a step repeated for the Abbot of Beaulieu in 1425. One Oxford layman, Sir Peter Bessels, bequeathed Frewin Hall for either a Cistercian or an Augustinian canons' house in 1424, but it was eventually assigned to the latter order.[13] However, in 1437 help came from a more powerful quarter. Henry Chichele, Archbishop of Canterbury, had taken an interest in the reform of the regular orders throughout his pontificate, and in particular in their education. Just as he proposed to sustain the flow of trained lawyers for public service through his foundation of All Souls College, so he evidently intended to restore the Cistercian contribution to the body of graduate clergy; whether he was prompted from some other quarter to give his attention to the Cistercians in particular is unknown. For the purpose he purchased two messuages on the east side of St Giles, on which a simple quadrangle was planned; a *mansum collegiale* seems to have been put up by February 1438 at the northwest corner, where the hall of St John's College now stands, though this was evidently a timber-framed building intended to be temporary, of which nothing now remains. At the same time the south range was being built, and perhaps part of the west range along St Giles.[14] In conformity with the Cistercian rule, Cistercian abbots were to be the visitors, and the head of the college was to be, as before, the provisor. A monk of Fountains, William Bramley, was to be the first of the new incumbents of this office.[15]

Chichele did not endow the subsequent building works, which were to be paid for from contributions from the English abbeys. Naturally, therefore, the old problems reappeared: the money proved difficult to collect, and there were complaints that it had not been spent on its proper purpose. In 1482, the buildings were 'only half-finished, if that', and in 1489 were compared to their disadvantage with the buildings of the unendowed mendicants.[16] It is notable, however, that the college was a constant source of concern to the English abbots, and was one of the principal subjects touched on in their letters to Cîteaux. The Abbots of Woburn, Stratford Langthorne and Fountains in turn attempted to effect the completion of the college's buildings. Eventually two energetic Abbots of Fountains, John Darneton and Marmaduke Huby, made some progress: the gate-tower must have been put up from about 1475 to 1490; between 1502 and 1517 the hall and chapel were completed and the east side of the quadrangle, designed to contain the library, had reached roof level.[17]

In spite of the slow progress of the building of St Bernard's, its foundation may have encouraged vocations. Stephen Herbert, a canon lawyer and principal of Eagle Hall in 1446, gave up what must have been a promising career to join the order two years later. That the provisor's control over individual Cistercians at Oxford was limited is indicated by the case of Richard Archebold, a monk of St Mary's Dublin who was Bachelor of Theology in 1451, but who remained in Oxford, residing for at least some time at Rewley Abbey and practising alchemy. He eventually took his doctorate in 1478, incurring great expenses for the order, and further displeasing his superiors by his alchemical pursuits.[18] Some of the monks of Rewley continued to take degrees, notably Henry Ryton, who took the degree of Bachelor of Theology about 1500, and became abbot by 1503. At St Bernard's, the flow of graduate monks was maintained at least at the level of the fourteenth century, and many of the graduates became abbots: John Pomfret, for example, who was resident roughly from 1449 to 1456, became Abbot of Rufford in 1458, while John Hornse, monk of Roche, who was a Bachelor of Theology by 1549 and doctor by 1464, was made Bishop of Ross in Ireland in the latter year, and acted as assistant to numerous English bishops up to his death about 1494. Some sixty-seven Cistercians are known to have studied at Oxford during the period 1500–1540. One of the most distinguished was Dr Robert Kyng, who was probably at St Bernard's in 1506, was Abbot of Bruerne and Thame, then

the first Bishop of Oxford from 1542 up to his death in 1557.
Another, Gabriel Dunne, monk of Stratford Langhorne, who
must have resided at St Bernard's up to 1521, combined
humanist and patristic learning with an individual career
path: he matriculated at Louvain in 1530, played a part in
the betrayal of William Tyndale to the imperial authorities,
was appointed Abbot of Buckfast, and after the suppression
of his house became a rich sinecurist in London and acted
occasionally for Cranmer. Surviving all regimes, he died in
1558 and left his books to 'the late Barnard Colledge', that
is, to St John's.[19] The Cistercians of these years were evidently under as tolerant a monastic regime as was accorded
to the Black Monks, allowing scope for individual aspirations
and talents, neither of which were lacking in their ranks.

The reformation and consequent dissolution of Rewley
and St Bernard's, in these circumstances, did not simply
excise a decayed or inert member from the body politic; the
Cistercians of this latest generation seem to have been as
active and intelligent as any of their predecessors. It must be
said, however, that to all appearances they were not a body
bound together by the inspiration of their Rule, and that
their several separate activities led many of them to co-
operate in, and benefit from, the dissolution of their communities. Rewley Abbey was dissolved in the summer of
1536; its last abbot, Nicholas Austen, had fought a rearguard
action, offering to turn it into a college, but accepted a
pension and continued his studies at Trinity Hall in Cambridge.[20] While St Bernard's retained a vigorous
arrangement for teaching its students logic and philosophy,
its lecturers were masters outside the order and little appears
to have distinguished them from lecturers anywhere in the
university.[21] No document records the college's surrender to
Henry VIII: it was still a community under the last provisor,
William Alynger, until his death shortly after 26 September
1539. The last inhabitants may have been the three monks
of Hailes (which was not dissolved until December 1539)
mentioned as scholars in Alynger's will; one of them, Philip
Brode, was referred to as 'purveyor' (provisor) of St
Bernard's as late as 13 May 1541. If he occupied that office in
Michaelmas term 1539, he must have shared the buildings

with secular masters such as the university scribe and vice-commissary, Richard Smyth, who had a room there, and in any case Brode acted for and took a pension from the government.[22] St Bernard's melted away into an academic hall, and was then, between 1554 and 1557, reborn as St John's College.[23] In practice, the long process of transformation from monastic to secular education had begun long before, with the modification of monastic observances to fit university life. Within that framework, however, the achievement of the Cistercian *moine universitaire* both at Rewley and at St Bernard's was substantial and, if only indirectly, a further witness to the fruitful and endlessly adaptable legacy of St Benedict.

FURTHER READING

M. W. Sheehan, 'The religious orders, 1220–1370', in *The History of the University of Oxford*, vol. i, ed. J. I. Catto (Oxford, 1849), pp. 218–19.

R. B. Dobson, 'The religious orders, 1370–1540', *The History of the University of Oxford*, vol. ii, ed. J. I. Catto and Ralph Evans (Oxford, 1992), pp. 544–6, 552–4.

C. G. Talbot, 'The English Cistercians and the universities', *Studia Monastica* iv (1962).

10

New Light on Uthred of Boldon

DAVID HUGH FARMER

Uthred, whose birthplace was probably in the county of Durham, has long been known as the most outstanding monk-scholar of late medieval England. The diversity of his achievements, his deep influence in his own community and outside it, not to speak of his Oxford writings in the fields of theology, monastic theory and history, make him an obvious choice for an article in this volume. But to do him justice, a whole book or a doctoral thesis would be necessary. The pioneer work on him was done many years ago by W. A. Pantin and others, but he deserves and still awaits a definitive biography.[1]

The chronology of his life is known in general, but there is still uncertainty about some details. His death was certainly in 1397, but his date of birth was about 1322. After living at Boldon until 1331, he moved to Newark (Nottinghamshire) until 1334, and then to London in 1338. In this year he went up to Oxford as a secular scholar. The minimum age was about fourteen, but Uthred could well have been some years older. He became a monk at Durham on 26 August 1341. Often the monastic novices were aged about eighteen, but Uthred's rather rapid promotion to the priesthood in 1344 might well suggest that he was a few years older than most. He certainly spent at least fifty-six years in the monastic life, towards the end of which (at Finchale) he was 'stricken by old age and weakness, and less capable of bodily work'. If he was born as late as 1324, he would have been seventy-five when he died, and needing a warden to handle the Finchale finances six years sooner. On the other hand, his vigour was commented on by contemporaries and he himself thanked God for it in his *Meditacio Devota.* His long life was spent in a period when the Black Death struck frequently, blighting England in 1348, 1361, 1369 and (in the North) 1379. A century later, both at Westminster and at Canterbury, the life expectancy of Benedictine monks was less than sixty years. Uthred, then, lived longer than many monks of his time, and escaped the considerable hazards of the plague.

Soon after his ordination, he was sent to the cell of Durham at Stamford. Founded in the twelfth century, this house never became strong or wealthy, but in the fourteenth century it had retained some distinction as a house which preserved a tradition of private scholarship and study. There Uthred spent three years before going to Oxford as a scholar at Durham College. It is a slight anachronism to describe thus the Durham house of studies on the site of the present Trinity College, Oxford, as it was not formally established as such until 1381, when Bishop Hatfield endowed it. Nevertheless Durham monks had lived there since 1280. In 1347 Uthred was a scholar there, and from 1349 until 1368 was periodically its warden. His chosen subject of study was theology, of which he was admitted as bachelor in 1353 and as doctor in 1357. During these years also, we may think, he began the monastic treatises developed after his departure from Oxford.

Fourteenth-century Oxford was a place where the questioning of received opinions and the working out of new theories were common in several subjects, such as metaphysics, ethics and theology. Owing to the Hundred Years War and later the Great Schism, Oxford was somewhat isolated from Paris and other universities. Thomist and Scotist views were being abandoned for those of William of Ockham, while John Wycliffe was an almost exact contemporary of Uthred of Boldon. Current controversies concerned dominion and grace, that is, whether the right to ownership was or was not dependent on the moral status of the owner. This had arisen in part from the Franciscan Spirituals, with their views on the poverty of Christ and its obligatory nature for his followers. Almost inevitably the

older monastic orders, now called 'possessioners', were on
the opposite side to most of the friars, who were later supported with characteristic and provocative invective by
Wycliffe. Uthred for many years opposed the friars, not only
in the somewhat sterile controversies over the claimed
antiquity in the Church of the various orders of canons,
monks and friars, but also over profound questions of grace
and predestination. His positions were attacked by the Dominican William Jordan and others.

Controversy raged so furiously that, following the public
attribution by the friars to Uthred of propositions on mendicants' poverty and, much more important, of his theory of
the clear vision of God at the moment of death, Archbishop
Langham intervened in 1368. He was also a Benedictine
monk, formerly Abbot of Westminster and on the point of
being promoted to cardinal. He imposed silence on both
parties and their followers, and censured thirty propositions
which he forbade to be defended in the schools. Twenty-two
of these are drawn from Uthred's known works, the other
eight are probably from his opponents'.[2]

The first proposition was the most important. This was his
view that all human beings of all ages and of all creeds or
none, enjoyed at the moment immediately preceding death
a clear vision of God. The soul would then choose or reject
God for all eternity. It was not itself the beatific vision but was
analogous to that experienced by St Paul and other mystics.
Apparently this was an original proposition by Uthred
himself; it has been restated in modern times, but with the
necessary corrections. At first sight, his theory seems attractive to readers of today. But in the way that he stated it, it
attracted criticism and was justly condemned. Many in his
time were concerned with the eternal destiny of unbelievers
and of unbaptised infants. Uthred tried to find a way for
God's salvific will to be realised as widely as possible, but with
due regard for the absolute gratuity of divine grace. This
grace, he held, was a relation, not a quality. Uthred gave
no hint that the final and irrevocable choice was decided
(absolutely or in most cases) by the person's previous moral
conduct, but made it clear that the wrong choice could be
made by one in a state of grace and indeed of innocence.

The consequences of the theory were also criticised. It seemed to make both faith and baptism unnecessary for salvation, to say nothing of the other sacraments, and even questioned the need for the life of the Church as a whole.

It is worth noting that the protagonists were not named in the condemnation, which described the propositions as erroneous but took no action against those who propounded them. This was doubtless because the good intentions were recognised and because the archbishop knew that Uthred had been or would be withdrawn from Oxford. The friars are seen exercising their traditional role as guardians of sound doctrine. There seems no doubt that Uthred had strayed into error through legitimate and praiseworthy concern for the salvation of the unbeliever. He had lacked neither daring nor pugnacity, but he submitted gracefully in 1368 and pursued occupations other than those of a controversial Oxford theologian.

These occupations were partly normal monastic ones and partly involvement in affairs of the Church as a whole. Well after his death a saying of his was quoted by a Prior of Durham to his students: 'It is not good to lose the substance for the sake of the accidents. I call the substance, saying and hearing Mass, saying the Divine Office at the proper times and fulfilling the other duties which befit monastic life primarily: but in the second place, as opportunity allows, to be free for books and teaching.'[3] With this scale of values it would have been easier to recover after the setback caused by the censure. Already he had attended the provincial chapter of the Benedictines in 1360, 1363 and 1366. In this last year he had been chosen to conduct the visitation of Whitby Abbey, then in a deeply divided and near-scandalous state. This was a difficult and taxing assignment, followed by the removal of the principal malcontent but not of the abbot. Uthred personally seems to have emerged with credit, and about ten years later visited other monasteries, including St Mary's York, Whitby again, as well as the churches of Howdenshire, and later still, as the assistant of the Bishop of Durham in visiting his own cathedral monastery. This last also must have been a supreme test of tact, integrity and the reconciling of conflicting interests.[4] The main offices he held alternately, were sub-prior of Durham (1369–73 and 1381–2) and Prior of Finchale.

Uthred's monastic treatises have been analysed and in part transcribed. Although he holds an important place in the development of this particular type of explanation and defence of the monastic order against attacks from Wycliffe and some of the friars, he was neither the first nor the last to undertake such a task. Not only Durham, but Bury St Edmunds, St Albans and Glastonbury all had an active part in the movement. Most of the treatises survive in manuscript only. The earliest contribution came from Bury, and focused on four themes: monastic origins, monastic saints, non-monastic orders and the defence of the older orders against the mendicants. Uthred's special achievement was the writing of the two treatises most discussed, namely the *De substantialibus regulae monachalis* and the *De perfectione vivendi in religione*, besides others on abstinence, on law as it affects monks, on St Bernard's treatise on precept and dispensation, monastic institutions and monastic saints. Leaving aside here such items, as well as the treatment of the long-standing controversy about eating meat, it seems useful to summarise the thought of the two principal treatises.

According to Uthred, monastic life is distinguished from those of other and less worthy individuals mentioned in St Benedict's Rule (ch. 1) by stability, obedience and 'conversion' or quality of monastic life, the last of which includes both poverty and chastity. These three substantial elements are binding, to some extent at least, on all Christians as well as all monks, and even on all men who are reasonable and discreet. Thus some sort of restriction on, or even abdication from, the total dominion over goods is required, because man has only a stewardship or a permitted use of goods which properly belong to God alone. Similarly continence in eating, drinking and sexual acts brings men under the control of reason over animal appetites. Obedience moreover, whether of nature, through inclination or by reason, belongs also to good living by rational creatures. These are called the *Regula Paradisi superaddita* (the Rule of Paradise augmented) in that it was necessary to supplement, after the Fall, the rule of reason alone.

Uthred also saw these substantial elements of monastic life being practised by the Old Testament prophets as well as by Christ, the Apostles and the early Church. Characteristically he saw no model of mendicancy in these three examples, although he did stress the poverty of Christ. A whole series of objections was proposed and answered. In this process it is insisted that the 'religion' of monks is not based on ceremonies but on obedience according to St Benedict's Rule, while this in turn is for the end of worship and charity. With a final word for other orders, Uthred emphasised that the monastic order adds no fresh perfection to the law of Christ, but strongly helps its observance. He too rejoiced in the variety of religious life: the supreme shepherd has many sheep of different colours with different fleeces. Not diversity, but indiscreet claims about the dignity and perfection of their state, are the real causes of envy and strife. With this final warning Uthred ended this treatise.

The second treatise, on the perfection of living, is a completion of the first. It starts with Matthew 19:16 which records Christ's words to the young man, beginning: 'If you wish to be perfect . . .' Along with the substantial elements of religious life studied in the previous treatise as well as the practice of the Apostles in the early Church, there was also the teaching of St Bernard that the rule of reason, which is the same as the rule of charity, binds all men. This is facilitated by particular monastic rules which flow from it. This treatise of St Bernard *On Precept and Dispensation* is found often in the same manuscripts as those which contain Uthred's other works. Perfection consists in the exercise of the three theological virtues of faith, hope and charity, and a man can be perfect in any of the three medieval callings of 'those who work, those who fight and those who pray'.[5] The most perfect state of all, he taught, is that in which the individual's perfection most closely accords with that of the Church militant. This means that the mixed life, or rather, the quadruple life, in which are found two contemplative and two active elements, to be pursued as opportunity offers, is the best of all. It is seen in the life of Christ and the Apostles and their successors, but also in all grades within the Church. Uthred then appeals to the work of Pseudo-Denys for further clarification. The three orders of purgation, illumination and perfecting are found in the monastic life, in the priestly ministry, and at the highest level in Christ himself.

This very brief summary, it is hoped, will introduce the reader to the content of Uthred's treatises. Their date and context should next be examined. The objections contained in the treatises seem to come both from Wycliffites and from the friars. It seems likely, therefore, that they date from 1374–6. If this is right, however, they would have been written, or at least completed, when Uthred had returned to Durham.

These treatises indeed contain a double element. On the one hand, they meet and refute current errors, but on the other they are of permanent value, stressing the value of the monastic life in itself and relating it (more or less convincingly) to the great figures of the Old and New Testaments. In spite of the controversial elements, they are on the whole remarkably moderate in tone. He kept the element of rivalry with the friars within reasonable limits, and stressed instead that perfection does not consist in either external observances or in any particular state of life, but rather in interior dispositions, attainable in any walk of life. These are the theological and moral virtues, but especially and above all, charity. Thus, a century before they appeared, Uthred refuted the assertions of the Reformers that monasticism consisted of formalism, superstition and ceremonial. He showed himself in short in full accord with monastic traditional writers, but restated their ideals in the style of an Oxford scholastic.[6]

Previous authors have stressed Uthred's interest in monastic saints as well as the need to defend traditional monasticism from various attacks by controversialists like Wycliffe. They have been more interested in the second than in the first. But recent study of Durham manuscripts links the two together. The fortress-like quality of Durham cathedral has often been noted; in it were kept safe the relics of Cuthbert and Bede, whose lives and teachings continued to inspire the monks of Durham, not only there but also in their various cells in the north of England. Most, if not quite all, of these cells were associated with these two saints. But the outlook of Uthred, as of his predecessors and successors, was far wider than a purely local one. In studying monastic origins he, like Philip Repingdon before him or John Wessington after him at Durham, and like the other monastic compilers mentioned above at Bury St Edmunds, Glastonbury and Westminster, rightly studied the great monastic figures of the past, not only from England but also from Europe, Egypt and Palestine. At Durham itself, in the chapel of St Jerome and St Benedict (now the Gregory Chapel) was a large screen which depicted a large collection of monastic saints. In the surviving Durham manuscript B.III.30 is found a collection of monastic history items, as well as the Lives of the Fathers, collected, it is claimed, by John Wessington, Prior of Durham 1416–46, and very probably written by him before he became prior. Most interesting for our purposes is a list with commentary on each person depicted on this screen, a particularly well-written item decorated with foliated capitals in red and blue. It cannot be proved at present that Uthred wrote the texts, but they were written at the time when his influence at Durham was at its height, while both the subject matter and the manner (writing summaries and giving exact references) certainly match just what he did elsewhere.[7]

This text has been known before, and part of it was printed by J. T. Fowler in his edition of *The Rites of Durham*.[8] But, as a local antiquary, Fowler was principally interested in the entries which described Northumbrian saints and worthies, but hardly at all in the European outlook displayed. This writer, on the other hand, was far more interested in the document as illustrating a wider outlook and interest in characters of Church and monastic history of other countries and other times. On the screen was an elaborate series of monastic saints of all times and places, including those who went on to become popes, bishops, even emperors. There too are found more 'normal' monastic saints who were abbots, teachers, doctors, writers or hermits. The selection of saints, each of whom had a recognisable image on the screen, is sometimes such as to baffle even a well-read student of monastic history. There can be no doubt that the screen and its accompanying text were designed for instruction as well as devotion and aesthetic satisfaction. Other examples are known to have existed at Worcester and Lichfield.

Among the monastic popes the first chosen is appropriately St Gregory the Great. The notice on him stresses the usual information about his family, his foundation of monasteries in Sicily and at Rome, the mission of St Augustine and St Paulinus to England, his institution of the Greater Litanies and his many admirable writings, including the *Moralia*. The next pope selected is the earlier Dionisius (260–8): the entry on him is taken from the Chronicle of Martin of Poland for the year 266. This source claims that he was a monk before consecration (hardly credible), that he established the parishes and cemeteries of Rome, and died a martyr under Valerian. Little of this entry corresponds with modern notices of this pope. The next entry on St Deodatus (672–6) is on safer historical ground. This pope was indeed a monk and a man of great kindness. In his time, the entry continues, the bodies of St Benedict and St Scholastica were translated from Monte Cassino to Fleury in the diocese of Orleans. This is taken from the same source.

Then comes Gregory VII, explicitly given his title of saint well before the full development of his cult in the periods of the Reformation and Gallicanism. His name of Hildebrand is used with the title of Prior of Cluny, his legacy in France mentioned, and a story about his detestation of simony added. This *exemplum* (a literary device often favoured by medieval writers) tells how Gregory confronted a suspected simoniac with the words: 'If you did not buy the Holy Spirit, say "Glory be to the Father and the Son and the Holy Spirit".' Three times the suspect began it, but three times he failed to complete it. Once demoted from the episcopate, however, he pronounced it clearly. This entry is taken from the *Historia Aurea* of John of Tynemouth.

Eugenius III's entry comes from the chronicle of Martin of Poland for 1147. His early life as a monk and abbot is mentioned, his council in France for the Second Crusade, and lastly his return to Rome and death there.

The next monk-pope on the screen was Adrian IV, the

Englishman from the monastery of Austin Canons at St Ruf, later Cardinal of Albano and legate in Norway, and thence promoted to be pope. He granted the bull to King Henry II enabling the conquest of Ireland. Next comes Celestine V, not described as a saint but called a monk and a hermit.

Emperors and kings are next considered. They include Lothar, Emperor of the Romans, and Michael, Emperor of Constantinople. Then comes the legendary Josaphat, 'converted by Barlaam and then a monk'. He is followed by Carloman, King of the Franks, Coenred, King of the Mercians, as well as Ethelred of the same dynasty who became a monk at Bardney. Next are the three kings of the East Saxons, Offa, Sebba and Sigebert. Ceowulf, who enriched Lindisfarne with land and other wealth and was buried there, comes next. His head, we are told, was translated to Durham after many years and was placed in St Cuthbert's Chapel with other relics. This entry is followed unexpectedly by one on Heraclius, King of the Bulgars (878) and one on Rachis, King of the Lombards (749). All these worthies were claimed to have been monks at some point of their lives; however, as with the popes, the information provided would not always satisfy modern historians, but was derived from contemporary monastic compilers.

The names of patriarchs follow: St Athanasius of Alexandria, St John Chrysostom of Constantinople and St Theophanius of Antioch (?Theopilus *c.* 120–185). Archbishops then follow: Martin, Basil, Boniface and Augustine of Canterbury. For the details of this last entry, Bede is the authority, with precise reference to chapters 23–26 of Book I of his *Ecclesiastical History.* Augustine is followed by Thurstan of York, who 'without any canonical subjection to Canterbury' was ordained archbishop and founded Fountains Abbey and eight other religious houses. David, King of Scots, was defeated by the barons of Yorkshire and by Thurstan at the Moor of Alverton (Battle of the Standard, 1138). Thurstan then took the monastic habit at the Cluniac monastery of Pontefract, where he died. The authority for this entry is Higden's *Policronicon, s.a.* 1141. Bartholomew of Lyons (like Thurstan not called a saint) comes next, his entry being taken from the same source. He is followed by St David of

Wales, 'popularly called Davy', attributed with the foundation of twelve monasteries, with a journey to Jerusalem by angelic intervention and with the gift of tongues for speaking in the countries where he travelled. Lastly, consecrated Bishop of Chester (instead of Menevia), he died at the age of 147. Other archbishops described include Rabanus of Mainz, Theodore and Dunstan of Canterbury; then Lanfranc, memorable as Abbot of Caen, Archbishop of Canterbury and author of the book *On the Body and Blood of the Lord*, as well as of the *Monastic Constitutions*. He is followed by Anselm, Leander, Honoratus of Arles, Odo and Elphege of Canterbury, Paulinus, Wilfrid and Oswald of York, Ildephonsus, Ausbert of Rouen, and Austregisilus and Sulpicius of Bourges.

Bishops described include far more from overseas than from England. Cedd and Ethelwold are there, but also Herculanus, Bishop of Perugia (559), Eutropius, Germanus of Auxerre, Theodulf of Fleury and Orleans, Lambert of Utrecht, Serapion of Thmuis (reputedly abbot of 10,000 monks) and Fructuosus of Tarragon (or rather of Braga, wrongly transcribed as 'Francis' in *The Rites of Durham*) and many more.

Turning to abbots, many famous names are found, but one entry of special interest to Durham is that of St Carilef, who founded the abbey of Anisole in Maine. The Bishop of Durham, who had invited monks to form the chapter of the cathedral in 1083, William of St Carilef (Calais), had been a monk of St Carilef and afterwards Abbot of St Vincent before becoming Bishop of Durham in 1081. He was described by David Knowles as 'an excellent representative of the observant and lettered foreign monasticism and a man of outstanding ability'. St Carilef (d. 536), some of whose relics might well have been brought to Durham by the bishop, is commemorated in this document as one who gave the King of the Franks, Hildebert, most abundant drinks of wine from a very small vessel, filled only once. He did not, however, allow the Queen of France to visit him, and also forbade women from entering his church with a perpetual ban. However, it is recorded that a woman in disguise had entered it with bold temerity and was struck blind at once.

This story comes from the *Historia Aurea*, chapter 62. It seems to provide an alternative explanation to the virtual exclusion of women from both the shrine of St Cuthbert and any close access to it. The Carilef story provides an example of a 'territorial' exclusion of women which could well have been at the origin of this Durham practice. Other explanations invoke the supposed dislike of Cuthbert for women, quite at variance with the evidence of the early Lives.

Didymus of Alexandria, Marianus Scotus and John Scotus Erigena head the list of monastic doctors. Also included are Vincent of Lerins, Cassiodorus, Ephrem of Syria and Bede. Hermits include Paul the first Hermit, Boisil, Neot and Guthlac. This last list recalls the abiding interest at Durham in the eremitical life, kept alive by members of the community seeking solitude, especially on the island of the Inner Farne. Here the example of the twelfth-century monk Bartholomew had been followed by John of Farne, author of several meditations, who had died in 1371.[9]

All in all, this commentary on the screen saints reveals a wide-ranging interest in monastic saints and monastic history. As in Uthred's treatises on their origins, this interest is not confined to Benedictines, nor to the local saints of Bede's Northumbria. If there had been some provincialism at Durham, and many have asserted it, by now it had been completed by a more comprehensive outlook.[10] Durham was quite rightly still devoted to its local saints, but the monks by no means thought of them as the only monastic saints in the Church. Their library too had long revealed supra-regional interests with its early and significant manuscripts of the works of both St Bernard and St Thomas Aquinas.

Uthred's known preference for what is substantial over what is accidental also found expression in another work of his. His *Meditacio Devota*, long in print but never translated, is the basis to the claim that he was a minor spiritual writer of the fourteenth century. This short work, which fills eleven printed pages, survives in seven manuscripts. Their provenance shows that it was read at Durham and its dependencies, at St Albans, Canterbury and Reading, as well as in the Carthusian monasteries of Hinton and Sheen and the Bridgetine house of Syon Abbey. One surviving copy belonged to a theologian who was an Austin friar. It was also almost certainly read by the great Abbot of St Albans, Thomas de la Mare, who became almost blind in his last years before he died in the same year as Uthred. The St Albans manuscript of this work was written in extremely large letters, suitable for someone of poor sight, and it mentions at the end the saints specially venerated there: Alban, Amphibalus, Oswin, Thomas, Benedict, Mary Magdalene and Catherine.[11]

Seemingly, this short work enjoyed a wider diffusion than Uthred's longer treatises: it is also arguably more deeply revealing of him. This is because it shows Uthred at prayer, looking back with humility and thanksgiving over his long and eventful life. He may well have written it in his later years when he was prior at Finchale (1367–9, 1375–80, 1382–3, 1386–96). The meditation is both conventional and personal. It is partly inspired by the works of St Anselm, which had been out of fashion in the thirteenth century but returned to favour in the fourteenth. The prologue indeed is a direct but amplified quotation from Anselm.

> Note that meditations are not to be read in tumult but in quiet, not cursorily and quickly but little by little with interest and leisurely thought. Nor should the reader plan to read through it completely, but rather as much as seems useful, under God's inspiration, to warm his affection for God's love, to stimulate fear of sin and examination of himself . . . Let him start and finish in such a way that length or frequent repetition do not cause torpor or aversion.[12]

Clearly this work was intended to be read repeatedly and not all in one sitting. It is both a traditional and a personal exercise in compunction. Uthred devoutly considered his own life as having 'a sad beginning and a worse continuation'. In order to avoid God's just judgement, a lamentable death and the deprivation of the company of the saints in eternal suffering of unbearable punishment, he implored God for 'an interval for penance' and asked to 're-think all my years in the bitterness of my soul'.

This soul-searching should acquit Uthred of any charge of complacency or self-satisfaction. It reveals him, on the contrary, as one deeply conscious of his own failings, and of his unworthiness for both monastic life and the priesthood. God, he acknowledged, preserved him from innumerable sins as well as many bodily dangers of 'rivers, fires, journeys and robbers'. Here he may have specially remembered his imprisonment in the Dauphiné, while an ambassador to the pope. He also acknowledged God's help when both awake and asleep, against evil spirits.

More can be gleaned about Uthred from the next paragraph.

> God gave me sense and understanding, talent and verbal fluency, with other virtues and qualities of the inner man. He also gave me in my body and members elegance and suitability, together with sufficient food, clothing and other strength and attractiveness of the outer man. God gave me, moreover, time and space for bearing fruit. He did not cut me down after three or four years like a barren fig-tree, but waited for a long time and each day stirred me through new benefits, so that I might exercise his gifts for his profit and praise. I would spend these for my own benefit and by this exchange acquire the reward of eternal happiness.

Uthred perceived himself as singled out for becoming one of the elect, but by God's grace, not his own merits, and this caused him a four-fold fear. These are fear of damnation, fear because of broken promises, fear of some actions, seemingly sinless but not so in reality, and fear of the loss of the beatific vision and of eternal punishment. However, Scripture provides examples of God's limitless mercy: Adam, David, Ahab, Manasses and the city of Nineveh, Mary Magdalene, Matthew, Peter and Paul. These all give him hope.

> Therefore, most merciful Lord, even if my sin is too great to deserve pardon, I also know that your grace is infinitely greater. Therefore, as you do not will my death but you give me an interval for repentance, inspire me with true repentance for my sins, not like the remorse of Judas. But as you looked on Peter who went out and wept bitterly, so also look on me with the eye of compassion, so that I may learn from my sins and never return to them. Kindle in me a sense of how momentary and false is pleasure in sin ... and how much greater is the exultation of not having committed it. Lastly you

have impressed on me, among other benefits, the gift of your secret inspiration. By this I recognize myself as yours, and glorify you for the supreme benefit of predestination, by which, I hope, you have called me from the beginning to your eternal glory. May the Trinity grant this, Father, Son and Holy Spirit, through the intercession of the glorious Virgin and St Cuthbert and all the saints. Amen.

From these diverse elements can be glimpsed a more complete and balanced picture of Uthred than that based too exclusively on his academic controversies. To be sure, Leland was right in judging that there was no monk of Durham more learned than he, while the Carmelite Bale stressed that he was, so to speak, no slouch in giving as good as he got in academic argument.[13] But Uthred was more than this. It was not for nothing that he was chosen as Warden or Superior of Durham Hall four times over: 1349–52, 1358–60, 1362–3 and 1365–8. He was thus responsible for the spiritual, as well as the academic standards of the house and the monks under his care. He was also repeatedly chosen as a member of the provincial chapter and, even more important, as Visitor of other monasteries, even when they were in a poor state. Throughout his life he had special responsibilities: at Oxford for the younger monks, and later, at both Durham and Finchale, for all those in his charge, not to mention the financial responsibility which has left more trace in the surviving records. Here one can note that consistently while in office, he seems to have failed to account for the sums received: it may be, that like Adam, Abbot of Eynsham in the early thirteenth century, he was a good academic but a poor administrator.

While his earlier writings show his deep interest in the Church with treatises on different but related topics such as Church–State relations and Church endowments, the Church and the Eucharist (against Wycliffe), on mendicancy and monastic origins (against the friars), not to speak of the salvation of those apparently outside the Church, his later ones are concerned with monastic origins, monastic saints and monastic compunction. But all in all, he revealed an attitude enriched by the wider and deeper training of his mind which he experienced at Oxford over twenty years.

The papacy, and especially Benedict XII (1334–42), the Cistercian monk, learned theologian and effective inquisitor, was deeply concerned with the quality of monastic life. Not only did he provide for regular chapters and visitations, but also with setting up houses of study. The intention of the legislator was not however to provide the universities with permanent teachers, but to improve the quality of life in the monasteries. Uthred, by staying twenty years in Oxford, had certainly contributed notably by his teaching to the faculty of theology there. But his stay in Oxford was a very long one; if not without parallel, it was longer than the average for most monks. When at the age of about forty-four he was withdrawn from Oxford following the censure of his teaching, it may well be thought that it was time for his long stay there to be ended, and that he was too valuable a member of his own community to be semi-permanently away from home. If his wider interest in Church affairs had led him to serve on a committee of national importance and unexpectedly to journey to Avignon and suffer temporary confinement in the Dauphiné, that could be seen as a consequence of his intellectual enrichment at Oxford.[14] Other consequences of this were seen in his treatises on monastic origins and in the wide-ranging choice of saints for the Durham screen with their commentary. Later in life, he did return to Oxford for some time between late 1383 and 1386.

Last of all, in the evening of his days, very likely at Finchale, where he lived, died and lies buried in the choir, he wrote a meditation which is characteristically monastic. In the exquisite setting of the priory, hallowed by the twelfth century hermit St Godric, he must have seemed far away indeed from the arguments of the Schools but close to the divine presence. The river Wear and its red sandstone cliffs, the church and monastery buildings (even though smaller than they had been in the thirteenth century), above all the presence of Durham monks coming in rotation to share the life of the small resident community, must all have contributed to the quality of life. The elderly academic who had relinquished his controversies and returned to contribute substantially to the good of his monastery, would

surely have been approved both by St Cuthbert and by St
Godric.

FURTHER READING

W. A. Pantin, 'Two Treatises of Uthred of Boldon on the Monastic
Life', in *Studies in Medieval History Presented to F. M. Powicke*
(Oxford, 1948), pp. 363–85.

W. A. Pantin, 'Some Medieval English Treatises on the Origins of
Monasticism', in *Medieval Studies Presented to Rose Graham*
(Oxford, 1950), pp. 189–215.

M. E. Marcett, *Uthred of Boldon, Friar Wiliam Jordan and Piers
Plowman* (New York, 1938).

11

Robert Joseph and his Letter Book

ANTHONY MARETT-CROSBY osb

In the year 1710, the historian and antiquarian Thomas Hearne visited the church of Sandford. The visit reminded him of an earlier experience in the same place, a conversation with 'the learned Mr Edward Lhuyd, since deceased'. Lhuyd had died only a year earlier, having been keeper of the Ashmolean from 1691 to his death and having used much of that time to collect a vast harvest of medieval manuscripts. At his death, there were 170 such manuscripts in Welsh and Latin alone, a vast resource 'to assist those who have a taste for the literary remains of the Ancient Britons'.[1] But in 1710 it was not this vast collection that Hearne remembered but a single manuscript, bought by Edward Lhuyd at St Asaph. Hearne describes it as 'containing diverse discourses, mostly by way of letter, written by Josephus Monachus Eveshamensis', Robert Joseph of Evesham. This letter book excited the imagination of Hearne and his friends, much as it did that of Edward Lhuyd himself. Lhuyd's handwriting is still to be seen annotating the pages of the manuscript, noting identifications of various of Robert Joseph's correspondents, and explaining words that he found unfamiliar or curious. But for all its interest, Hearne could write that 'the matter of it seems mean and trivial and not fit to see the light', even though he acknowledged that it was 'penned in a pretty good Latin style, far better than might be expected from a man bred in a cloister'. Hearne's judgement on the latter point is unimpeachable; his view of the content of Robert Joseph's letter book is surely inadequate. There are few sources available to the historian of English monasticism comparable to his letters, written by an otherwise shadowy monk of Evesham between 1530 and 1533. Robert Joseph was both monk and scholar, a student at Gloucester College, Oxford and a lifelong lover of that university. Writing 250 years after Thomas Hearne, David Knowles described it as 'a window on the monastic world', a window into Oxford and into the last generation of monastic students to attend that university before the Reformation.

Almost all that we know of the life of Robert Joseph is extracted from these 176 letters, preserved in a single volume now held in the National Library of Wales.[2] The text is written in one hand, very probably that of Robert Joseph himself, and there can be little doubt that it was one of his most prized possessions. He did lend it to others, but in a letter to Richard Smith in December 1530, he made clear that its absence affected him deeply. Turning to the kind of classical allusion he loved so much, Robert Joseph compared his sense of loss to that of Chaerea, the lonely lover in Terence's *Eunuch.* He begs Smith to collect the letter book from Thomas Tucke, and such is his impatience that within a month he is writing to Smith again, castigating him for failing in the task he had been set.[3] However parochial its content, it was clearly very close to his heart.

THE LETTER COLLECTION

The contents of his beloved book are mixed, more mixed than the title of 'letter book' given to it by Aveling and Pantin would suggest. Alongside real letters sent to real friends, there are imaginary letters, joke letters, poems and a number of lectures given by Robert Joseph to his students in the novitiate at Evesham. This range of material has something of the commonplace book about it, and we know from begging letters sent to friends that the author put together the contents by copying material he had sent out. On occasions, he asks friends to return letters already sent purely for the purpose of being copied into the book, and in a letter to Robert Dorning in November 1530 this request is

accompanied by the promise that copies of other letters will
be sent back in return.[4] This apparently haphazard method
of proceeding made the possibility of losing letters very real,
and we know of at least one letter sent by Robert Joseph that
never made it back into the letter book. In a letter to his
friend Humphrey Chester at the Cistercian abbey of
Combermere he asks that a letter be returned, and then
gives a brief summary of the contents of that missing letter.
From all that he says of it, it is quite clear that the letter was
either never returned or never made it into the manuscript,
for there is no letter to Humphrey Chester that corresponds
to the contents described.[5] We are therefore dealing with a
selective collection, in which the process of selection was
primarily governed by chance, and by the vagaries of
message carriers to and from Evesham. Thus Robert Joseph
complains of the difficulty of finding letter bearers, and in
his only letter to a Master of Cambridge University, he complains that it has taken him two years to find a way of
conveying any message to that university from Evesham.[6]

Difficulties such as these were only part of the problem.
On two occasions, Robert Joseph makes clear that he wrote
his letters in the face of considerable opposition from those
in authority, most notably the abbot. In a letter of April 1530
to John Cadecraft, he expresses his incomprehension of so
obscurantist a position, describing it as an improper use of
the Rule of St Benedict. He clearly has in mind the provisions of Chapter 54 of the Rule, where it is ordered that on
no account should a monk be allowed to receive letters
without the permission of the abbot. It may be that at
Evesham this provision was used to stop excessive letter
writing, and as in the same letter Robert Joseph admits that
he was writing them immediately after Matins, we may
understand why this was thought important. But Robert
Joseph can see no reason for so restrictive an interpretation,
and it is entirely consonant with his understanding of the
Rule that so direct an attempt to enforce it would seem to be
simply superstitious. He notes in passing that its enforce-
ment was of a severity comparable with the rule preventing
monks from frequenting brothels. Nevertheless, he feels free
not to abide by it, but the fact that the restriction is men-

tioned in a later text serves to remind us that letter writing was to some degree a covert activity.[7]

The final selection of letters underwent at least some process of editing. A glance at the manuscript reveals a series of corrections, and at least one word has been corrected every time it appears in the manuscript. When he first wrote the letters, Robert Joseph seems to have been happy with the spelling *zenolium* to render the English word 'present', but every time this word appears there is, above the line, a correction to alter the initial letter of the word to form *xenolium*. As he does this five times in the course of the manuscript, it is likely to be more than accidental, and almost certainly represents some kind of re-editing of the whole.[8]

Other features of the text suggest a less careful approach. Although Robert Joseph was very anxious to obtain letters for his book, once obtained they were not always copied into the volume with great care. The text is peppered with crossings out, respellings and the adding of phrases at the foot of the page or in the margin. He himself admits that he frequently wrote his letters in the dormitory after Matins,[9] and this may have extended to the writing of the letter book itself. This may account for all the indications that suggest it was written in a hurry, and without great care for the visual impression of the letters. There are occasions when he attempts to draw more elegant capital letters reminiscent of a scriptorium style, but the attempts are usually failures and very often they have been scored out in the manuscript and replaced with his more usual writing.[10] We are not in the presence of a master of monastic scribal beauty.

Anyone attempting to use the letters of Robert Joseph as a historical source must also accept that there are grave difficulties in dating the originals. Many letters do contain dates, but others do not, and their position in the manuscript cannot be used as a guide. It seems almost certain, for example, that the first letter preserved cannot have been written before letter 75, since it refers to John Feckenham as a priest, and elsewhere it seems that Robert Joseph has inserted short letters into blank spaces in the manuscript. Letters 62 and 89 show signs of having been thus inserted, and the writer has also used a different kind of pen to that of the letters around them. There is no reason to suppose that they were added by a different hand, but they warn against assuming the letters sit in a neat chronological order within the whole.

We are therefore faced with a manuscript with distinctive and apparently contradictory characteristics. On the one hand, there is clear evidence that it was written without particular care for the final product, while on the other hand there are suggestions that it underwent at least some process of checking or editing. These conclusions pose an obvious question: why was the manuscript written at all? Many of the letters are, after all, of little more than personal interest, and few if any of them deal with the great events of Robert Joseph's era. For the historian accustomed to thinking in terms of great men or great events Robert Joseph will prove a disappointment, for his world was confined largely to the monastic and academic, to Evesham and Oxford, and only vague rumours of the vicissitudes of Wolsey remind us of the high politics of the period.[11] Moreover, there are letters among the collection whose preservation seems surprising. It includes some which were clearly misunderstood by their recipients, and others contain expressions of loneliness or frustration that an author might not want to be remembered. There are indeed three occasions within the corpus of letters where Robert Joseph expresses anxiety over their contents falling into the wrong hands, and in a letter to Master Henry Wyllys in September 1530 he notes that some letters have come back to him without ever finding their recipient, for which he is grateful. In an earlier letter to a Cistercian friend John Winchcombe he urges him to keep the letters private, and to use only a trusted messenger when sending a reply back to Evesham.[12] Though not letters that would shake kingdoms or princes, Robert Joseph does not spare those around him from criticism if he feels it to be justified. In the wrong hands, his letters would have done nothing to advance his reputation.

Despite these concerns, there can be little doubt that the letter book was intended to be read, and to be read by others. It has already been noted that the book was sent by Robert Joseph to his friends, and in one place he includes

an explicit preface to a letter in order to warn the reader of
what is to follow. This preface, letter 113 in the printed
edition, was never intended as a letter to be sent to anyone
else, for where other letters have the name of the recipient,
this letter simply reads '*ad lectorem Iosephum*'. Addressing his
'honest reader', Joseph writes that the letter following is a
comic invective, not to be taken seriously under any circumstances. We know from elsewhere in the letter book that
Joseph's attempts at humour could go seriously wrong,[13] so a
warning has been inserted to make it obvious that the text
which follows, the longest letter in the series, cannot be
taken at face value. This consciousness of an audience is an
important guide in understanding the nature of the work.

It is as a book of examples that the letter book of Robert
Joseph was conceived. His desire for privacy and secrecy was
subservient to the higher need of providing models of good
letter writing for his friends. In this sense, the purpose of the
book is didactic; Robert Joseph clearly hoped that his letters
might enable those to whom they were sent to compose
letters more skilfully themselves, and it is this purpose which
explains two of the most persistent themes in the letters.

Firstly, Robert Joseph frequently deprecates his own style,
describing it as '*scribendo infantia*' to an anonymous friend in
1530. The vulgarity of his style is a constant concern, and
in letter 57 to John Tucke of Gloucester Abbey he goes so far
as to list various possible styles and ask his correspondent to
choose the one he prefers: 'Therefore I beg you to tell me as
quickly as you can which kind of literary style pleases you
most, and then you will find that your Joseph is no parsi-
monious writer of letters.'[14]

Parallel to this concern with his own style is a readiness
to comment on the style of others, and where necessary to
recommend changes or improvements. A necessary first
stage for all his correspondents was to write in Latin, and in
one of the earliest letters in the volume he castigates
Thomas Lovewell for writing in English.[15] The value of letter
writing for improving the Latin style of his correspondents
is frequently emphasised, and it is in the context of these
exhortations that we can understand his concern with the
correct spelling of Latin words. On more directly stylistic

issues, he shows a marked dislike for flattery as a literary convention, which he describes in hostile fashion as 'gnathonism' after an unappealing character in Terence's *Eunuch*. In a letter to Richard Eslond he explains that his dislike of excessive praise stems from his fear that it can all too easily look like mockery, and he opts instead for restraint of language, writing to Thomas Tucke that expressions of kind feeling are much more valuable than any exaggerated praise. Indeed, his sense of the danger inherent in overmuch praise seems to have been one of the principal reasons for writing his first invective against Richard Smith in letter 81. It was an invective intended as a joke, but the joke had a serious purpose, for 'by these incriminating letters I hope Smith's intemperate praise will be cured.'[16]

As a series of exempla the text is a long way from many other monastic letter books, and we may ask whether to describe it as such is to clarify its nature or conceal it. Robert Joseph's own day certainly did see the production of other monastic letter books, and most of the great abbeys and cathedral priories of England have registers of letters dating from the early sixteenth century. But these contemporary texts have a very different purpose to Robert Joseph's; they are almost entirely concerned with administration, registers of the chapters, and letters of superiors, and they form part of that wider history of the organisation of monastic administration dating back to the thirteenth-century General Chapters. Robert Joseph's collection of letters is clearly distinct from this body of material, not only because it does not reflect a particular department of monastic administration, but also because it is not the product of a religious superior or of that superior's deputy. It is in this context unhelpful to see Robert Joseph's letters as a product of his time as abbot's chaplain, a post he held for about a year from 1529 until the middle of 1530. Abbots' chaplains did keep letter books at Gloucester, Worcester, Peterborough and other houses, but practice in this matter varied widely, and there is no immediate evidence to suggest that at Evesham it was the practice to work in this way.[17] The letter book as we have it is not the product of any monastic official, but the product of a mind, a mind formed in the habit of letter writing by both remote and recent tradition.

By Robert Joseph's day, the great centuries of medieval monastic letter writing were long past. His was not the age of Boniface or Anselm or Peter of Celles, but for all that monks had not lost their interest in the epistolary art, and throughout the late Middle Ages there continued to appear treatises on letter writing or *dictamen* from monastic theorists.[18] The Westminster monk Thomas Merke, Bishop of Carlisle from 1397–1401, wrote a characteristically elaborate and formalised handbook on the subject, and many such texts included worked examples of the kind of letter that the author wished to inspire his readers to write. An anonymous fifteenth-century treatise on the same subject contains a full section of letters, with correspondents ranging from popes and kings to canon lawyers, monks and students. The very range of the authorship of these texts suggests a wide interest in correct style, and even if some of the letters are fictitious many others are almost certainly not. Thus the text preserves an early example of a *prior studentium* writing to an abbot about the studies of one of the monks in his care, and from the initials of the monk included in the text we can identify him as William Pygot, a monk of Selby who studied at Oxford between 1397 and 1398.[19] That the letter of the prior and the abbot's reply should have been preserved suggests that Robert Joseph was not the first monk of Oxford whose letters could be taken as appropriate models of style.

There is indeed evidence that monks of Oxford had preserved their correspondence in letter books before the sixteenth century. One such is the collection put together by the Canterbury monk William Glastynbury, who kept eight letters sent to him by different correspondents in the year 1432.[20] Their subject matter is very close to that of Robert Joseph's correspondence; we hear of the lending of books and the desire for their return, of plans to give a new year's present to the Prior of Dover, and above all of the difficulties experienced by monks in Oxford over money. There is no indication that the Glastynbury letters were preserved because of the fineness of their style, but they add further weight to the impression that there was something natural to monks in the sending and keeping of letters, letters which conformed to the canons of medieval epistolary theory. Well into the sixteenth century, letters characteristic of his late medieval style were being produced; it is a background we cannot afford to neglect.

HUMANISM

But Robert Joseph is not simply an exponent of the medieval art of *dictamen*. He himself expresses his own profound debt to another more recent tradition, that of humanism. It is as a humanist that Robert Joseph is generally understood as a product of sixteenth-century Oxford, where the values of the continental humanists were beginning to show themselves in new foundations and new studies very different from the traditional corpus of learning embodied in the *Sentences* of Peter Lombard. Thus humanism has been described as 'a disturbing force beneath the surface of a traditional curriculum', a force which worked to break down the structure of the medieval university from within.[21] Robert Joseph's letters have frequently been taken as proof positive that this new humanism embraced even the oldest of the religious orders, demonstrating that even at Gloucester College it was possible that 'a monk might learn a great deal of Erasmian humanism'.[22]

We should not underestimate how remarkable a conclusion this is for our understanding both of late medieval monasticism and late medieval Oxford. In its favour, there is the undeniable importance that Robert Joseph attributes to Erasmus, whose works are quoted directly on eighty-nine occasions within the corpus. In a letter to his Cistercian friend John Winchcombe, Robert Joseph is uncharacteristically prolix in his praise of Winchcombe's defence of Erasmus against detractors, and he then goes on to note how he himself refutes such detractors by the use of a phrase extracted from the *Antibossicon* of William Lily.[23] Lily had been a leading English humanist, and had been appointed by Colet as the first High Master of St Paul's in 1512. Renowned for his knowledge of Greek and Latin, he had been a close friend of Erasmus, and his works became well known amongst late medieval English Benedictines. Early editions of his grammatical works are found amongst the early printed books of both Peterborough and Westminster, and Robert Joseph so valued him that he used another of his texts in his opening lecture to the novices at Evesham in 1530. Lily was primarily a grammarian, and represents that part of the humanist tradition in which the love of good Latin was always a concern. This was very much the humanism of Robert Joseph, who uses a series of Erasmian texts on letter writing to justify his own interest in the subject, and shows a particular predilection for the *Vulgaria* of William Hormann.[24] This extraordinary work was published in London in 1519, and comprises a list of Latin phrases with English translations, divided into a series of thematic chapters. The reader could consult the work to find the appropriate classical Latin phrase for any one of a number of subjects from erudition and scholarship to marriage and the kitchen. In letter 24 Robert Joseph asks for a copy of this book to be sent to him, and shortly afterwards we hear that he has sent Feckenham a series of 'lubrications' from the book.[25] We can only presume that by this Robert Joseph means that he has sent Feckenham some particularly appealing extracts from the work.

It is nevertheless dangerous to assume that the new learning had too great a hold over the university in the early sixteenth century. However much it was a 'disturbing force', it nevertheless existed at a time when scholastic theological discourse remained in the ascendant. Robert Joseph and his friends went to Oxford to study a theology that was entirely medieval in its outlook, and his dislike of some of its ways only reflects its unchallenged supremacy.[26] The basic cursus of Robert Joseph's theology was probably not greatly changed from that of an earlier English Benedictine monk, John Lawerne, who studied at Oxford around the year 1448. By chance, his notebook of jottings and lectures survives,[27] and is a privileged insight into the world of monastic scholasticism some eighty years before Robert Joseph. His book contains notes, copies of documents and sermons, and an extensive refutation of the Lollard heresies. His main work, however, is a traditional commentary on the *Sentences*, which begins with a eulogy of Peter Lombard based on a text from Hosea 11:1. The Lombard is the 'builder of a city set on a hill' which will withstand the attacks of any heretic, and among the doctors of the Church he is 'like the shining of a star among other dim lamps'. Lawerne is a thorough-going scholastic, and the tradition of theology that he imbibed did not die easily.

The caution of sixteenth-century Oxford humanists is amply demonstrated in the prehistory to the foundation of the flagship humanist college of Corpus Christi.[28] Its founder was Richard Fox, a graduate of Magdalen who had built his ecclesiastical career upon service to the Tudor dynasty. In 1511, it became known within Oxford that he was planning to make a new foundation, plans which eventually bore fruit in the foundation of Corpus in 1517. But in 1511, his first proposal was to found something entirely familiar to Oxford, a monastic house of studies. It was to be a dependent cell of the cathedral priory of Winchester, modelled on those already serving the monks of Durham and Canterbury, and it was a project that received the enthusiastic support of Oxford's great men. Writing to Fox in 1511, the chancellor and the masters had described his scheme as not only a work of benefit to the university, but a work that will ensure the salvation of his own soul. We do not know why Fox changed his plans, though an unsupported anecdote records how the Bishop of Exeter dissuaded him by a less than flattering description of monks and a dire prediction of their imminent disappearance. By 1516, Fox's plans had changed, but the very fluidity of his proposed scheme allows us to see both the hesitancy of early Oxford humanism and its close relationship with the institutions of an altogether older system of learning.

If humanism in Oxford was a gradual affair, merging with the medieval system rather than confronting it, then much the same can be said of the humanism espoused by Robert Joseph. In this sense he is very much the product of the Oxford of his day. Despite his enthusiasm for Erasmus, and his desire to defend him against all comers, there is in practice little humanist theology in Robert Joseph's outlook. His

admiration is in fact confined to the theory of letters rather
than to any wider humanist gospel. It is Erasmus' love of
Latin that Robert Joseph finds compelling, that love of a
beautiful and polished style that had lain behind the
humanist endeavours at Magdalen College School in the fifteenth century. By the sixteenth century, Erasmus' concern
for Latin was somewhat passé, for many Italians of his day
were now writing in the vernacular tongues that Robert
Joseph so elegantly despised. Erasmus' preoccupation with
the Latin letter form was by 1520 a byway of the humanist
endeavour,[29] and from the mid-sixteenth century his letters
came to be neglected by the collators of its achievements.
Robert Joseph probably knew some Greek, but Latin always
remained his language. His was not the learning of a
Richard Reynolds, the Bridgetine monk who at the Reformation was thought to be the only *Vir trilinguis* amongst the
English monks.[30]

If Robert Joseph was a humanist, then he was a selective
humanist, and in his letter book the new is merged with the
old. It is difficult to believe that the medieval letter collections were not very much in his mind as he put together his
compendium of a new Latin style. Even the eloquent calls
for simplicity of language are not unknown amongst characteristically medieval treatises of *dictamen*, one of which
recommends that 'if you are asking a friend for money, what
right have you to begin with the Incarnation of the Word?'[31]
Robert Joseph's Erasmian sympathies are real enough, but
his was a piecemeal humanism mediated by the tradition of
the cloister. To see him as a humanist and this alone is to
miss much of the richness contained in the world he
describes.

OXFORD

That world was dominated by two places, places which
Robert Joseph frequently saw as being radically opposed.
The University of Oxford and his own abbey of Evesham
were at the centre of his life, and if most of his letters are
concerned with Oxford, it is worth remembering that all bar

twelve were written at Evesham.[32] It is the interrelation of Oxford and Evesham, of monasticism and learning, that makes Robert Joseph's witness so exceptional.

But we should be careful before assuming that his experience of Oxford was anything typical. Perhaps, indeed, there is no such thing. Of the sixty-two letters attributed to Oxford correspondents with certainty by Aveling and Pantin, forty-three are addressed to monks, twenty-one of whom are monks of Evesham. Of his remaining Oxford correspondents, none belonged to any other religious orders, a striking fact when one considers the significant role played within the university by the orders of friars and the physical proximity of his college to the houses of other orders. Of his letters to non-religious, sixteen are to Oxford Masters, and even including letters of uncertain attribution to Oxford there are only three correspondents whom we can describe as lay students. These figures warn us against assuming that Robert Joseph's Oxford was everybody's Oxford. Rather, all that follows must be based on the understanding that his experience of the university was critically determined by his monastic identity.

This is in one way a paradoxical statement, for there can be no doubt that Robert Joseph's view of Oxford was dominated by the desire to escape from his monastery and to return there. Writing to a monk of Abingdon in 1530, he declares that 'I would prefer Oxford to the richest of all offices', and this sentiment is expressed so often that it forms a leitmotiv for the whole collection.[33] To his friend Edmund Rougham he states that his desire to return to Oxford is both desperate and unceasing, and in a later letter to John Feckenham he compares this to Aeneas' earnest search for Italy as described by Virgil. There could be no more poignant an image for any cultured man of letters.

The very insistency of this desire requires some explanation. It has already been noted that Robert Joseph's letters stem from a period between two stays in Oxford, from 1530 and 1533. He had been in Oxford for six years before returning to Evesham, and when he first came back he occupied the post of abbot's chaplain, very probably an obedientiary office that Robert Joseph himself much prized.

It is not clear whether Robert Joseph was brought back from
Oxford specifically to fill this office. It is not mentioned as
among the major obedientary offices in the list compiled by
Thomas de Marleberg in the thirteenth century, but the
evidence of other comparable monastic houses suggests that
it would have been a not unimportant monastic appointment. It would not, however, have been conceived as a long-
term job. The statutes of the General Chapter of 1444 had
decreed that chaplains were to change every year, and
though this did not always happen, few could have imagined
it as a lasting office.[34]

But Robert Joseph probably held it for only a few short
weeks. In November 1530, the disputed election of a new
prior was followed by a redistribution of offices, and those
who had spoken out too freely for the losing side suffered.
Many of Robert Joseph's friends found themselves with new
posts, but to him came an appointment that deeply embitt-
ered him, that of teacher of novices. It meant that he
became bound by the cloister more tightly than before, far
too closely for his liking.

In this context, his desire to return became all the more
insistent. It also encouraged an ever more desperate search
for support. In a letter to the schoolmaster of Evesham,
Edmund Fyld, written soon after he became teacher of
novices, he describes how the Abbot of Pershore had promised to write to the Abbot of Evesham in support of his
return, and later in his campaign he elicits the help of
Richard Kidderminster, a former Abbot of Winchcombe
renowned for his support for learning. These and others are
urged to write to Robert Joseph's abbot, Clement Litchfield,
who gradually assumes the role of adversary in the growing
campaign for freedom.[35]

This very campaign inevitably colours Robert Joseph's
view of Oxford. His is not the perspective of the dispassionate observer, but of the former student whose hope
of returning is fading, and whose view of Oxford and its men
is becoming increasingly jaundiced. There is something of
the 'old member' about Robert Joseph, seen most clearly in
his reaction to news of a freshman, William Lyttleton. In a
letter to an Oxford monk, Thomas Penthecost, Robert

Joseph assumes the attitude of a defender of tradition in condemning the new generation for their failure to observe the custom of 'salting' a new arrival.[36] The end of this tradition seems to him reprehensible, a sign of how things are changing. There is a sense throughout the later letters that Oxford is slipping out of his grasp, not merely because of the intransigence of his abbot but because times are changing, people are changing, and he is becoming forgotten. Thus there are frequent complaints that Oxford men fail to keep in touch with him, that news is all too slow in making the journey from Oxford to far-away Evesham. This gap is expressed most clearly in a letter to George London, a monastic contemporary at Evesham, wherein Robert Joseph describes rumours that have reached him of his being labelled as '*rusticus*'.[37] So soon after his return from the university, the monk in his rural abbey is being distinguished from the monks in the cosmopolitan university, and it may be that one of Robert Joseph's primary motivations in writing so many letters was precisely to prevent this label from sticking.

However much this desire to return to Oxford dominates Robert Joseph's thinking on the university, the glimpses he gives us of monastic life at Gloucester College remain very valuable. They provide what one might label as an 'undergraduate monastic' perspective on the university, and it is therefore no surprise to find that money is the greatest concern.

A concern with money amongst monastic students is the most consistent feature of all evidence from such students during this period. Amongst the letters received by William Glastynbury, the two related issues of the paucity of his grant from the sub-prior and the need to buy presents for the Prior of Dover dominate, and amongst the letters received from monastic students by Henry of Eastry, eight out of ten include at least some request for financial help. Robert Joseph too was asked for such help, though the money at his disposal was undoubtedly less than was available to the Prior of Canterbury. On numerous occasions we hear that he has sent 2d., or some other sum, to a correspondent, and it is also clear that other correspondents sent Robert Joseph money at Evesham. There is ample evidence within the letters to suggest that living at Oxford was an expensive business, and the demands of life there clearly made money in short supply, such that Robert Joseph could coin the phrase of Oxford students that 'whoever comes up to Oxford with money goes down penniless'. He describes Humphrey Chester's desire for wealth as equivalent to that of Cardinal Wolsey, and in his last extant letter to John Feckenham the cloistered monk can sign himself as 'yours pennilessly'.[38]

This concern with money is at one level surprising, but the consistency with which it appears reminds us that money was very much part of the monastic system by the end of the Middle Ages. Although *Summi Magistri* had banned the personal money allowance in 1336,[39] there continued to be a great deal of money at the disposal of relatively junior monastic officials. During Robert Joseph's time as abbot's chaplain, it is likely that he handled considerable sums, and such a post could be amongst the wealthier of the obedientiaries. Thus at Selby Abbey the chaplain was paid an annual fee of over 13s. in 1399, more than either the prior or the sub-prior, an income parallel to that of the most respectable of the abbey's employees. As well as this fee, the chaplain handled 52s. worth of presents to be given to various persons on behalf of the abbot,[40] a custom which Robert Joseph certainly picked up from somewhere, and continued to exercise after his term as chaplain. Thus we hear that he had sent a bracelet to a monastic colleague at Ramsey, and in a letter to Edmund Fyld he complains that his lack of money prevents him from giving the presents he regards as customary at Christmas time. Such were the sums that he handled that on one occasion we hear of him receiving a set of scales for the weighing out of gold coin.[41] There can be little surprise, in a system such as this, that there was a considerable overspill into the life of the academic monks.

But money sent to Oxford very often had a specific purpose, that of the purchase of books. The letter collection is full of evidence that points both to the need for books and to the sharing of books between monks and monasteries, in which practice Robert Joseph was a considerable master. He frequently asks his friends to send books unobtainable at

Evesham, and many of his letters contain eloquent thanks for such loans. Equally, Robert Joseph was assiduous in writing to those to whom he had lent his own books, always desiring their speedy return. Indeed, when a volume written by Thomas More became lost, Robert Joseph was quick to pass the blame onto someone else.[42] His is a world in which books played a huge part, and he and his friends clearly regarded the possession of books as very important.

Their subject matter was, moreover, wide-ranging. As well as Bibles and some works of contemporary theology, Robert Joseph was keen to acquire the works of classical authors, to be placed on his shelves alongside the great humanist writings of Erasmus or William Hormann. We even know that Robert Joseph had a copy of Theophrastus' *On Plants*, which he lent to John Gabriel and which was then lent on by John Gabriel to a monk of Hyde. Robert Joseph writes to John Feckenham demanding its return, writing that 'it would be inhuman thus to lose so elegant a volume.'[43]

An author such as Theophrastus, however elegant his study, could not have been regarded as central to Robert Joseph's theological education. Its presence, however, is not particularly surprising, because he had little respect for that education, at least as narrowly conceived. We should not assume that Robert Joseph's desire to return to Oxford was fuelled by a desperate wish to immerse himself more deeply in theology or Scripture.

Studies

Yet it was on account of theology that Robert Joseph had presumably been sent to Oxford in the first place. This point is easy to overlook, especially if one pays too much attention to his apparent criticisms of the Scotist method of theological discourse to be found within the letters. Robert Joseph's theological education was entirely that of the scholastics, and it is therefore surprising at first sight to find him using Scotism as almost a dirty word. Robert Joseph was clearly well known for this, and in a humorous letter to Robert Tailer he recounts stories told at Oxford in which his own dislike of Scotism, and preference for the learning of antiquity, formed an important part.[44] There is indeed a certain undercurrent of criticism in his letters, perhaps even a sense of frustration with the limitations imposed by the scholastic method, but nowhere does Robert Joseph actually disavow his medieval theological formation. Rather, he chooses to defend it when pressed, and in a letter to Thomas Ethelstan at Oxford he offers a vigorous defence of the Scotist system against one of its detractors.[45] Ethelstan, later a monk of the restored community of Westminster, had written to Robert Joseph a letter full of complaints at what he was studying. He had described the teaching of the Scotists as 'dirty puddles', and clearly expected Robert Joseph, with his reputation before him, to agree with him. In this he was disappointed, for in his reply Robert Joseph does not share in his scorn, but offers a middle way between it and the learning of the ancients, asserting not a radical choice between the one and the other but a fusion of the two. Thus he writes, 'I always consider Scotus and his followers, in order to take ideas from them, but I find my pure Latin from other more cultured works.'

This is the synthesis of one in whom theological discourse and the demands of humanism were able to coexist. His complaints against scholasticism are not to do with its theology, but to do with the time that it took to study it. Thus when writing to John Feckenham at Oxford in 1532, he derides its questionings because they stop his favourite friend from writing enough letters, and elsewhere his complaint is that it takes people away from the study of decent Latin.[46] It is the complaint of a purist, one who perceives that scholastic Latin is not all that Latin could be and who prefers to see his friends reading the ancient writers whose Latin will enable them to write the kind of letters that he loved. In this sense, we are back to the very purpose of the letter book. It is only anti-scholastic insofar as it contains within it an implicit appeal for a style of Latin writing unknown to the medieval theologians, whose constructed vocabulary was something that the humanists frequently abhorred. Apart from this, there is no reason to suppose that Robert Joseph's theology, and the spirituality that flowed from it, were anything other than typical of an Oxford where scholasticism continued to flourish well into the sixteenth century. For all the flurry of interest in his letters in the new learning, Robert Joseph's Oxford was not one which had yet rejected the canons of medieval scholarship.

In many ways, the view of Oxford that Robert Joseph advances is conventionally medieval. It is a monastic Oxford, an Oxford where the curriculum continued to be dominated by a theological method centuries old that coexisted with new learning. A conclusion such as this raises an obvious question, for his Oxford was soon to be overturned, and his monastic generation was to be the last to have an Oxford education for many centuries. We may therefore expect to find some sign of this impending calamity within the pages of such an observer.

THE NEW AND THE OLD

Enough has been said to suggest that Robert Joseph was not the type to be found at the forefront of change. His was a conservative mind, but he was not immune to what was going on around him, and there are in his letters plenty of references to suggest that he was living at a time of increasing theological ferment, ferment which he himself despised. We first come across this in a letter to Master Henry Wyllys of September 1530, when he asks to hear about the case of William Tracey.[47] Tracey's will had been examined by Convocation and been found to express Lutheran theology; it had therefore been condemned and Tracey's body exhumed and burned at the stake. To all this, Robert Joseph's reaction is entirely straightforward. Tracey is like the Old Testament judge Samson, doing more harm by his death than he had ever done in his life, even though his views in life had themselves been pestiferous and misguided. His request to hear of Tracey's fate is not that of the dispassionate or interested theological student, but rather of one who wishes the affair had never started and was soonest over. He clearly regards Tracey's opinions as an unwelcome intrusion into a settled theological pattern, and he retains this view remorselessly in the face of other attacks on the Church. In a letter to Richard Bedell he asserts that God's love for the Church saves it from error, and he therefore rejects criticisms he has heard of three pillars of medieval devotional practice, devotion to Mary, fasting and pilgrimage.[48] During his years at Evesham, it appears that Oxford correspondents put him in the way of various doubtful texts, but to each one Robert Joseph's response is the same – he rejects them out of hand, and longs for a time of peace. Thus in a letter to Edward Grexson almost at the end of the collection he laments the degree to which learned men now seem to disagree over matters of theology, and hopes that in time the different theological views will come to a synthesis again. If they do not, the result will be clear, and he predicts for the Church a future like that of Sodom and Gomorrah.[49] It is the closest he gets to prophecy.

Such a view of the tumult of his own times reflects a settled spiritual pattern within Robert Joseph's own life. He is not someone who wears his spirituality on his sleeve, but for all his evident frustration with the minutiae of monastic observance, there is a strong sense of what is important in his faith. At the end of the same letter to Edward Grexson he writes that 'for Joseph it is enough to join with Paul and confess Christ crucified', and all that we see of his piety tends to reinforce this impression of simplicity. Requests for prayer abound in his letters, even to the extent of asking others to pray that he might return to Oxford, and he is happy to send images of saints and rosary beads to his friends. We may assume equally that his friends were happy to receive them. In a letter to Humphrey Chester, Robert Joseph advises that prayer is the best cure for fever, and he has no doubt as to the efficacy of the Mass as a form of petitionary prayer.[50]

Above all, what is important for Robert Joseph is the priesthood. In a letter probably addressed to Robert Dorning he advances a high view of the life of priests and their need to be free of scandal. Within a conventional piety, priesthood assumed a large part, and it is the very centrality of this priesthood which contains some clue as to Robert Joseph's fate after the tumult of the dissolution of the monasteries.

For Robert Joseph comes at the end of a story. His monastic world and the Oxford that existed within it were to vanish, and the prosopography of Robert Joseph's correspondents reflects the many ways in which the last medieval monastic generation sought to cope with this change. For some, change itself was welcome; among Robert Joseph's friends were two monks of Bury St Edmunds with decided Lutheran sympathies,[51] and in his wider circle of monastic acquaintances there were some for whom the chance to preach the royal supremacy came as very welcome. One such is John Placet, mentioned by Robert Joseph among a list of friends, who in 1535 wrote to Cromwell to ask that he 'may be commanded to preach the supremacy every Sunday . . . and that I may compel every monk to preach it and teach it to others.' In Placet's mind, this preaching was allied to a radical dissatisfaction with the ceremonies of the monastic life, most notably the 'heaping of psalms'. Robert Joseph also found such endless recitation irksome,[52] but there is no suggestion that he was ever tempted down the path of radical advocacy of the new cause.

On the other hand, Robert Joseph had no connection with the attempt to refound monasticism during the brief reign of Mary. Amongst his friends were several who joined the new foundation of Westminster, but Robert Joseph's name does not appear among them, despite the fact that its abbot was his once closest friend John Feckenham. For Robert Joseph himself, there was as always a middle way, and what little we know of his life after 1540 suggests that he served as a parish priest until his death. This fits in well with what we know of his spiritual outlook, for in one of the last letters in his collection he extols the life of the secular priest in terms of high romanticism. That life is one such that none more tranquil can be found, a way of life that is chaste, holy and endowed with human virtue. The letter was written in the early part of 1532,[53] when the future seemed to revolve around the question of returning to Oxford. The life of the secular priest was perhaps then a dream, but it became a reality and Robert Joseph accepted that reality apparently placidly.

That so conventionally a medieval monk should so happily

slip into this new role is deserving comment. The fact that so medieval a figure as Robert Joseph could become so absorbed into the new ecclesiastical order tells us something important about that new order. It suggests to us that it was perhaps not so different from the old.

There is a postscript to Robert Joseph's story, pointing back towards the medieval but also forward into another new age. Amongst his friends, Robert Joseph counted William Lyttleton, the monk of Evesham whose failure to be greeted with the usual customs reserved for freshmen had so upset him.[54] Lyttleton may have been the youngest of Robert Joseph's friends; certaintly, he outlived most of them, for in 1603 we find his name again in monastic circles. But now the composition of that circle has changed, for we are in the era of the monastic Counter-Reformation. In that year, there arrived from the continent an Englishman who had been clothed with the monastic habit in Spain. He had come to begin a mission in support of recusant Catholics, and at a country house in Worcestershire, this representative of the new monasticism met an aged survivor of the old. Father Augustine Bradshaw was introduced to William Lyttleton, 'who had formerly been a monk of Evesham and was now best known by the nickname of Parson Tinker.' There followed a kind of reconciliation that is the stuff of the new spirit of the seventeenth-century mission and Lyttleton died at peace with the Church. Lyttleton's story makes good party reading, but we will search in vain for such an ending in the case of Robert Joseph. He died as he had lived since 1540, a parish priest at All Saints, Evesham. In the 1830s, the historian George May recorded the inscription on a tomb thought to be his, and after giving the text he described it as containing 'Romish solicitations . . . [such that] we may infer that his religious sentiments were moulded by the vacillating religion of the state.'[55] This may serve as an epitaph to the middle way of the sixteenth century, the way of Robert Joseph.

12

Benedictine Monks at the University of Oxford and the Dissolution of the Monasteries

PETER CUNICH

The Benedictine order, with its three colleges and fifty monk-scholars at the time of the dissolution of the monasteries, was the most conspicuous of all the religious orders at Oxford in the early sixteenth century. Not only were the Benedictines numerically dominant, but they also produced both the largest number of graduates and a greater number of doctors than any other order between 1500 and 1540.[1] Statistics such as these do not tell us much about the quality of learning of the monks, nor do they allow us to gauge their performance against that of the seculars studying at the university, but they should nevertheless alert us to the peril of putting too much faith in the opinions of nineteenth-century writers who characterised the monastic colleges of Oxford in this period as having 'very little importance in the history either of learning or of education'.[2] Such negative assessments of the performance of monk-scholars at the universities have been accepted by most twentieth-century commentators and have been further reinforced by doubts as to the desirability and utility of a university education for monks. Even Professor Knowles was critical of the practice of sending monks to the universities, and his judgement has been highly influential since the 1950s.[3] Negative assessments such as these have been refuted by several scholars during the last twenty years,[4] but there is still a lingering

suspicion among some historians of the English Reformation that the monks of sixteenth-century Oxford were
probably not a very scholarly lot, and even those who
were academically distinguished would have been better off
in the cloister where they belonged. Monastic Oxford has
therefore provided for historians a convenient example of
the more general decline into which the monastic regime in
England is supposed to have fallen by the 1530s.[5]

It is rather difficult to test the assertions of either the
detractors or the champions of Oxford's Benedictine alumni
in the early sixteenth century. There are a number of works
which provide a glimpse of the lives led by Benedictine
monks and the University of Oxford in the later Middle
Ages, at none of them more impressive in its scope and
scholarship than Professor Dobson's recent contribution to
Oxford's own *History,* but the question of the state of the
Benedictine colleges at the time of the dissolution has never
been adequately addressed. Some of the insights into Benedictine Oxford are quite telling. We know, for example,
that monk-scholars returning from Oxford to Norwich
Cathedral Priory sometimes proved to be arrogant and dis-
dainful of their confrères, but Dr Greatrex has assured us
that the positive influence of the Norwich graduate 'filtered
through the cloister and also extended beyond the
enclosure to the community outside'.[6] Professor Dobson has
likewise asserted that the Oxford graduates at Canterbury
Cathedral Priory formed a small academic élite within the
convent 'whose influence was quite out of proportion to its
numbers'.[7] Some historians have questioned the quality of
the learning of the Benedictine monks at Oxford, but we
have now become well acquainted with Robert Joseph's talented circle of monk-correspondents who had undoubtedly
been inspired by the humanist intellectual trends of the
age.[8] That academic distinction was to be encountered
among the Black Monks at Oxford is evident from the fact
that several of them undertook expensive postgraduate
studies at overseas universities. William Gillingham and two
other monks of Canterbury College are known to have completed their studies at Paris between 1512 and 1540, and
Thomas Goldwell, the future Cathedral Prior of Canterbury,

took his doctorate at Turin in 1511 before proceeding to Louvain for further study. It must, therefore, be assumed that these were men of considerable academic attainments and not simply the conservative relics of a medieval scholasticism which had been overtaken by Renaissance humanism within the wider intellectual community of Oxford.[9]

It has always been recognised that a university education presented certain difficulties in the formation of a Benedictine monk, but we should not be too quick to condemn the Oxford experience as being inherently destructive of regular conventual life and the Benedictine ideal of stability. By the beginning of the sixteenth century the pattern of university life for English Benedictine monk-scholars was well established along lines which sought to maintain regular observance and stability, even though an individual monk might spend the larger part of his monastic career away from the cloister of his mother-house. While it is true that by living away from their monasteries for periods of up to eight or twelve years these monk-scholars developed both a physical and an intellectual independence which St Benedict certainly never intended for his monks, it would appear that long-standing arrangements were, to a large extent, successful in maintaining a sense of extra-claustral stability within the wider community of monk-scholars at Oxford. There is no better example of the success of these arrangements than a day-trip to the village of Islip by Thomas Barton of Westminster and four of his confreres on 14 October 1522. While at Islip for their autumn picnic the Westminster monks celebrated the feast of their monastery's patron, St Edward the Confessor, in the parish church which their abbot had known as a boy. These sorts of activities must have been common enough among the many small communities of monk-scholars who attempted to maintain their vow of stability while outside the cloister for long periods.[10]

It might be argued that university monks posed a serious threat to the peace and tranquillity of their convents when they returned home from their studies, and there is no shortage of evidence to support this claim. There can be no doubt that university monks did cause problems when they returned to their cloisters, and the conflicts for which they were responsible were often destructive of community spirit. The example of Richard Norwich and Thomas Norton of Norwich Cathedral Priory is well known. At the episcopal visitation of the priory in 1532, these two monks who had recently returned from Oxford were found to be *inflati spiritu alti cordis et indebitantur in universitate.*[11] Haughtiness may also have been at the root of the difficulties caused by Hugh Egwin (*alias* Cooper) at Winchcombe between 1534 and 1539.[12] This was probably a more common complaint within the English Benedictine cloisters on the eve of the dissolution than the surviving evidence allows us to state with any degree of certainty. Robert Joseph provides us with another example of a monk whose actions in the chapter house, even though they may not have been intentionally subversive, nevertheless caused discord within the convent and brought abbatial retribution upon his own head.[13] A similar fate befell William Kendall of Gloucester in mid-1531, so we are probably safe to assume that university monks tended to be more outspoken and less compliant than their non-university brethren when they eventually returned to the cloister.

Given the frailties of human nature, it was probably unavoidable that divisions between the *claustrales* and the *scholastici* would eventually occur within even the best disciplined monasteries, but it is also likely that most monastic communities would have developed mechanisms for coping with opinionated or otherwise difficult university graduates within the convent. This was perhaps the case at Durham Cathedral Priory where many monk-graduates became priors of dependent cells almost as soon as they returned from Oxford. This was a relatively painless solution for both monk and convent where potential difficulties arose from interpersonal conflicts. The means by which conflicts involving monk-scholars were resolved within Benedictine monasteries have left scant evidence in the visitation records of the early sixteenth century, and this perhaps indicates that the difficulties which did arise were overcome relatively quickly. Unfortunately, the dearth of visitation records relating to monks studying at Oxford or to the problems which monk-graduates caused when they returned to their convents makes it as difficult to assess the negative impact of university education on the individual houses of the Benedictine order as it is to evaluate the academic achievements of those monks.

The evidence, then, appears to be contradictory. While the type of university education envisaged by Benedict XII's Constitutions of 1336 sometimes threatened the cultivation of a humility and 'unhesitating obedience' which St Benedict exhorts in his Rule, the arrangements at Gloucester, Canterbury and Durham Colleges nevertheless provided an extra-claustral environment in which monks from the various Benedictine houses were protected from the most serious temptations which Oxford had to offer the innocent undergraduate while pursuing his studies there. This problem was not, however, peculiar to the early sixteenth century. It was one which had to be faced by any abbot sending young monks to the university, and this was as true for the medieval period as it is today in the twentieth century. There were serious dangers implicit in allowing a monk to be away from the rest of the *conventus* during the later years of his formation, but these perils had to be weighed against the many benefits which a university education bestowed upon both the individual monks and the monasteries to which they returned at the end of their studies. The academic preparation which the monk-scholars received in theology was as invaluable for the religious life of the monastery as their training in canon law was for guarding and extending the ecclesiastical privileges of the great Benedictine abbeys. A university training also seems to have been of some value in the more secular concerns of estate administrations and the legal obligations which the monasteries had as prominent landowners. In an age of expanding educational opportunities the Benedictines of sixteenth-century England must also have realised that in order to maintain their status they had to take university education seriously. Such a realisation is clearly evident in Robert Joseph's letters and its impact may be seen ranging from the changing emphases in the academic exercises of the monk-scholars to the considerable expenditure on the buildings in which those studies took place. By 1500 the Benedictine order already possessed some of the best collegiate accommodation in Oxford and, even though some of these buildings had now been standing for more than a century, they appear to have been kept in good repair right up until the dissolution. Early in the reign of Henry VIII Bishop Fox of Winchester even proposed that a fourth Benedictine college should be built at Oxford to house eight monks from Winchester Cathedral Priory. This plan was only abandoned in 1513 and the fact that Corpus Christi College was ultimately founded for secular students says more about the need to educate the secular clergy than it does about the fitness of the 'bussing monks' of Winchester for studies at Oxford.[14] Another new development which was taking place at this time was the provision of scholarships for lay students at Oxford from funds administered by the Abbot of Glastonbury and the Cathedral Priors of Canterbury and Durham.[15] There was, then, much interest and activity in the field of higher education among the monks of the Benedictine order in England on the eve of the dissolution.

One thing which also becomes clear from a reading of the contemporary evidence is that young monks continued to covet the opportunity of studying at Oxford until the suppression of the Benedictine *studia*. During the episcopal visitation of Glastonbury Abbey on 15 July 1538 several of the monks complained that the prior's favourite, Dom John Neot, had been at Oxford for nearly a decade without even having learnt to preach properly and was therefore preventing other qualified brethren from going up to Gloucester College. From other evidence we know that Neot was in fact a rather more accomplished student than his brethren led the visitor to believe, so it is clear that his long tenure of a Glastonbury scholarship at Oxford was greatly resented by the other young monks left in the cloister. The complaints appear to have been effective, for by the autumn of that year Neot had been recalled to the cloister and a new batch of monks had been dispatched to Oxford for a chance at university life.[16] But perhaps the best example of a monk who wanted more than anything else to study at Oxford is Robert Joseph of Evesham. From the time he was recalled from Gloucester College back to his monastery in 1530 until the day he returned to Oxford in early 1532, Joseph used every opportunity and marshalled all his contacts in an effort to persuade his unco-operative abbot that Oxford was the best place for him.[17] For the English Benedictine monk-scholars themselves, then, it seems that there was no doubt as to the value of a university education in the years immediately before the dissolution.

It is also evident that only the most promising novices were sent up to Oxford for advanced studies in philosophy, theology and canon law. The novice-master at Durham kept a close eye on his charges and chose those who were 'apte to lernyng, and dyd applie his booke, and had a pregnant wyt withall' to fill the fellowships falling vacant at Durham College.[18] A detailed investigation of the Benedictine monk-scholars of the early sixteenth century would ideally take into account the academic attainments and religious commitment of each monk who studied at Oxford in this period. It is virtually impossible, however, to make a satisfactory assessment of either the intellectual or the spiritual attainments of these monk-scholars. The surviving evidence simply does not allow for this type of detailed prosopographical study.

What is possible, however, is a reasonably thorough general survey of those Benedictine monks who are known to have studied at Oxford in the early sixteenth century. A broad outline of the career paths of these monk-scholars both within the cloister and after the dissolution will help to provide a clearer picture of how a university education influenced the life of a Benedictine monk in the period immediately before the dissolution. This may in turn enable us to arrive at some firmer conclusions concerning the state of the Benedictine colleges in Oxford in the forty or so years before the dissolution. The biographical materials necessary for a survey such as this have been available since the publication more than twenty years ago of the final volume of Dr Emden's *Biographical Register of the University of Oxford*. In this volume Emden provides short biographies of the 241 Benedictine monks whom he found at Oxford during this period. Further research has produced evidence of another twenty-five Benedictine monk-scholars, and it is probable

that Dr Greatrex's forthcoming *Biographical Register* will
identify even more monk-scholars from the monastic
cathedral priories.[19] It has therefore been possible to supplement Emden's biographies with much additional
material from numerous sources, among which the voluminous records of the Court of Augmentations have
proven to be particularly rewarding.[20] The picture which
emerges from this survey is much more positive than that
which has been painted by the critics of monastic Oxford.
What has become clear from the quantitative evidence is
that the majority of sixteenth-century Benedictine monk-scholars at Oxford were both learned and successful. While the
quality of their learning is not easy to assess and the evidence
of their religious convictions has for the most part proven
elusive, the fact that many monk-scholars were both intellectually distinguished and deeply religious may nevertheless
be argued from the surviving evidence of their later careers.

It is not possible to determine exactly how many Benedictine monks studied at Oxford in the early sixteenth century,
even though the university's records are much more reliable
in this period than they are for the fifteenth century. Virtually all graces for degrees are recorded after 1505, but
degree-taking alone cannot be used for determining the
total number of Benedictines at the university. Many monk-
students (and perhaps a majority of those who passed
through the Benedictine *studia*) did not take degrees at the
conclusion of their studies. Emden's *Biographical Register* lists
143 Benedictine monks who together took 177 degrees
between 1500 and 1540, and further research has provided
the names of another six monks who took degrees at this
time, giving a total of 149 monks taking 184 degrees at
Oxford in the early sixteenth century.[21] In the same period,
however, there were at least another 105 Benedictine monks
who studied at Oxford but who did not take degrees. Our
knowledge of these non-graduate monks rests almost
entirely upon the chance survival of documents which were
not produced by the formal record-keeping procedures of
the university. These sources include college accounts, monastic obedientiary rolls, personal correspondence, wills,
inventories of books, legal papers and visitation records. The

survival of these types of records is very uneven, however, and it seems likely that many more Benedictine monks than are mentioned in the surviving records were actually studying at Oxford in the first forty years of the sixteenth century. Indeed, it is probable that considerably less than half the monks who went up to Oxford stayed in residence long enough to take degrees. In the case of Canterbury Cathedral Priory, for example, only eighteen of the forty-three monk-scholars who are known to have studied at Oxford in this period took degrees. The same is true for Westminster, Glastonbury and Bury St Edmunds, but several other large monasteries such as Gloucester, Evesham and St Albans had higher proportions of graduates among their monk-scholars.[22] While these differences may simply be a result of the uneven survival of records, it may also indicate that there was a certain degree of variety in the policies regarding degree-taking among the larger Benedictine monastic houses.

There were, of course, many other reasons for what at first appears to be a rather poor completion rate among monastic scholars. A large number of monks died while studying at Oxford,[23] and some were no doubt found to be unsuited to university study and returned to their cloisters after completing only part of the formal requirements for a degree. Others were probably called back to their monasteries after a longer period of study but before they had taken degrees,[24] and it seems likely that a smaller number lost their Oxford scholarships as a punishment for unbecoming behaviour either while at Oxford or else during return visits to their monasteries.[25] It may sometimes have been necessary for monks to leave Oxford because their monasteries were experiencing financial difficulties. University study was an expensive undertaking, as those monks who lost their scholarships at the time of the dissolution quickly discovered. Most of these monks found it impossible to complete their degree studies, even though they were supported by relatively generous state pensions, and in general only those monks who were granted exhibitions by the Crown continued their university studies.[26] For whatever reason, then, the number of monks recorded as having studied at Oxford in the early sixteenth century is far greater than the number who ultimately took degrees.

It should be noted that failure to take a degree was not unusual among university students at the time, and even seculars for whom a degree was often a prerequisite for clerical preferment are known to have left the university in large numbers without any formal qualification.[27] For the regulars, a degree was more often considered to be an expensive privilege rather than a necessary preparation for future duties within the cloister, so the fact that approximately half the Benedictine monks at Oxford did not take degrees cannot be taken as necessarily indicating ineptitude or lack of commitment to their university studies. For a monk it was the study of theology or canon law which was most important rather than the act of taking a degree at the end of those studies. This is not to say that a degree was of no assistance to a monk's claustral career. It clearly was. Monk-graduates normally rose quickly through the ranks within their convents, regularly being appointed to the most responsible obedientiary offices (especially as cellarers, sub-priors and claustral priors), to the priorships of dependent cells, and many Benedictine graduates were eventually elected by their confrères to rule their monasteries as abbots and priors. During the early sixteenth century twenty-nine monk-graduates from Oxford became heads of monastic houses and another fifteen Cambridge graduates achieved the same status.[28] A university degree was therefore of inestimable value in securing a successful career within the English Benedictine Congregation in the sixteenth century. But there are also numerous examples of monks who did not take degrees at Oxford but who nevertheless pursued highly successful careers within their cloisters.[29] We should not therefore be too surprised to discover that only half the monk-scholars completed the long and expensive studies which ultimately led to the conferment of degrees in theology or canon law. What is perhaps surprising about the Benedictines in the sixteenth as in the earlier centuries is that so many monks did take degrees despite the expense and time involved.

The English Benedictine commitment to university education was not limited to the larger and wealthier houses of the order. Statistical evidence shows that a large number of houses, both great and small, sent monks to study at the order's colleges in Oxford and Cambridge. A total of at least 324 monks from forty-two houses attended the two universities during the early sixteenth century, but the number of Benedictine monasteries sending monks to Oxford and Cambridge was probably even larger because the origins of thirty-eight monk-scholars is not known. Oxford was clearly much more popular than Cambridge as a place of study. This was probably because of the heavier concentration of Benedictine monasteries in the West and the greater provision of Benedictine college accommodation at Oxford rather than having anything to do with the educational merits of one or the other university. Eight of the houses (mostly in East Anglia) sent their scholars exclusively to Cambridge, while seven used both the Oxford and Cambridge *studia.*[30] Twenty-seven monasteries placed all of their monk-scholars at the three *studia* in Oxford, with most residing at Gloucester College, the Oxford *studium generale* for the English congregation. A total of thirty-five known monasteries therefore sent 247 monk-scholars to Oxford during this period (see Appendix).

Canterbury Cathedral Priory had the largest number of monks at Oxford (43), all of whom were fellows of the priory's own *studium,* Canterbury College. At any one time there were normally six monks from the priory (a warden and five monk-fellows) in residence at Canterbury College.[31] Durham Cathedral Priory was likewise sending up to eight monk-scholars at a time to its Oxford *studium,* Durham College. The names of only twenty-eight of these monks have survived, but there were probably many more who made their way to Oxford during this forty-year period.[32] These two colleges were relatively small and remained aloof from the Benedictine *studium generale* under the authority of the *prior studentium* at Gloucester College, but both colleges provided rooms for 'sojourners' from other monasteries who could not be accommodated at Gloucester College. The Warden of Canterbury College rented rooms to Benedictine monks from Battle, Reading, Winchcombe, Winchester,

Rochester and Peterborough, and he also provided accommodation for a group of Cluniac monks from Lewes and a number of senior secular members of the university.[33] Durham College probably provided a similar arrangement for monks from the great northern monasteries such as Whitby and York St Mary's, but the names of only two of these monks have survived and neither of them took degrees.[34] Despite lacunae in the evidence, it has been possible to identify seventy-one of the monks from Canterbury and Durham Cathedral Priories studying at Oxford between 1500 and 1540. This represents approximately one quarter of all known Benedictine monk-scholars and is indicative of the lead which these two houses took in monastic higher education during the sixteenth century.

The only other monastery which came anywhere close to Canterbury and Durham in sending monks to Oxford was Westminster, with twenty-five known students at Gloucester College in the sixteenth century. Westminster's policy of sending such large numbers of scholars to Oxford seems to have been forced upon the abbey by its patron Henry VII, who insisted on having university-educated monks serving at his splendid new chantry chapel. We are particularly fortunate to know the names of the twenty-five Westminster monk-scholars of Oxford. Gloucester College has left very few written records of its existence, but it has been possible to use the surprisingly large number of surviving obedientiary rolls at Westminster to fill the lacunae in the university's records.[35] Considerably fewer records have survived from the other Benedictine monasteries and it is therefore impossible to make complete lists of all monk-scholars from those houses. Despite the incompleteness of these lists we do know that at least six houses sent more than ten monks up to Oxford between 1500 and 1540, and another seven houses sent between five and eight.[36] The remaining nineteen houses, all of which had less than five monk-scholars during these years, were generally much smaller monasteries, and many of them were not even formally required to send monks to the universities. Only communities with twenty or more monks were subject to this requirement under the 1336 constitutions of Benedict XII, but at least eleven Benedictine monasteries which consistently had convents numbering less than twenty monks are known to have sent monk-scholars to the Oxford or Cambridge *studia* in the early sixteenth century.[37] Likewise, it was unusual for larger houses to shirk this responsibility. Only three abbeys with convents of more than twenty appear to have neglected to send scholars to the universities, and even in these cases the apparent lack of enthusiasm for university studies may simply be a result of the poor survival of evidence rather than a failure on the part of these communities to send their quota of monks to Oxford.[38]

What is clear, however, is that a number of monasteries were sending far more students to the universities than was required of them. Canterbury and Durham led the list, but Westminster, St Albans and Bury St Edmunds were not far behind, and even smaller houses such as Evesham and Hyde were consistently sending more than their quota.[39] Hyde and Evesham are particularly noteworthy in this respect. Hyde Abbey, with its convent of only twenty-one monks in 1539, usually had four scholars studying at Oxford at any given time in the late 1530s, and two of its graduates, Andrew Alton and Thomas Wells, were appointed as *priores studentium* in 1535 and 1538 respectively. At its surrender in April 1539, the abbey had no less than seven university-educated monks, a third of the convent. Such a high proportion of monk-scholars in a monastery with so few members was unusual and can probably be attributed to the election of the highly talented theologian John Capon (*alias* Salcot) as abbot in 1530.[40] At Evesham, a much larger house than Hyde, there were eleven university monks in a convent of thirty-four when the house was surrendered in November 1539. This was obviously another house which placed a high value on university studies, which is perhaps why it produced three *priores studentium* in the last ten years before the dissolution.[41] When the figures for the order as a whole are considered, it becomes clear that a very large number of Benedictine monks had been up to one or other of the universities by the time of the dissolution. In 1540, approximately one in seven Benedictine monks had spent some time at either Oxford or Cambridge, at least one in thirteen had taken degrees, and one out of every five monk-graduates held a doctorate in theology.[42] These figures are, by any measure, impressive. But it is the attainments of individual houses such as the cathedral priories of Canterbury and Durham, with ten and fourteen graduates respectively, or smaller Evesham with eleven, which give a better indication of the truly healthy state of learning within the English congregation in the years immediately prior to the dissolution.[43]

While these statistics certainly provide evidence that Benedictine monks studied at the universities in large numbers between 1500 and 1540, it has nevertheless been argued by some that the academic attainments of the regular clergy in England were in fact falling during the late fifteenth and early sixteenth centuries. It has been suggested that the minds of even the most intellectually adventurous of the Benedictine monks were in fact 'conventional and unexciting' and relatively uninformed of the great affairs of Church and State. The fundamental conservatism of Benedictine monks combined with an instinctive obedience to established authority have been seen as being responsible for their failure to respond fully to the challenges of Erasmian thought which so agitated both Oxford and Cambridge in the 1520s and 1530s.[44] While it is true that the Benedictine order produced few radical or even truly creative thinkers at that time, this does not mean that the Black Monks at the universities were totally uncritical and uncreative. Robert Joseph's correspondence indicates that he had wholeheartedly embraced Erasmian humanism, but his approach to the new learning was one of moderation rather than extremism. Joseph therefore advises his correspondents that 'the middle course is best. Just as those are wrong who spend their whole life weaving syllogisms out of Scotist subtleties, so those also are wrong who point the finger of scorn at scholastic arguments and think Scotus has nothing worth having.' The Benedictine monk should therefore 'season Scotist wiliness with good Latin' so as to be of equal merit in both the faculties of letters and theology.[45] In seeking a 'middle way' between scholastic and humanist learning, Robert Joseph's approach is completely consistent with the experience of a whole generation of Oxford and

Cambridge scholars who sought to make use of both traditional and new ideas as part of an orthodox reform movement during the early decades of the sixteenth century.[46] It is impossible to gauge the extent to which other Benedictine monks shared Joseph's enthusiasm for humanist literature, and it is clear that some older monks and superiors discouraged too great an interest in the new learning, but the general impression remains that a large number of younger monks who had studied at Oxford were actively engaged in exploring the opportunities offered by new intellectual trends.

Not all Benedictine monk-scholars were as cautious as Robert Joseph in avoiding controversial and at times heretical ideas. Several Benedictine monks embraced Lutheranism during the Reformation period and one was even executed as a heretic. William Jerome of Canterbury Cathedral Priory was burned at Smithfield on 30 July 1540 and is the best known of the small number of Benedictines who became Lutherans. That Lutheran books and ideas were circulating within the monastic *studia* at Oxford in the late 1520s seems likely. A number of monks were suspected of reading heretical books during the Garrett scandal of 1527–8, and Edmund Rougham of Bury St Edmunds was accused of preaching an heretical sermon at Oxford in the same year. Rougham evidently learned his lesson, for in 1545 he was to be found preaching against Lutheranism at Kirby's execution for heresy. Roger London of Reading was less circumspect. In 1538 he was inhibited from lecturing in theology within the cloister at Reading after three monks accused him of heresy, and by November 1539 he had been incarcerated in the Tower.[47] One of the Benedictine graduates of Oxford who embraced Protestant ideas (Humphrey Charity of Westminster) was forced to flee to the continent during Queen Mary's reign, and at least two were deprived of their livings for marriage, but these men appear to have been exceptions.[48] Very few Benedictine monks fully embraced Luther's teachings in the 1530s and this too is consistent with the general response by members of the two universities. It was not until the reign of Edward VI that it became safe to espouse such radical beliefs openly.

It is perhaps because of their conformity to the traditional teachings of the Church that it has been suggested that the Benedictines of sixteenth-century Oxford lacked the intellectual creativity of their medieval predecessors.[49] While it is true that Benedictine monks tended to be followers rather than leaders in the intellectual trends of the Henrician age, there are nevertheless many examples of Benedictine creativity in the last four decades before the dissolution. Robert Joseph offers a good example of some of the literary work which Benedictine university graduates were attempting in the early sixteenth century. His Latin verse compositions and the concern which both he and his correspondents show for imitating good literary style in their letters is indicative of a literary creativity searching for a means of expression beyond the choral duties of the cloister.[50] While Joseph and his correspondents spent their time in literary and epistolatory endeavours, other Benedictines turned their attention to musical and liturgical pursuits once they took up residence in Oxford. Robert Holyngborne introduced polyphony with a 'book of pricksong' at Canterbury College during his wardenship (1501–4, 1506–8), and John Dygon of St Augustine's Canterbury was distinguished not only through having studied under Vives in Paris but also by producing a number of musical compositions.[51] Preaching was a creative activity within the Benedictine monasteries which was highly prized by monk-graduates, and once again Robert Joseph shows us one monk's sincere concern to collect particularly effective examples of the oratorical art to help in preparing his own sermons. Benedictine monks were well represented among the university preachers at Oxford in the thirty years before the dissolution, and the episcopal registers of the 1530s make frequent references to Benedictines who were licensed to preach both within and beyond the cloister.[52] The Black Monks had been famed as chroniclers during medieval times, but there appears to have been a waning of interest in historical studies among the Benedictine monks in the latter Middle Ages. The sixteenth century nevertheless produced William Malvern's rhyming history of Gloucester Abbey, and Robert Wells of Ely was responsible for writing the continuation of the *Historia Eliensis* from 1486 to 1554. William Malvern was also a great builder in the perpendicular style during his abbacy at Gloucester, and in this he was followed by a number of university-educated abbots in the years before the dissolution.[53]

Observations such as these cannot be extended too far because so little is known of the intellectual attainments of individual monks. At best these examples can only give a partial impression of the university-educated élite within the Benedictine order in the early sixteenth century, but this impression is one of high quality if not original scholarship. A more quantitative approach to the attainments of these monk-scholars has the advantage of providing some idea of the sheer scale of degree-taking among the English Black Monks at the time. The statistics for degrees taken by Benedictine monks at both Oxford and Cambridge tell a rather unexpected story. In the case of Cambridge, there seems to have been a surge in degree-taking by Benedictines in the twenty-five years prior to the dissolution of Buckingham College, and this produced perhaps the most distinguished group of graduates in the college's history.[54] In Oxford, the three Benedictine colleges were also producing large numbers of highly qualified graduates. In the thirty-year period for which the university's records are most complete (1510–39), the number of degrees taken by Benedictines is surprisingly consistent in each of the decades before the suppression of the *studia*: 58 (1510–19); 56 (1520–9); and 54 (1530–9).[55] While it is clear that there was a small decline in the number of degrees being taken over this period, it must also be noted that degrees in canon law were not conferred after 1534, and this certainly had a detrimental impact on the number of Benedictines being admitted to degrees in the last five years of the 1530s. The most surprising feature of these figures is the fact that the five years to 1539 saw more Benedictine monks taking degrees than at any time in the previous forty years. In fact, it was the final two years in which the Benedictines maintained *studia* at Oxford (1538–9) which saw the highest number of degrees taken by monks, with sixteen bachelors and five doctoral degrees in theology. This no doubt represents something of a rush by monk-scholars to take their degrees before Cromwell's plan for a complete suppression of the English monasteries had been implemented, but it is also obvious that there were many monk-scholars ready to incept at this time. This indicates that until the very last moment Benedictine monks were prominent members of the intellectual élite at Oxford.

Most monk-scholars ceased their university studies after the dissolution, but a number of the newer students of the late 1530s did continue with their studies, and some even managed to take bachelor's degrees in the five years after the dissolution, while four monks incepted for their doctorates in the decade after 1540.[56] One former monk-scholar of Canterbury College, John Throwley, who had taken his B.Th. in 1528, returned to Oxford after the dissolution and eventually qualified as a physician, while a monk of Ely, Thomas Wilburton, transferred from Cambridge but does not appear to have taken a degree.[57] Even though these monks continued their studies after the dissolution, only one of them (George London of Evesham) appears to have settled permanently at Oxford as a career academic. Even the Oxonophile Robert Joseph chose to remain in the vicinity of Evesham as a poorly paid curate rather than return to the university. While this at first seems surprising, especially considering the internationally recognised talents of a number of English Benedictines, it is probably explained by the fact that most of those who were best qualified for academic careers after 1540 were either too old to return to Oxford or else had lost touch with the university. It must also be remembered that these were the men who were the most highly qualified of the former monks and were therefore in a position to pick up the wealthiest livings in the post-dissolution job market, so it is not surprising that they shunned the relatively poorly paid life of an Oxford don. Of those monks who remained in Oxford, only George London had any long-term connection with the university, residing there until at least 1560, but even he never managed to take his doctorate in theology. When Nicholas Marley of Durham eventually returned to the academic life in 1563, it was at Louvain after he had been deprived of his livings by Elizabeth's commissioners and forced to flee to the continent.[58] It seems, then, that only a few of the former Benedictine monk-scholars considered the academic life as a viable career after the dissolution.

When the dissolution came in the late 1530s, those Benedictine monks who had studied at the universities found themselves in a considerably more advantageous position than their confrères. University monks (whether graduates or not) were members of privileged élites within the powerful Benedictine monasteries and generally held the most important obedientiary offices within their convents. They were therefore in a position to take full advantage of both local and national patronage networks in securing post-dissolution employment and pensions. Their educational qualifications must also have been of enormous assistance in launching them into secular careers. Of the 158 Oxford-educated Benedictines who were still alive at the time of the dissolution, 102 held degrees and twenty-one of these had doctorates. These degree-holders received preferment much more quickly than the rank and file of the ex-monks, a fact which is clearly demonstrated in the appointments made to the new cathedral chapters established to replace the former cathedral priories. Thirty-seven, or approximately one-quarter, of the surviving university monks were appointed to prebends and canonries in these new foundations. Such appointments normally included stipends of at least £10 per annum, lodgings in the old monastic cloisters and an allowance for commons. The monk-scholars who were able to secure prebends and canonries in the new cathedral chapters not only continued to enjoy the peace and security of familiar monastic precincts but quite often found themselves living in far greater style and comfort, and with much greater independence of movement, than they had known as mere monks. Those monks who were fortunate enough to be appointed as deans of the new cathedrals continued to live in much the same style and with similar privileges to those which they had enjoyed as cathedral priors before the dissolution.[59] In addition to the prebendaries and canons, a further eleven monk-scholars were either granted exhibitions to continue their studies at Oxford or else were provided with scholarships within the new cathedral foundations.[60] For nearly one-third of the Oxford-educated Benedictine monks, then, post-dissolution life as members of the clerical élite in Henry VIII's reformed Church differed little from their life in the cloister before 1540.

Those monks who did not receive Crown appointments immediately after the dissolution were provided instead with state pensions, and the former monk-scholars fared particularly well in securing very generous pensions from the Crown's dissolution commissioners. The average pension for a Benedictine monk was somewhere between £5 and £6 per annum, which in the early 1540s provided a basic living wage for a priest in rural England. Virtually all of the former monk-scholars did much better than this average. Only two Oxford-educated Benedictines were granted pensions of less than £6 per annum, and this action was probably intended to be seen as a punishment for having been members of the ill-fated Glastonbury community.[61] Of the 110 monk-scholars who did not receive Crown appointments and therefore had to rely on state pensions to support themselves, nearly half (44) were granted pensions in the range of £6 to £9 per annum, but another thirty-one received pensions of £10 per annum or more, and four had pensions exceeding £20 per annum.[62] These monks had fared much better than their confrères, and this they owed almost entirely to their university training. A small group of sixteen graduates received the greatest prizes of all. These were the men who had risen through the ranks to become abbots and priors after their return from studying at Oxford. As heads of the great Benedictine houses they were considered to be members of the baronial class and therefore had to be compensated for the loss of status and income which surrendering their monasteries entailed. The largest pensions of all went to John Melford, Abbot of Bury St Edmunds, and Robert Wharton, a former monk of Bury who in 1525 had been elected as abbot of the Cluniac monastery of Bermondsey. They each received £333.6s.8d. per annum. The Abbots of St Albans, Tewkesbury and Ramsey, were granted pensions of £266.13s.4d. per annum, while the Abbot of Abingdon had £200 per annum and the Abbot of Eynsham received £133.6s.8d. per annum. Such large pensions allowed these men to live in a style approximating to that of a pre-Reformation abbot.

The monk-scholars drawing Crown pensions also appear to have had much better fortune than the non-university monks in gaining preferment to clerical livings in the years after the dissolution. It has not been possible to trace the careers of all the 158 surviving Oxford Benedictines, but it is known that at least thirty of the 110 monks who were not appointed by the Crown to capitular livings in 1540 found parish or chantry livings within five years of the dissolution. This is an impressive figure when it is considered that fifty-one of these former monks already had pensions of £10 per annum or more and therefore had little need of securing parish livings. When this factor is taken into account it may be concluded that approximately half of the monk-scholars who were in need of employment after the dissolution were able to find preferment within a very short time. This is a remarkably high percentage when compared with the average employment ratio of non-university monks after the dissolution (5–10 per cent).[63] It also says much for the superior qualifications of these former monk-scholars in a market for parish clergy which was flooded with ex-monks, canons and friars throughout the 1540s.

The former monk-scholars who secured preferment after the dissolution found employment in every level of the Church's ministry. At the top end of the career spectrum there were several Oxford-trained Benedictine bishops who rose to prominence in the post-Reformation English Church. Robert Wharton had already been elevated to the episcopate as Bishop of St Asaph in 1536 and was later translated to Hereford during the reign of Mary (1554–7); John Wakeman of Tewkesbury became bishop of the new see of Gloucester (1541–9); and Anthony Kitchin of Eynsham had the dubious distinction of being the only Marian bishop to retain his see after Elizabeth's accession (Llandaff, 1545–66).[64] Four Oxford Benedictines were appointed by Henry VIII as suffragans: John Stonywell of Pershore (Bishop of Pulati *in partibus*, suffragan of York, 1524–6, and Worcester, 1526–51); John Salisbury of Titchfield (Bishop of Thetford, suffragan of Norwich, 1536–54 and 1559–70,

Bishop of Sodor and Man, 1570–2); Thomas Sparke of
Durham (Bishop of Berwick, Suffragan of Durham,
1537–72); and Richard Thornden (Bishop of Dover, suffragan of Canterbury, 1545–56). Seven bishops in so few
years is an impressive performance for any Oxford college,
but when these seven are added to the five other Benedictine bishops who were educated at Buckingham College in
Cambridge it becomes clear that the English Benedictine
university colleges were in some respects more successful in
the early sixteenth century than they had ever been in the
previous two centuries.[65] Former monk-scholars were also to
be found among the ranks of senior church office-holders
during the later years of Henry VIII's reign. Loys Ferrers
of Wymondham was Archdeacon of Suffolk (1542–8) and
William Este was Archdeacon of St Albans (1544–5). Este was
later made a canon of St George's Chapel, Windsor under
Queen Mary, while John Feckenham was appointed to canonries at both St Paul's and Canterbury (1554–6) before
resuming his Benedictine habit in 1556. Other former
monk-scholars became parish priests, curates, chantry
priests, itinerant Mass-sayers, and at least two (but probably
more) secured employment as domestic chaplains.[66]

It has already been noted that some Benedictine monk-
scholars embraced Lutheranism while at Oxford and one
was even burned as a heretic in 1540. It is more difficult to
determine how many of the former monks accepted the
changes in religion which took place during the reign of
Edward VI, but there are clear indications that several
of them did. Humphrey Charity of Westminster appears to
have been the only Marian exile among the former monk-
scholars of Oxford, but he only stayed on the continent for a
short time and conformed upon his return to England in
1556. He was later made a canon of Elizabeth's new foundation at Westminster after accepting the settlement in
1559.[67] Two other former monk-scholars lost their livings
because they had married. John Clifford had to wait until
1559 before again finding preferment, but John Salisbury,
the pluralist Dean of Norwich and Suffragan Bishop of Thetford, quickly complied with the return to Catholicism under
Mary and was appointed to the chancellorship of Lincoln in

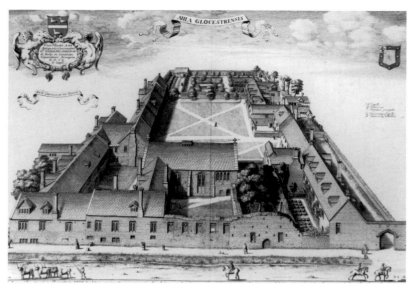

1. *(above)* Gloucester Hall. Engraving by Loggan from *Oxonia Illustrata* (1675), p. 40 (Richard Sharp).

2. *(below)* Trinity College, formerly Durham College. Engraving by Beerblock (1566) from Oxford, Bodleian Library, MS Bodl. 13 fol 14r. (The Bodleian Library, Oxford).

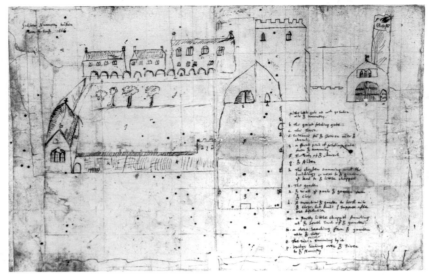

3. *(above)* Godstow Nunnery. Drawing by Anthony Wood from
Oxford, Bodleian Library, MS Rawl. B.408, flyleaf
(Bodleian Library, Oxford).

4. *(below)* Oriel Square, showing Canterbury College on the left.
Inscribed Edw. and Mich. Rooker, *Oxford Almanack* (1770)
(Ashmolean Museum, Oxford).

5. *(above)* The Old and the New. Above, a design for Worcester College. Below, a group of founders, benefactors and allegorical figures admire the new Worcester, with the old Gloucester College behind. Inscribed G. Vertue, *Oxford Almanack* (1741) (Ashmolean Museum, Oxford).

6. *(below)* The Old Destroyed. Canterbury building, Christ Church, in the process of demolition with Tom Tower behind. A landscape by I. B. Malchair (1783) (Ashmolean Museum, Oxford).

7. Dom Oswald Hunter-Blair, in the habit of the Beuronese Congregation (St Benet's Hall).

1554. He was restored to his other livings in 1559. Other monks with Protestant leanings such as Gabriel Morton of Gloucester conformed under Mary in order to keep their livings, but still clung to their beliefs. Morton, for example, was living in the Protestant household of Sir Anthony Kingston in the early 1550s.[68] Many of the former monk-scholars complied with all the religious changes which took place after the dissolution and managed to hold on to their livings, no matter what the religious policy of the day demanded of them. Thomas Richards of Totnes was rector of St George's, Exeter from 1535 until his death in 1564; Thomas Sparke of Durham continued to enjoy the fruits of his many benefices from 1541 until his death in 1572; John Warham lived quietly as a prebendary at Canterbury from 1542 until 1565; and Anthony Kitchin was the only bishop who succeeded in retaining his see under all four monarchs until his death at the ripe old age of eighty-nine in 1566.[69] Kitchin is probably representative of the great majority of former monk-scholars whose later careers show an uninterrupted tenure of parish livings through all the religious changes of the 1540s and 1550s. They were happy enough to conform to the wishes of their prince in return for the peace and security of a country parish.

There were, however, several very determined Catholics among the Benedictine graduates of Oxford. Of the eight members of the order who were executed during the 1530s four were former Oxford scholars, but the only Benedictine whom Professor Knowles considered to be a true martyr for the Catholic faith was Hugh Cook, Abbot of Reading, who does not appear to have studied at either university.[70] The other Benedictines who suffered for their faith did so during the reigns of Edward VI and Elizabeth. Five of the ex-monks who were prebendaries of Durham were deprived of their livings between 1560 and 1572, and Richard Ramsey lost his canonry at Gloucester in 1559 for refusing the Oath of Supremacy.[71] Many of the most conservative ex-Benedictines were spared the penalties which these men suffered because they died before the settlement of 1559. Richard Thornden, described by Cranmer as the 'false, flattering, lieing and dissimuling monke', who had led the Prebendaries Plot at

Canterbury in 1543, reintroduced the Mass into the cathedral in 1553, and presided at the trial of the Protestant martyrs of Kent in 1555, succumbed to a 'palsy' in March 1558. Robert Wharton, translated to the see of Hereford by Queen Mary early in 1554, served on the commission for the deprivation of married bishops later in that year, but died in September 1557. William Courtmill of Hyde lost his rectory of Hartley Mauditt in 1548 but was restored to it in 1554 and died early in 1557. These men would certainly have been deprived of their livings in 1559 had they refused to accept the Oath of Supremacy, but it is also likely that some of them may have forsaken their Catholic faith, as was the case with several conservative prebendaries at Durham who complied in 1560 rather than lose their livings. Not all conservative ex-Benedictines suffered persecution under Elizabeth. George London of Evesham does not appear to have had a living of which he could be deprived after the settlement of 1559, and he continued to reside in Oxford in relative peace, despite having given evidence against Cranmer and preached against Lutheranism in the Worcester diocese.[72]

The one group of Benedictine scholars which stands out in terms of both adherence to their Catholic faith and determination to return to the monastic life is the ageing band of former monks who restored the monastic life to Westminster Abbey during the reign of Queen Mary. When John Feckenham gathered together the remnants of English monasticism to form the new convent at Westminster late in 1556, a remarkably large number of his monks were former Benedictine colleagues from Oxford. Of the twenty-three ex-religious who resumed the monastic life in November 1556, thirteen were former Benedictine scholars and at least one other Oxford monk joined the community before its dissolution in May 1559.[73] Many of them had given up wealthy livings in order to return to the cloister, so their reasons for resuming the monastic life must have been sincere.[74] The other thing which is striking about this group is that virtually all of them had been resident in Oxford in the 1530s, and all but one of the seven graduates had been admitted to their degrees after 1534. This perhaps explains why the monastic life at Westminster has been described as being more 'col-

legiate' than 'monastic'. The leading lights of the convent
had all spent more time living in Gloucester College than
within the monasteries to which they owed their stability.[75]
These men nevertheless represented the final flowering of
the last group of Benedictine monks to study at Oxford
before the Reformation, and it seems that they did their
alma mater proud in the final years of their lives. While
most of the elderly monks at Westminster were satisfied to
conduct the daily round of ceremonies in the royal abbey
church, John Phagan and John Neot decided to lead a small
group of former Glastonbury monks in trying to bring about
the restoration of their old abbey. They wrote to Queen
Mary's lord chamberlain requesting that they be given
nothing more than the site of the monastery and some of the
customary rents so that

> with our labour and husbandry, we may live there a few of us
> in our religious habits till the charity of good people may
> suffice a greater number; and the country there, being so
> affected towards our religion, we believe we should find much
> help amongst them, towards the reparations and furniture of
> the same; whereby we would happily prevent the ruin of
> much, and repair no little part of the whole, to God's honour
> and for the better prosperity of the King and Queen's
> majesties.[76]

The plan did not come to anything, but the sentiments
expressed in their petition are surely worthy of the noblest
aims of both the early Benedictine missionaries to England
in the sixth century and the later missionary priests who
bravely ministered to the embattled recusant community
during penal times.

The restored monastic community at Westminster was
doomed to suppression after the accession of Queen Elizabeth in November 1558, and the monks were eventually
dispersed in July 1559. Some fled abroad while others went
into hiding. John Feckenham and John Langdon were
imprisoned, but Langdon managed to escape and went into
exile in Flanders with a number of his confrères.[77] Feckenham was not so fortunate. He was kept under close guard,
spending more than twenty years in the Tower of London

and under house arrest before being consigned to the 'vile and foetid' prison for Catholic priests at Wisbech Castle in 1580. He died there five years later, but not before founding a hospital for the poor of Bath and paying for the construction of a causeway across the dangerous fens of Wisbech. His influence among Catholic recusants was feared by Elizabeth and her government, and his importance as a rallying point for English Catholics was appreciated throughout Europe. What is perhaps more indicative of the man, however, is his stoicism and unfailing generosity in the face of personal hardship, which provided an inspiration for his fellow-sufferers at Wisbech.[78]

John Feckenham was undoubtedly an extraordinary character and cannot therefore be considered as being representative of the majority of monk-scholars who passed through the three Benedictine *studia* at Oxford in the first forty years of the sixteenth century. He does, however, embody many of the attributes which we would expect to find in the most outstanding graduates of a Renaissance university: a noted scholar and talented preacher, an energetic parish priest and respected counsellor to his prince, a generous benefactor and champion of the weak, steadfast in his beliefs and faithful unto death. In fact Feckenham was exactly the sort of priest that John Fisher was hoping to produce when he supported the introduction of a more humanist curriculum at Cambridge early in the sixteenth century.[79] But Feckenham was not the only Benedictine monk-scholar of Oxford who had been influenced by the new learning of a sixteenth-century university education. Many of his fellow scholars aspired to the ideal which he embodied and some of them were able to achieve a great deal in their secular careers after the dissolution of their monasteries. It is true that few of the Oxford monk-scholars were capable of achieving this lofty ideal, but in both quantitative and qualitative terms it appears that a great many of them nevertheless left an impressive record of service to Church and State during their later careers. That these achievements are not better known by our present generation of Reformation scholars is a testament to the success of the suppression of Gloucester, Canterbury and Durham

Colleges during the late 1530s. None of these Benedictine houses were ever restored as monastic *studia*, and for this reason later generations of Oxford students have not read of their achievements in college histories, nor have they listened to the praises of long-deceased alumni being sung at chapel services marking the commemoration of benefactors, as is the case in colleges with an unbroken history. The centenary of St Benet's Hall is therefore a fitting occasion on which to remember the truly remarkable attainments of the last Benedictine monk-scholars of medieval Oxford.

APPENDIX: English Benedictine monk-scholars at Oxford and Cambridge, 1500–1540

| Monastery | Number of monk-scholars at | | Total |
	Oxford	Cambridge	
Abingdon	5	–	5
Athelney	3	–	3
Battle	3	–	3
Burton-on-Trent	1	–	1
Bury St Edmunds	13	2	15
Canterbury Christ Church	43	–	43
Canterbury St Augustine's	8	–	8
Cerne	2	–	2
Chester	2	–	2
Colchester	–	1	1
Coventry	2	–	2
Crowland	–	3	3
Durham	28	2	30
Ely	–	9	9
Evesham	12	–	12
Eynsham	1	–	1
Glastonbury	15	–	15
Gloucester	13	–	13
Great Malvern	1	–	1
Hereford St Guthlac	1	–	1
Hyde	6	–	6
Malmesbury	3	–	3
Merton	1	–	1
Norwich	3	8	11
Peterborough	5	1	6
Reading	2	–	2
Ramsey	6	4	10
Rochester	2	–	2
St Benet of Hulme	–	1	1
St Albans	12	–	12
Sherborne	1	–	1
Selby	–	1	1
Spalding	–	1	1
Tavistock	2	1	3
Thorney	–	1	1
Tewkesbury	7	–	7
Totnes	1	–	1
Walden	–	1	1
Westminster	25	3	28
Winchcombe	6	–	6
Worcester	10	–	10
York St Mary's	2	–	2
House unknown	19	19	38
Total	266	58	324

PART II

Monks and Oxford
from Dissolution to Return

13

Benedictines of the Seventeenth Century Who Studied at Oxford

PHILIP JEBB OSB

This paper examines eleven English and Welsh Benedictines of the seventeenth century known to have studied at Oxford. In order of their deaths, well spread across the century, they were: Blessed Mark Barkworth, alias Lambert (1601), St John Roberts, alias Mervin (1610), Ralph Francis Antrobus (1626), Archbishop William Gabriel Gifford (1629), John Leander Jones (1635), Roland Thomas Preston, alias Roger Widdrington (1640), the Venerable David Augustine Baker (1641), Nicholas Fitzjames (1652), Hugh Serenus Cressy (1674), Richard Wilfrid Reeve (1693) and Charles Sumpner (1702). Short biographical details will be found in an Appendix at the end of this chapter.

On any showing they were a remarkable collection of men: eight of them have entries in the *Dictionary of National Biography*, and two of these have had full-length biographies written about them; two of them are honoured as martyrs, executed for their faith, while four others suffered imprisonment in England for their faith, and one in addition was imprisoned in Rome by the Inquisition; one appears to have been held in 'protective custody' in England, as at one stage he was in fear of his life from his fellow Catholics; all by the fact of their monastic profession were exiles; one was an archbishop, one was President General (the first) of the restored English Benedictine Congregation, and four were superiors of English Benedictine Congretation houses; six were authors of important published works; two held important preferments in the Church of England before their conversion to Catholicism; between them they held important clerical and academic posts in England, France, Spain and Italy, and several were involved in significant diplomatic or political missions.

They not only span the seventeenth century, but were between them involved in all the major traditional works of the EBC: teaching in schools and universities; writing spiritual, controversial and learned works; working on the Mission; caring for the nuns. Several were involved in the early beginnings of the EBC and represented the two main streams of the Cassinese and Spanish Congregations, as well as coming from all parts of England and Wales.

This paper will attempt to consider their influence on the foundation of the EBC and their governing of it; their persecutions, martyrdoms, imprisonments and exiles; how these particular men affected the early history of the EBC; the crucial timing of the martyrdoms of Mark Barkworth and John Roberts; the foundation of the first two houses; the Spanish and Italian influences; the setting up of the Union; their literary output and the mystical tradition transmitted through Augustine Baker and Serenus Cressy; the influence they had on public affairs on both sides of the Channel.

As it was not possible during the period under consideration for Catholics to attend the university, it follows that all of these monks were received into the Catholic Church after their time at Oxford. The appearance of the majority of them in the earlier part of the period is an indication of how unsettled were the minds of so many of the young with regard to the Catholic Church under Queen Elizabeth. Oxford was, however, much more lenient in its application of the penal laws against Catholics than were the authorities in many other parts of the country.

Until 1606 anyone from England or Wales wanting to follow a monastic vocation would have had to enter a foreign monastery on the continent, and considerable numbers were clothed and professed in the 1590s and early 1600s in Spain and Italy, while others attempted to maintain the continuity of the old EBC through Father Sigebert Buckley, the sole known survivor of the Westminster community re-established by Queen Mary. This is not the place to go into the history of these various movements to restart English monasticism, but it is to our purpose to show the influence of the Oxford men on the refounding of the EBC, which was finally achieved in 1619.

THE CONGREGATION

It is significant that John Roberts, at least twice during his expulsions from England as a secular priest, stayed at St Gregory's, Douay, and is regarded as a founder member of that community. Also the martyrdom of Mark Barkworth came at a crucial moment in the negotiations for the setting up of St Gregory's at Douay, convincing the authorities of the value of the Benedictine contribution to the English Mission. It is no coincidence that his picture appears among the five Benedictine martyrs (along with John Roberts) depicted on Abbot Philip de Caverel's Deed of Foundation of St Gregory's.[1]

Probably the most important of those involved in the restoration of the EBC was Dom Leander Jones, who after his profession in the Spanish Abbey of St Martin at Compostella was sent to England to work on the Mission. But on his way to England he stayed at St Gregory's at Douay and acted as novice master within a year of its foundation. Then as vicar general of all the monks from Spanish monasteries living outside Spain he took a prominent part in the negotiations, and was the first of the nine Definitors appointed in 1617, to draw up the terms of the Union of the Spanish, Cassinese and those affiliated to the old English Congregation. When the Union was finally achieved in 1619, Dom Leander was appointed the first President of the EBC in the place of Dom Gabriel Gifford, who had just been promoted to bishop before he could take up that office. Gifford had himself been one of the nine Definitors, having been originally clothed at Rheims but then professed for St Lawrence's, Dieulouard, of which he was prior (1609–11), having been influential in obtaining the property for the English Benedictines. He was then prior of the new foundation at St Malo.

Of the Italian Cassinese Congregation the most important of the Oxford men was Dom Augustine Baker, who with his legal background worked out (to the satisfaction of the Cassinese at least) the legal implications of Dom Sigebert Buckley as the sole survivor of the refounded Westminster community. Baker was himself 'aggregated' to Westminster and the old English Congregation, thus claiming for himself and for the others aggregated with him all the 'rights, privileges, ranks, honours, liberties and graces' formerly existing in the Abbey of Westminster, and so of the old English Congregation. Whatever the merits of this contested claim, at least Dom Augustine was the one with the legal training who achieved the physical continuity of the one Congregation from the other.

Nicholas Fitzjames was the first novice clothed at St Gregory's, Douay in 1606 before going on to be Superior of St Lawrence's at Dieulouard and novice master of Gabriel Gifford.

Gabriel Gifford had ecclesiastically by far the most eminent career of all these Benedictines from Oxford: chaplain in turn to Cardinals Allen (in Rome) and Borromeo (in Milan) and then Chancellor of the Diocese of Rheims. Within a year of his clothing as a Benedictine novice he was appointed superior of that house, before helping to found and to be superior of the house at St Malo. Finally he was appointed Archbishop of Rheims, a Duke and First Peer of France.

The others who were superiors were Francis Antrobus, of Dieulouard and Douay; Leander Jones, who besides serving two separate terms as President General was also twice Prior of St Gregory's (1621–8 and 1629–33); Thomas Preston, who was superior of the Cassinese monks in England, while his counterpart for the Spanish was Leander Jones.

MISSION AND THE CARE OF NUNS

It is arguable that the great influx of the English and Welsh into the Benedictines in the early seventeenth century was inspired not so much by the desire to lead the regular monastic life (though many of them did, and were an example to other laxer communities) but to go into England in order to bring help and support to the Catholics, and at the same time to be free of the influence and control of the Jesuits. It is certainly true that from its earliest beginnings the EBC had this 'missionary character', and looked back consciously to the decision of Pope St Gregory the Great to send St Augustine and his monastic companions to convert the English at the end of the sixth century. It is not therefore surprising that all but one of these eleven Oxford men spent at least part of their monastic life, illegally, in England working to maintain, and in hope of restoring, the Catholic faith in their native land.

Mark Barkworth had entered as a novice at the Abbey of Yrache while on his way to England after ordination at the English College at Valladolid. He was allowed to complete his 'novitiate' in England. He was quickly arrested and condemned as a seminary priest, but asserted that he was a Benedictine and contrived to be dragged to Tyburn and executed in a Benedictine habit in 1601.

John Roberts was imprisoned and banished four times for being a Catholic priest, and was especially noted for his work among those stricken by the plague in London. After his fifth illegal entry into England he was executed at Tyburn in 1610. He was canonised by Pope Paul VI in 1970 among the Forty Martyrs of England and Wales. Mark Barkworth was beatified by Pope Pius XI in 1929.

Dom Francis Antrobus was sent to England in 1621 and was for a time in prison before his death in Staffordshire in 1626.

Dom Leander Jones, as already noted, was superior of the Spanish monks in England and frequently visited this country. He finally died in London in 1630, although in his case it would appear that his friendship with Archbishop

Laud and others at court protected him from being molested.

Dom Thomas Preston was superior of the Cassinese Benedictines in England and died in the Clink prison in 1640. However, while dealing with such religious persecution two considerable ironies might be noted: Thomas Preston was for a time held in prison as a protection against the threat of death from his fellow Catholics because of his defence of the Oath of Allegiance, and Francis Antrobus, who before his conversion had been a minister of the Church of England, was for a short time imprisoned by the Inquisition on his arrival in Rome.

Dom Augustine Baker was twice imprisoned in England as a priest, and at the time of his death in 1641 he was working among those afflicted by the plague. He had earlier done much of the research for the *Apostolatus Benedictinorum in Anglia.* Later, in 1636, he composed his *Treatise of the English Benedictine Mission,* in which he had changed his attitude and endeavoured to dissuade young monks from leaving their monasteries for the Mission because of the spiritual dangers which could threaten the contemplative life. At the end of this treatise he writes that any English monk is liable to be sent to England, but that this will not now happen to himself 'whose body is so extreamly decayed, that if it intended such a thinge it would not suffice for it but would faile by death ere it could well reach halfe way.' But then there is added in the margin of the Ampleforth manuscript: 'The Authour himselfe, contrary to expectation, is now gone by obedience.'

Nicholas Fitzjames, that first novice to be clothed at St Gregory's, died in 1652 on the Mission at Stourton in Wiltshire at the age of 92 after working there for many years. Serenus Cressy also died in England at West Grinstead in Sussex in 1674, having been on the Mission since 1660, working as chaplain to Queen Catherine of Braganza at Somerset House.

Charles Sumpner also spent some time on the English Mission in the south province, though he returned to Douay in 1683 and died at Cambray in 1702 acting as vicar to the English nuns there.

This care of the nuns was of course (and remains) another important element of the priestly work of the monks, and besides Charles Sumpner, Augustine Baker was for many years confessor at Cambray, giving the nuns a great many spiritual treatises, many of which were collected by Serenus Cressy to produce *Sancta Sophia.* This same Serenus Cressy was himself for a time vicar of the nuns in Paris.

TEACHING

From the very start of the English Benedictine revival, monks were involved in teaching in universities in France and Spain as well as in the school attached to St Gregory's, which was certainly in existence before 1620. Once again, this small group of Oxford men can be shown to have contributed more than their fair share to this important work.

The most distinguished in this, as in much else, were Leander Jones and Gabriel Gifford. The former, after gaining his doctorate at Salamanca, was for twenty-five years Professor of Theology and Hebrew at the Colleges of Marchiennes and of St Vedast in the University of Douay. Gabriel Gifford, having left Oxford and graduated at Louvain, studied divinity for four years under Robert Bellarmine. He then moved to the Sorbonne, and so to Rome. After this Cardinal Allen (himself a graduate of Oxford) had him lecturing on the *Summa* at the English College at Douay. Having gained his doctorate, he taught theology at intervals for twelve years at Rheims, where he was later nominated rector of the university. He was esteemed to be one of the most eloquent preachers in the French language in the Paris of his day, and had many eminent people attending his sermons, from King Louis XIII down. Earlier he had given Latin orations at Lille, including one at the inauguration of the Archdukes Albert and Isabella as sovereign Princes of the Netherlands.

Richard Reeve suffered from severe lameness as a result of an illness as a very young child, so his parents 'bred him up to learning', which stood him and his many pupils in good stead. After gaining his degree at Oxford he was appointed

Usher of Magdalen College School in 1668 and Master in
1670, but had to leave three years later because of his Catholicism. Having become a monk at St Gregory's he taught
the boys in the school at Douay for ten years 'Classics, poetry,
rhetoric and Greek'. Bossuet is said to have held him in high
regard while he was for two years at the priory of La Celle in
the diocese of Meaux. In 1688 he was recalled to England
on the authority of King James II and by royal mandate
was nominated Master of the Bluecoat School in Gloucester,
where he was to instruct 'Popish youths'. Wood writes of
him: 'He was accounted a perfect philologist, admirably well
versed in all classical learning, and a good Grecian; and had
been so sedulous in his profession of paedagogy that he
had educated 60 ministers of the Church of England and
about 40 Roman priests.'[2] Reeve was never ordained a priest,
but was imprisoned for a time in 1688 as a 'priest and a
Jesuit', though released after nine months, as both charges
were false. He continued in England until his death in
Westminster in 1693.

LITERARY WORK

It was almost inevitable that such a group as we have been
examining, in the period in which they were active, should
have produced a considerable body of literature. But the
range and quantity of their output is remarkable when it is
remembered in how much else they were engaged and the
peculiarly difficult times in which they lived, which by no
stretch of the imagination could be said to be positively
conducive to literary work. But six of these eleven had books
published, and there remain extant over 100 works printed
or in manuscript: Baker 70, Cressy 19, Gifford 7, Jones 15
(massive works in 29 volumes), Preston (Widdrington) 13,
Reeve 7.

They cover a wide range, from the purely spiritual *Sancta
Sophia* (a digest of Augustine Baker's treatises compiled by
Serenus Cressy), through great tomes of ecclesiastical history
by the same Augustine Baker and Leander Jones, from the
apologetics of Cressy to the sermons of Gifford, the Latin

poems of Reeve and the learned editions of earlier writers edited by Jones, Baker and Cressy.

The most important of all these writers, for the originality of his work and the continuing relevance of his spiritual doctrine, is Augustine Baker of whom Dom (later Abbot) Justin McCann could write in 1933, justifying the publication of the *Life of Baker* and a list of his manuscripts:

> Turning to the biographical items which are concerned primarily with Fr Augustine Baker and his work, it is proper that we should offer some explanation of their inclusion among the historical documents of the Catholic Records Society's volumes. It might be urged in the first place, that Fr Baker is a striking, if not unique, figure in the history of post-reformation English Catholicism. The fourteenth century in England, with Richard Rolle, the anonymous author of *The Cloud of Unknowing*, Walter Hilton and Dame Julian, produced original spiritual writings of the first quality. If we look for any parallel to their work in post-reformation Catholicism, we find one book, and one only, Fr Baker's *Sancta Sophia*, which can be set beside it. That book resumes and completes the teaching of the most substantive of the fourteenth century writings, Walter Hilton's *Scale of Perfection*. It is recognised on all hands as the work of a spiritual master. On this ground, therefore, Fr Baker deserves very special notice. But if that were all, it would not be enough, for the Society is not concerned with spirituality as such, and Fr Baker would have no special claim upon it. But there is more than that. For the record of Fr Baker's life is a record also of the times in which he lived and throws a direct light upon the fortunes of English Catholicism and English Benedictinism in those times. We learn from him what was the state of religion in Monmouthshire at the end of the sixteenth century, of Papists, Church-Papists and Protestants. We have his valuable account of his years at Christ's Hospital and at Oxford, with his judgement on his experiences in both places. And then we have the whole history of his life as a Benedictine and a missionary priest. No other such comprehensive account of a priest's life, lived in that period, has come down to us. For its whole tenour, and for the important particulars which we have mentioned, it deserves to be regarded as of historical value.[3]

This points to another significant contribution of Baker and

Cressy in particular: they were actively concerned, at a time when their reforming countrymen were engaged in a wholesale destruction of the medieval spiritual tradition, to preserve this tradition for their own contemporaries, and so in fact for posterity. It was these two men, Cressy following Baker, who were at pains to obtain and publish the works of Hilton, Rolle, *The Cloud* and Julian of Norwich. Without their perseverance and far-sighted determination it could well have been that such works would have been lost forever, and the present-day 'industry', especially with regard to Julian, could never have started, let alone have inspired so many of such differing religious backgrounds around the world.

It is ironical, even amusing, to note in the Protestant Bishop Parker's preface to his reprint in 1843 of Cressy's edition of Julian's *Revelations*, the following:

> The spiritually-minded reader will meet with some few statements in the course of the following pages, in which he will not be able to acquiesce; but in the main he will meet with much amply to repay a careful perusal. The Authoress, a pious recluse of the name of Juliana, was contemporary with Wiclif; it does not appear that she had any connection with his party; the work before us bears independent witness to the truth, and is peculiarly interesting as a devotional treatise of the fourteenth century. I do not venture to pass any judgement as to how far these Revelations may be imputed to a fevered imagination: to whatever cause we attribute them, the overruling hand of God for good must be recognized. Viewed as a religious composition, the present volume comprises much of deep Christian doctrine and experience; affording us a fresh testimony to the fact that the Spirit of God is able to lead His people into all saving truth under the most disadvantageous circumstances: it gives us additional cause to rest assured that in all ages God has had a seed to serve Him; and confirms our belief that even during the worst corruptions of the Romish Church there was a generation within its pale, who, though unknown to history and labouring under many imperfections, yet held the Head Christ; and formed a part of that vital bond which connected the Apostolic Church with the revival of primitive Christianity at the times of the Reformation. It is

very interesting to trace the strugglings of the writer's mind against preconceived and erroneous opinions.[4]

With his concern for the worst corruptions of the Romish Church, the Bishop is unable or unwilling to see that these Revelations were both nurtured by, and then preserved to his own time, simply thanks to the adherents of that same Church.

Dr David Rogers, in a paper read to the EBC History Symposium in 1990 entitled 'The English Recusants: Some Medieval Literary Links', said:

It will be appropriate to draw attention to a feature of the English Recusant body which seems to have been little studied. Its members formed, in actual fact if not by conscious design, a cultural bridge in two directions, one lateral and the other vertical. The lateral resulted from their continuing immersion (if the mixed metaphor may be pardoned) in the full tide of Catholic life, at an exciting and expansive period of the Counter-Reformation, through the movement to and fro across the sea of exiles and the setting up of English seminaries, schools and religious houses in continental Europe. I call this the lateral bridge because it caused a sideways movement, chiefly of religious ideas, influences and styles, which were (in part at least) mediated through the recusants to their home country, whose rulers had chosen to strive for an intense national unity at the expense of an increasingly insular mentality. At the same time the recusant also formed a natural bridge backward, across the break caused by the Reformation, to the habits of thought and the pieties of the Middle Ages and earlier. This is what I have chosen to term the vertical bridge, and it formed an understandable preoccupation in the minds of English Catholics, who felt that the changes in religion amounted to an attempt to sever them from a past that was still their heritage.[5]

Cressy's own independent Catholic writing started with the *Exomologesis,* or full confession of his reasons for becoming a Catholic, and it is nice to note that the *Oxford English Dictionary* quotes this title among its references for the use of the word. This book, running in the first edition to 655 pages, is an important apologetic, notable in a violent and condemnatory age for the liberalism of its attitude to the Church of England and a sensitivity to the Church which had nurtured his religion in his youth. Indeed it is noteworthy that Hugh Cressy should take Serenus for his name in religion, which has been seen as a conscious reference to the peace which the Tew Circle took as a paradigm of that peace enjoined of all Christians.[6] Such works of controversy seldom remain relevant for very long, but they are important at the time, and this work was clearly an encouragement to the embattled Catholics to continue to hold to their faith. 'This was the golden calf,' wrote Wood, 'which the English Papists fell down and worshipped. They bragged that book to be unanswerable, and to have given a total overthrow to the Chillingworthians and the book and tenets of Lucius Lord Falkland.'[7]

Cressy engaged in several other works of controversy (including a second and considerably revised edition of the *Exomologesis*), and these also were effective, judging by the number of replies they elicited from members of the Church of England. He also wrote *The Church History of Brittany or England*, though little of this is the fruit of his own original research.

Returning to the works of Augustine Baker, although none was published during his lifetime, more than seventy titles are extant in manuscript, the great majority of them spiritual treatises written for the benefit of the nuns of Cambray, who preserved them with great care until the chaos of the French Revolution, when they appear to have been destroyed. Fortunately all but a few survive in copies made by the nuns and others. Among these copyists few were more assiduous than Richard Reeve, of whose copies nearly twenty are still in existence.

Besides these purely spiritual treatises Augustine Baker also produced, as noted above, a long and detailed autobiography and at least three books concerned with the life and writings of Dame Gertrude More. There were also his materials for the *Apostolatus*, which were copied from libraries in England. He also produced copies and translations of several books of other spiritual authors, of the Fathers, the medieval mystics and some contemporary French and Italian works. It has been noted that he does not appear to have had any knowledge of the works of St Teresa of Avila or of St John of the Cross.

It was perhaps inevitable that at the time when he was writing (and when the *Index* was at its most extensive) his more pioneering spiritual work should come under question. This resulted in some works by Baker in defence of his teaching, which was promoted with equal vigour by his supporters, especially the nuns of Cambray. And it should be noted that none of his works was finally condemned.

Beside these two writers the other four have nothing like the same significance in the variety or range of their literary work. Leander Jones does not appear to have produced any book which was his own original work, but he was assiduous in producing versions and translations of others, including commentaries on the Bible, theological and philosophical works, and also a rendering into 'elegant Latin' of the *Apostolatus*, for which the material was largely collected by Augustine Baker. In all fifteen titles are known to have been published by Leander Jones, but they amount to nearly thirty massive volumes.

Gabriel Gifford has seven works ascribed to him, two of which are apologetical, arguing against aspects of the Protestant schism, and the rest collections of prayers or printed sermons. All no doubt useful in their day, they do not appear to be of perennial significance.

Of Richard Reeve, the schoolmaster 'bred to learning', there are extant half a dozen volumes of poems composed in Latin for various persons and occasions and a life of St Wilfrid.

Finally, from a very different stance come the works of Thomas Preston, who wrote under the alias of Widdrington, probably as a protection against his co-religionists. This was because most of his writing, largely done from prison (where he seems to have spent most of his adult life), was in support of the Oath of Allegiance proposed by King James I, but which was condemned as unacceptable to Catholics. He was an acknowledged expert in canon law, which he had studied while he was a monk at Monte Cassino, and he was not afraid to attack the propositions of Bellarmine, Suarez, Lessius and others. He published appeals to Pope Pius V, and also wrote a fierce attack on the Jesuit Fr Garnet 'to make it evident that it is no new thing for Jesuits to curse and ban to justifie a lie.'

WIDER CONTACTS

It is not surprising that among such a group of impressive men there should be found important contacts with leading figures in Church and State on both sides of the Channel and as far as Rome. What is remarkable is the diversity of such work.

John Roberts during his time at St John's College shared rooms with John Leander Jones who was himself a close friend of Archbishop Laud. It was possibly in this connection that in 1634 Dom Leander was sent to England by Pope Urban VIII to try to open diplomatic relations between Britain and the Holy See. Jones was also in correspondence with Barberini about the deposing power of the Pope. He was also believed to have come to negotiate a reconciliation with the Church of England and to have been in active consultation over this with Laud. Although Laud denied this at his trial, the fact of the accusation points to the status of Dom Leander in such matters. In 1636 he died in London, working as chaplain for the Catholic Queen Henrietta of France, the wife of Charles I.

Something of the exalted positions of Archbishop Gabriel Gifford of Rheims has already been noted: Duke of Rheims, First Peer of France, preacher to the French King, chaplain to Cardinals Allen and Borromeo, a student under Robert Bellarmine, friend and client of the Duke of Guise. But in England also he had influence: in 1586 he wrote to Secretary Walsingham thanking him for permission to return to England, and expressing his loyalty to the Queen. In 1603 he carried to James I a despatch from the Nuncio in Brussels assuring the King of the Pope's anxiety that English Catholics should submit peaceably to his government. Later he persuaded the Cardinal of Lorraine to grant the empty priory at Dieulouard to the English Benedictines.

Hugh Serenus Cressy's early career, before his conversion,

was impressive enough: Fellow of Merton College, and after taking orders in the Church of England chaplain to Thomas, Lord Wentworth while he was President of the Council of York, and later, when he was Lord Deputy of Ireland, at which time Cressy was installed as Dean of Leighlin, and later appointed a Canon of Windsor. By 1638 he was chaplain to Lord Falkland and an active member of the Circle of Tew, which included among its members Sir Edward Hyde, later Lord Clarendon, who wrote in his autobiography:

> His house, [i.e. Lord Falkland's] where he usually resided (Tew or Burford in Oxfordshire), being within ten or twelve miles of the university, looked like the university itself, by the company that was always found there. There was Dr Sheldon, Dr Morley, Dr Hammond, Dr Earles, Mr Chillingworth, and indeed all men of eminent parts and faculties in Oxford, besides those who resorted thither from London, who all found their lodgings there, as ready as in the colleges ... So many came thither to study in a better air, finding all the books they could desire in his library, and all the persons together whose company they could wish, and not find in any other society.[8]

After the death of Falkland, Cressy was tutor to Charles Berkeley, later Earl of Falmouth. He clearly had a great future ahead of him in the Church of England, and was always regarded by its leading figures with great respect. After Cressy had made his recantation of Protestantism before the Inquisition in Rome, Hyde wrote of him:

> It is a great loss to the Church, but a greater to his friends dead and alive ... If we cannot keep him a minister of our Church, I wish he would continue a layman in theirs, which would somewhat lessen the defection.[9]

While in Paris Cressy was befriended by Queen Henrietta, and on the marriage of Charles II to Catherine of Braganza he was one of her chaplains at Somerset House. In 1669 he was consulted by Clifford of the cabal about reunion before the secret Treaty of Dover.

Dom Thomas Preston seems to have spent a great deal of his adult life in various prisons in England, and while at the start this was because of his being a Catholic priest, later, when he was supporting the controversial Oath of Allegiance and writing of this with his knowledge of canon law under the name of Roger Widdrington, he was for his own preservation 'lying quiet in the Marshalsea prison with his life threatened by the rigid Papalins'. Secretary Conway wished some safeguard to be devised for him, who having taken the Oath would be in danger if he left the king's protection. Indeed Widdrington later wrote to the king thanking him for his care and asking that he be forbidden to leave the country for fear of falling under a personal excommunication. James I, at the time of negotiations with Spain for his marriage, granted Widdrington a pardon for all offences and a dispensation to exercise in private houses 'the rites and ceremonies of divine worship according to the custom of the Church of Rome'. A copy of the pardon was handed to the Spanish Ambassador, and it was confirmed by Charles I.[10]

Dom Augustine Baker, before his conversion, was appointed Recorder of Abergavenny. He was a friend of Sir Robert Cotton, and a letter survives in the Bodleian asking Sir Robert to supply him with copies of the English mystics such as Hilton and Rolle for the use of the nuns at Cambray.

CONCLUSION

It might perhaps be thought that these eleven men were outstanding in EBC affairs only because they had so few contemporaries, and that it was inevitable that all who were part of the Congregation at its frail and uncertain beginnings would have to shoulder such major responsibilities. But in fact there were over 450 English and Welsh monks active during the seventeenth century, and the Oxford group makes up less than three per cent of the total. And perhaps a Cambridge man could be excused for pointing out that there were at least seven from Another Place, where the Protestant Reform had taken a firmer hold, and two of these gained the martyr's crown.

There were other equally outstanding men who were members of the Congregation and who showed similar vision, vigour and courage through the seventeenth century, and who together co-operated in forming a body still full of life 400 years later. But the achievements of these eleven cover all the main characteristics of that body, and it would have been very much the poorer and less significant in matters spiritual, pastoral, educational and constitutional had they not played their part. And the Church at large would have been the poorer by two martyrs and several courageous confessors who helped to keep alive the Catholic faith in this land and to preserve the continuity of centuries of monastic tradition.

APPENDIX

Biographical details of the eleven Oxford Benedictines of the seventeenth century:

Blessed Mark Barkworth, alias Lambert, born in Lincolnshire. Dom Bede Camm says he was at Oxford, but gives no authority, and he is not mentioned in Foster's *Alumni Oxonienses*. Converted at twenty-two at Douay College, studied at Rheims and Valladolid, professed as a Benedictine at Yrache. Hanged at Tyburn on 9 March 1601. Protomartyr of the English Benedictines. Entry in the *DNB* and a chapter in *Nine Martyr Monks*.

St John Roberts, alias Mervin, born in London 1575, but of Welsh descent, attended St John's College. Received into the Church in Paris 1598. Entered English College, Valladolid, left and professed as Benedictine at St Martin's, Compostella. Imprisoned and banished four times as a priest in England, worked tirelessly through the plague in London. Helped with the foundation of St Gregory's, Douay. Executed at Tyburn on 10 December 1610. Entry in *DNB*, biography by Dom Bede Camm.

Ralph Francis Antrobus, born at Chester 1576, at Brasenose College 1596. A minister in the Church of England, but later converted and went to Rome, where he was imprisoned for a time by the Inquisition. Professed at Onia in Spain and novice master there. Acted as 'President' of Dieulouard in 1612. Was first Prior of St Gregory's after the Union in 1619. Imprisoned in England and died in Staffordshire on 10 June 1626.

William Gabriel Gifford, born in Hampshire in 1554, at Lincoln College, then Louvain, then Professor of Theology at Rheims and then chaplain to Cardinals Allen and Borromeo in Rome and friend of St Francis de Sales. Clothed in Rheims for Dieulouard. First Prior of St Malo, elected first President of the EBC but appointed Archbishop of Rheims. A great preacher and author of several works. Entry in *DNB.*

John Leander Jones, born in Llanfrynach, Brecknockshire, in 1575, Fellow of St John's College, shared chambers with the future Archbishop Laud. Professed at St Martin's, Compostella, DD at Salamanca. Prior of St Gregory's, First President of EBC. Sent by the Pope to Charles I at time of his marriage to Henrietta Maria of France. Significant author and editor of major works. Entry in *DNB.*

Roland Thomas Preston, alias Widdrington, born in Shropshire in 1567, attended Magdalen Hall. Professed at Monte Cassino and became a master in canon law. Superior of the Cassinese monks in England. Acquainted with Sigebert Buckley and arranged for the 'aggregation' of Cassinese monks to Westminster and the old English Congregation. Imprisoned and died in the Clink 1640, where he had written many works under the name of Roger Widdrington defending the Oath of Allegiance. Allanson lists thirteen titles. Entry in *DNB* under Widdrington.

David Augustine Baker, born at Abergavenny in 1575, studied at Broadgates Hall and then at the Inns of Court. Clothed at St Justina in Padua. Confessor to nuns at Cambray. Twice imprisoned in England and died in London 1641. Mystical and spiritual writer, Volume 33 of *CRS* lists sixty-eight titles and gives his autobiography and a life. His *Holy Wisdom* is still in print. Entry in *DNB.*

Nicholas Fitzjames, born at Redlynch in Somerset about 1572, at Gloucester Hall, now Worcester College. First novice at St Gregory's, superior at Dieulouard and novice master to Gabriel Gifford. 'Of undaunted spirit in a diminutive body.' He died on the Mission at Stourton in Wiltshire in 1652.

Hugh Serenus Cressy, born at Thorpe Salvin in Yorkshire in 1605, Fellow of Merton College. Anglican chaplain to Strafford and then Falkland, and in the Circle of Great Tew. Professed at St Gregory's 1649. Chaplain to Queen Catherine of Braganza. Consulted by Clifford of the cabal about reunion before the Treaty of Dover, died 1674. Considerable author and editor, including *Sancta Sophia*. Entry in *DNB*.

Richard Wilfrid Reeve, born in Gloucester in 1642, at Trinity, MA for Magdalen, Master of Magdalen College School. Professed at Douay but never ordained because of severe lameness. Master of the Bluecoat School at Gloucester on the invitation of King James II. Eight months in prison in 1688. Said to have educated sixty Protestant ministers and forty Catholic priests. Entry in *DNB*.

Charles Sumpner, born at Hellingly Castle in Sussex in 1645, studied at Trinity College, professed at St Gregory's 1672, and Prefect of Studies there 1683–1701. On the Mission and later Vicar of the nuns of Cambray. Died 1702 at Cambray.

FURTHER READING

B. Green OSB, *The English Benedictine Congregation: a short history* (*CRS*, no date).
D. Lunn, *The English Benedictines 1540–1688* (London, 1980).
CRS 33 (1993) for the writings of Augustine Baker.
B. Camm OSB, *Nine Martyr Monks* (London, 1931).
B. Camm OSB, *The Life and Times of John Roberts* (Sands, 1897).
T. P. Ellis, *Welsh Benedictines of the Terror* (Cardiff, 1936).

14

Oxford and the Benedictines:
From the Restoration
until Catholic Emancipation

GEOFFREY SCOTT OSB

It has to be admitted that, as far as Benedictines educated in the university are concerned, this period was largely one of hibernation, but the English Jesuit, C. C. Martindale, writing in 1925 about the poor showing of Catholics generally in Oxford in this period, took heart from God's word to the prophet, 'Who hath despised the day of small things?' There were only a dozen Oxford-educated men who were professed as monks between the end of the sixteenth and end of the seventeenth centuries, and none professed throughout the entire eighteenth century. These Oxford Benedictines fall into two meagre groupings: firstly, the nine converts and cradle Catholics who were professed before the mid-seventeenth century, who included a martyr, an archbishop and a President of the English Benedictines among them, and, secondly, the tiny band of three convert Oxford men who were professed as monks between 1649 and 1676.

The relationship between Benedictines and the University of Oxford in the early modern period is best highlighted by understanding the impact which monks possessed of an Oxford background had on the English Benedictine Congregation itself and on the English Catholic community, and, secondly, by emphasising the continuous attraction which the Benedictine historical and intellectual inheritance held for certain members of the university. Monks in and around Oxford throughout the seventeenth and eighteenth centuries occasionally exploited this latter sympathy, though it is perhaps surprising how rarely, in fact, they took advantage of it. One should always remember in any discussion of the involvement of post-Reformation Benedictines in the university that these monks lived and worked within the confines of English Catholicism and approached the university through that context. They had the same suspicions of Protestantism and the same missionary aspirations as their fellow Catholics; they were English Catholics first and Benedictines second. Given this, what is worth concentrating on in some detail, then, is any evidence for a unique Benedictine contribution to Oxford in this period, slim though it may be, which distinguished the monks, to some extent, from their Catholic compatriots.

We have glimpses of monks in university circles from the early seventeenth century, and positive evidence of a Catholic congregation in the city and its environs which was occasionally served by monk chaplains. The turbulent John Barnes, for instance, professed as an Anglo-Spanish Benedictine in 1605 at Valladolid, was known to have resided privately in the University of Oxford to pursue his studies during a time of renewed proscription of Catholics in the 1620s. In his later life, he was mentally deranged, but at Oxford he consulted the libraries in pursuance of his ecumenical aim 'to mince the Catholic truths that the Protestants might digest them without choking, and so likewise to prepare the Protestant errors that Catholic stomachs might not loathe them'. At the same time, the monk Justus Edner had established a missionary base, and a degree of independence from his monastic superiors, by purchasing a house and land close by the city at Temple Cowley where he died suddenly in April 1635.[1]

The promulgation in June 1636 of the Laudian Statutes at Oxford, which demanded subscription to the Thirty-Nine Articles and the Oath of Supremacy as a prerequisite for matriculation, considerably reduced the possibility of Catholics becoming fully involved in university affairs. However, informal contacts continued after this time. The presence of the Benedictines serving as chaplains and tutors to recusant households within the neighbourhood of Oxford, such as those of the Hildesleys at Little Stoke and the Brownes at Kiddington, where Fr Robert Sherwood died in 1665, might have made little impression on Oxford, but the redoubtable Elizabeth Cary, Lady Falkland, certainly did. She acted as a catalyst, creating a patronage network which brought certain monks and nuns to the acquaintance of Oxford and vice versa. Her translation in 1630 of Cardinal du Perron's answer to King James I's attack on Catholicism was partly motivated by her determination to make converts of 'the scholars of Oxford and Cambridge who did not generally understand French'.[2]

If there was one single aspect of contemporary Benedictinism which interested some Oxford scholars in monasticism, it was the revival of mystical writing among English Benedictines during the seventeenth century. It is noteworthy that this thin thread of interest ran through the entire Stuart period and was not to be submerged by that febrile clamour of anti-popery which has, in its turn, tended to distort our contemporary perceptions of seventeenth-century Oxford's attitude to Catholicism. For the revival of this literary and spiritual culture, possibly stimulated in part by the crisis of Civil War and Commonwealth, was to remain soundproofed to contemporary religious passions throughout much of the century.

Lady Falkland had been converted to Catholicism in 1626 by a Benedictine and was henceforth served by a line of monk confessors, among whom was numbered Fr Cuthbert Fursden. Fursden was a disciple of the renowned English Benedictine mystical writer, Fr Augustine Baker, who had been educated at Oxford and had died in 1641. Fursden had met the Oxford Anglican, Hugh Cressy, at Lady Falkland's house and was partly responsible for his later conversion to Catholicism in 1646 and for introducing him to the teachings of Baker after Cressy had been professed as a monk in 1649. Before he turned to Rome, Cressy had been a member of the scholarly circle of Great Tew, just outside Oxford, which had met during the 1630s and which had been convened by the second Viscount Falkland. The Great Tew circle was frequented by a number of Oxford

academics, its leading theologian being William Chilling-
worth, Fellow of Trinity College, who had become a Catholic
briefly in 1630 and is reputed to have lodged with the Benedictines at Douai 'where not shining so much as he
expected ... he returned to Oxford a Protestant' and published his famous *Religion of Protestants* in 1638 to rebut
Catholicism. Cressy was to drop out of the Great Tew Circle,
but later became Anglican chaplain in Ireland to Lady Falkland's son, Lucius Cary, second Viscount Falkland.

As a Catholic, Cressy had thought of becoming a Carthusian, but was then attracted to the Benedictines. His main
claim to fame rests on his editions of the classics of English
medieval mysticism, which made these writings available to a
wider English audience. Cressy had derived his version of
The Cloud of Unknowing from another Oxford man, Maurice
Chauncey, the last Carthusian of the London Charterhouse.
In pursuit of his interest in mysticism and spirituality, he
published at Douai in 1657 *Holy Wisdom*, the principal digest
of Augustine Baker's spiritual teachings. He was chaplain in
1651 to the English Benedictine nuns in Paris which two of
Lady Falkland's four daughters who became Benedictine
nuns helped to found. Her two younger sons had tried their
vocation as Benedictine monks, having escaped in 1636 from
the clutches of their Anglican brother, the Viscount, at Great
Tew by means of a kidnap organised by their mother, which
involved tiptoeing through Oxford and rowing from
Abingdon to London. It was the four Cary nuns at Paris and
Cambrai who helped propagate the spirituality of Baker by
defending him against his critics and through transcribing
his works. Like Cressy and other converts, they had 'fled
from reason to that peculiarly Benedictine blend of tradition, authority and mysticism which in different ways, was
to be responsible for the Catholicism of Dryden and Charles
II'.[3]

During the 1650s and 1660s, the Benedictines' reputation
at Oxford continued to be based on their spiritual teachings
and, more publicly, on the medieval Benedictine inheritance, for during this and the following century, the
endeavour of antiquarians like William Dugdale and
Thomas Hearne was beginning to expose the architecture

and learning of the medieval monastic world to their contemporaries' gaze. In 1659, too, we find the Oxford
antiquarian and gossip Anthony Wood, himself just about to
embark on his medieval researches, purchasing engravings
relating to Benedictine history. That same year there was
published in London *The Scale of Perfection* written by the
fourteenth-century mystic, Walter Hilton. With other mystical treatises, this had been taken abroad by English
recusant exiles, and was used extensively by English Benedictines such as Augustine Baker and Dame Gertrude More, a
nun of Cambrai. The responsibility for publishing Augustine
Baker's manuscript of *The Scale* in 1659 rests either with
Serenus Cressy, or with the Oxford convert, Abraham Woodhead, who had been ejected from his fellowship at University
College in 1648. The subject and the date make Cressy pref-
erable as the editor, since the bulk of Woodhead's numerous
religious books were to appear only in the 1670s and 1680s.
Whoever was responsible, however, the edition was the work
of an Oxford man and is indicative of the level of interest in
Benedictine spirituality and its sources by scholars with an
Oxford background.

Because of the restrictions imposed on Catholics
becoming members of the university and because of the
underlying anti-popery endemic in English society
throughout the seventeenth century, Benedictine involvement in the university tended to be the result of informal
contact between individuals who shared common intellectual pursuits, and, more rarely, some similar religious beliefs.
From the 1640s, the Stuart Court's lengthy sojourns in
Oxford appear to have increased the level of interest there
in Catholicism, and certain monks thus found themselves
drawing nearer to university circles. In July 1643, Charles I
had been joined at Oxford, which had virtually become his
capital, by his Catholic queen, Henrietta Maria, who lived at
Merton for three years. Later, in 1663, Charles II and his
Catholic queen, Catherine of Braganza, had been welcomed
to the city by the Chancellor, Edward Hyde, Earl of Clarendon, himself once a member of the Great Tew Circle, and
'an old friend' of Serenus Cressy, having 'been acquainted
nearly fifty years' with him, though saddened by his 'odious

alteration' to Catholicism. On a return visit in 1665, to avoid the plague in London, the King lodged at Christ Church and the Queen at Merton, whilst the Spanish ambassador stayed at New College and the French ambassador in Magdalen, Mass being said in Oxford for Catholic members of the Court.

Many of Cressy's apologetic works were written whilst he lived at Somerset House, where Catherine of Braganza normally had her Court, and where he officiated as a royal chaplain. The Oxford scholar, Anthony Wood, paid him a visit in Somerset House in the summer of 1669, although he admitted that in his conversation with Cressy, he did not find his expectation satisfied. It is possible that Cressy returned to Oxford when the Court visited the city during the 1660s. Whatever the case, it certainly seems that such royal visits facilitated the entrée to the university of other monks attached to the Stuart Court. In 1669, two of them, John Huddleston and Vincent Sadler, were to be found living, significantly, in the centre of the city in 'back-side housing' at Amsterdam Court, adjoining Brasenose. This university involvement and the fact that they were not attached to any specific Benedictine missionary enterprise suggests that they had lingered in Oxford after the Court had returned to the capital. In 1671, they were again in Oxford, this time publicly to attend the solemnity of the Act (as Encaenia was called) and to witness graduation. The interests of these two monks, and, in Huddleston's case, prestige, prompt one to surmise that they were, as Benedictines, labouring to make Catholicism more acceptable to the university.

Huddleston had claims to fame and royal patronage. As a secular priest chaplain to Thomas Whitegreave at Moseley in Staffordshire, he had been instrumental in saving the life of King Charles II after the battle of Worcester in 1651. He had been professed as a Benedictine after the Restoration and became attached, through royal gratitude, to the Court of Somerset House where he was, like Cressy, chaplain to Queen Catherine. He later reconciled the King to Catholicism on his deathbed in February 1685. As a mark of the high esteem in which he was held within Court circles, Huddleston was exempted from the penalties of the laws against Catholics which were resurrected during the Popish Plot in the 1670s. In July 1671, Timothy Nourse, a Fellow of University College, who knew both Huddleston and his monk companion, Vincent Sadler, took Anthony Wood, his fellow drinking-companion, to meet Huddleston. Wood persuaded the monk to set down in writing his version of the King's flight after Worcester. Nourse was himself soon converted to Catholicism, presumably through the encouragement of the Benedictines, and hence lost his fellowship in January 1674 when he refused to subscribe to the oaths and take the sacrament.

Vincent Sadler mixed in the same royal and aristocratic circles as Huddleston, but seems to have made a more useful contribution to Oxford scholarship. Whilst his many popular books on the spiritual life were practical rather than mystical, and largely derivative, those which collected together 'the marrow of the Ancient Fathers' would have attracted Anglican readers. Others were written specifically for the Confraternity of the Rosary, an aristocratic lay fraternity established by the Benedictines which had its chapel in the Earl of Cardigan's house in London. Sadler was its dean and dedicated the books written for it to the Earl of Cardigan, Queen Catherine of Braganza, and to William Sheldon of Beoley in Worcestershire and Weston in Warwickshire, and his wife, Elizabeth. The Sheldons of Beoley, especially William's son, Ralph Sheldon, played, in turn, a central role in making Oxford aware of contemporary Benedictinism. It seems likely from the book's dedication to William Sheldon that Sadler had been chaplain to the family in the early 1650s and Sheldon was himself probably a confrater of the Rosary, although the list of members is no longer extant. It was William's son, Ralph senior, who built up the magnificent library at Weston and was well known in Oxford, especially through his patronage of Anthony Wood, but the collection of specifically Benedictine material in his library seems to have been pre-eminently due to the efforts of Sadler. Through Ralph Sheldon these valuable Benedictine records were gifted to Wood and eventually found their way into the Bodleian.

The Sheldons had grown close to the Benedictines during

the seventeenth century. Ralph had a brother who was a monk of Douai and a sister who became a nun of Cambrai, and two cousins who were also Benedictines. Ralph Sheldon's library at Weston contained Benedictine Constitutions, and the precious Cartulary of Glastonbury Abbey (the *Secretum Abbatis*) executed between 1340 and 1342. Had the Cartulary, one wonders, been preserved with the relic of the crown of thorns, which had also come from Glastonbury and which, together with the relic of Christ's cross taken by Abbot Feckenham from Westminster Abbey, were the two prized possessions of the Confraternity of the Rosary? Wood had little interest in Benedictine mystical treatises but was greedy for material on Benedictine history which might go into his forthcoming book, the *Historia et Antiquitates Universitatis Oxon.* (published in 1674), which was to establish his reputation as 'the historiographer of the University of Oxford'. Serenus Cressy was instrumental in aiding Wood's antiquarian endeavours in this respect. In July 1671, Cressy had met Ralph Sheldon in London and pointed Sheldon towards Wood, giving Sheldon a book on St Scholastica published in Rome in 1659 which he might use as a passport to make Wood's acquaintance. The two met each other a few days later in the Mitre in Oxford, where Ralph Sheldon tended to lodge when he visited the city, and a close friendship was thus sealed between these two great lovers of antiquity, Sheldon promising to help Wood in whatever way he could to forward the book on Oxford's history. In return, Wood promised to deliver Catholic books to the Oxford booksellers, one being *The Rule of Faith*, which Sheldon's Benedictine uncle had translated in 1660.

Until Sheldon's death in 1684, Wood was a constant visitor to Weston, where he read and catalogued the library, met other Benedictines, like Augustine Latham, also a Queen's Chaplain, and where he often overstayed his welcome. During these visits, Sheldon handed him judicious presents of papist books, including one by Cressy. Through Sheldon's generosity, books and important manuscripts which had been owned by Benedictine chaplains to the family were borne away by the magpie Wood to Oxford and eventually found a safe home in the Bodleian and in other Oxford libraries. The largest historical item which Sheldon offered to Wood for his research on the university's history and antiquities was the Benedictine Augustine Baker's historical collections of transcripts of documents from medieval monastic houses, probably compiled by Baker in the 1620s to use in the work *Apostolatus Benedictinorum in Anglia* (Douai, 1626). These collections once belonged to the English priory of St Laurence, at Dieulouard in Lorraine, the forebear of modern Ampleforth. Probably through the agency of Serenus Cressy, who had himself made use of these Baker transcripts in 1668, this collection was to be found in Sheldon's library between 1677 and 1681, and Sheldon thus offered it to Wood to help with the English translation of the *History and Antiquities*. Four of the six volumes are now in Jesus College Library. Wood, incidentally, was impressed by the exhaustive research displayed in the *Apostolatus Benedictinorum*, especially in regard to the foundation in Oxford of the Benedictines' Gloucester Hall. Among other Sheldon books which came into Wood's hands were the sole surviving copy of the Benedictine Vincent Sadler's *The Childe's catechism* (London, 1678) and a manuscript of supreme worth for a study of post-Reformation Benedictine history, Thomas Woodhope's *Obital book of Eminent Benedictines since the schisme*, a commonplace book which Woodhope, a Benedictine, had in his pocket up until near his death in 1654. This 'obital' was a prized possession in Wood's 'little library' because not only did it list the obits of monks, it also contained notes on Benedictine history, a useful resource for Wood in his research for his history of the University of Oxford. Woodhope, as chaplain at Beoley, had been Ralph Sheldon's tutor 'in juvenile and grammaticall learning', and his obit list was enlarged and continued by the later monk chaplain, Vincent Sadler, in a 'Catalogue' which Wood himself inspected in 1675 and made use of in his *Athenae Oxonienses* (Oxford, 1691) but which no longer survives. Wood's diligence and specialist antiquarian research incline one to overlook material of a more spiritual nature which he extracted from Sheldon but its presence continues to highlight that persistent interest in spiritual and mystical matters in those Catholic tassels attached to Oxford's hem.

Thus, Woodhope's 'obital book' contains English prayers from Blosius, and an extant manuscript of *The Prick of Conscience*, now at Douai Abbey, which belonged to Woodhope in 1633, suggests that he had been collecting English medieval works of a devotional nature even before he entered the Sheldon household. Woodhope knew of a similar copy of this popular vernacular theological poem in the library at St Gregory's, Douai, which had been donated by his near contemporary, Leander Pritchard, the 'socio' and biographer of Augustine Baker. The Sheldons appear to have preferred chaplains who were attracted to the works of the mystics. The Benedictine Gregory Mallet, whose death at Weston in 1691 Wood records, had been chaplain to the Cambrai English Benedictine nuns in 1653, and whilst there translated Spanish and French mystical works 'that meaner capacities as well as the sublime wits may have their share in the Treasure'.[4]

Through the agency of the solitary and eccentric antiquarian Anthony Wood we derive most of our knowledge of Benedictine involvement in Oxford during the last decades of the seventeenth century. Wood was acquainted with Richard Reeve, an Oxford convert, who became a monk in 1674, taking the religious name Wilfrid. Among the few Oxford Benedictines of the time, Reeve remained the closest to his old university, and his deep interest in mysticism and the spiritual life reminds us once again that this aspect of Benedictine monasticism held a particular fascination for some members of the university. Reeve was educated in Gloucester, matriculated at Trinity College in 1661 and graduated BA in 1665. In 1668 he became an usher at Magdalen College School, and was made chief master there in 1670. During his schoolmastering, he converted to Catholicism in 1667, being received into the Church in the chapel at Holywell in north Oxford, which belonged to the Napier family. Reeve was an accomplished teacher, 'a perfect philologist, admirably versed in all classical learning, and a good Grecian and . . . sedulous in his profession of Paedagogy'; he was praised for his child-centred teaching methods and in great demand among the students. The scrawl on one of his pupil's books, 'Mr Reeves the best grammarian in the world', reflects this respect. Since an attack of palsy had left him lame on his left side, he would say that he had been 'taken off from the rambles of the world [to] spend most of his time altogether in studies and devotion'.[5]

Whilst Reeve was teaching at Magdalen College School, Anthony Wood completed his draft of the History and Antiquities of Oxford, and it was accepted in 1670 for publication in a Latin translation by the university's delegacy for printing books, 'for the honour of the University in forreigne countries' and so as to recover 'the words themselves' of original documents. In 1669, the press had been installed in the newly completed Sheldonian Theatre, and in 1671, its management came into the hands of Dr John Fell and three others. Fell was then Dean of Christ Church, and was to become Bishop of Oxford in 1676. Richard Reeve's scholarly reputation, in spite of his popery, encouraged Fell to employ him on the translation of Wood's history of Oxford, and Reeve began work on the section dealing with Lincoln College in June 1673, before moving on to Christ Church in August of that year. It was through this commission that Reeve was introduced for the first time to Wood himself, and the two henceforth became fast friends, exchanging books and queries with each other. The work of translation was, however, snapped off in the bud, since Fell and others became anxious following rumours of Reeve's attempts to pervert members of the university to popery, and of his refusing to subscribe to the oaths and take the sacrament, as demanded by a recent statute. Reeve was forced by the President of Magdalen in December 1673 to resign his post.

The charges which led to Reeve's resignation have generally been accepted at face value and, in the tense atmosphere of that decade which was to explode in the Popish Plot, he was easily put into the category of militant popish proselytisers like the Jesuits. One rumour maintained that he had educated in his teaching career 'sixty Protestant ministers and forty Catholic priests', which is possible, but another conflated this with a further story that he had been paid a yearly pension to make converts at Oxford. There is no evidence for this accusation: who, in any case, would pay him such an annuity? Reeve, as we shall see, held strong political opinions, but he was at home in Oxford circles, and any preaching he did was quietly performed by way of discussion and recommendation of useful reading. The immediate cause of his ejection seems to have been over Walter Harris of New College, who had 'a Worm in his Pate' and became a Catholic after being beguiled by the 'lively memorials of Popery in statues and pictures on the Gates and in the chapel of New College' and by reading the Oxford convert, Abraham Woodhead's *The Guide in Controversies* (published in 1667 and 1673) on the Council of Trent. Reeve was engaged in a heated dispute at the time of the conversion with Harris' parson brother over the mission of St Augustine and adopted the view taken by the Benedictine, Serenus Cressy, in his *The Church History of Britany,* published in 1668. Reeve was blamed by his opponents for Walter Harris' conversion, even though this was the work of the Jesuit, Francis Goldie. Harris soon reverted to Anglicanism during the Popish Plot scare, but it is significant that in later life he continued to maintain the value of the discourses and example of Reeve, 'whom he could never afterwards name but with a particular respect'.[6]

In January 1674, Anthony Wood, himself accused of popish tendencies, saw Reeve off at Abingdon. Reeve's last request was that Dr Fell, 'whom I have been more beholden to ever since I came to Oxford', should allow him to continue with his translation of Wood's *History of Oxford,* which was, in fact, published in July of that year and contained, to Wood's fury, 'many base things put in by Dr Fell to please his partial humour and undo the author'. Wood immediately set out to rewrite his *History* in English. Serenus Cressy, corresponding at the time with the Benedictine chaplain at Weston, also expressed his unease with Fell's action, and Reeve, who was living in London 'at a glass-shop over against Somerset house', hoped Wood would secure him a copy, with 'the most material wrongs . . . done you' noted by Wood in the margin of the printed text. By the end of July 1674, Reeve's bags were packed for Douai, where he would be lodged as a *convictor* at the English Benedictine priory of St Gregory, whither all the Oxford converts of his generation who became monks had finished up. Douai, with its English

College founded in 1568 by Catholic refugees from Oxford and its numerous British colleges and religious houses, possessed a thriving university, and would not have been too unlike Oxford for someone of Reeve's temperament and gifts. Before leaving England, Reeve invited Wood to use him in 'in any way servicable' after his arrival in France, and in return, looked forward to news from Oxford, 'which is a place I must forever love and honour before all the world'. He packed Wood's book into his luggage and requested another copy for the Jesuits in Antwerp.[7]

Reeve found the English monastery of St Gregory at Douai congenial. The community was housed in part of the university's Vedastine College, founded by the Benedictines of St Vaast in Arras for its monks studying at Douai, and as such, resembled the monastic colleges in Oxford before the dissolution. 'Hardly out of his riding clothes', Reeve wrote immediately to Wood, enthusing about the 'well-furnished library' containing books Wood would be glad to see. Prior Alexius Caryll was eager to see Wood's *History of Oxford,* and Reeve hoped Dean Fell might be prevailed upon to send over a copy with 'cuts in it for their sakes, who have no other means of seeing our famous University'. Reeve's apparent rejoinder to Oxford's recent 'censure' on his Catholicism was to quote from 'a certain Poet': 'Great men 'gainst poor to anger still are prone. It is not well, but profitably done', for he had now at Douai 'something better to think on'.[8] Even before Reeve was professed a monk on St Benedict's Feast, 11 July 1676, his declamatory and literary skills were being exploited in his new home. From his pen flowed a significant collection of encomiastic Latin verses to be recited publicly on festivals and commemorations, often by students in St Gregory's College. Other poems revealed his contemporary political preoccupations, like those celebrating James II, Louis XIV and his Revocation of the Edict of Nantes, and those attacking William III and his wife, the 'Princess of Orange'.

Reeve took the religious name 'Wilfrid' on his clothing, and celebrated the event with a history of the 'English Apostle', St Wilfrid, information about whom he culled from Serenus Cressy's *Church History of Brittany.* As Cressy died in

1674, it cannot be proved that Reeve ever met him, but Reeve's reputation as a Benedictine rests on him assuming Cressy's mantle as the editor and translator of the mystical treatises of their predecessor, Augustine Baker. Baker, Cressy and Reeve were, as we have seen, all Oxford men, and with the monk, Wilfrid Reeve, we see the continuity of an Oxford interest in the seventeenth-century English Benedictine school of mystical writing and its predecessors. His passion for transcribing these manuscript works, helped along by his lameness, continued unabated until the end of his life. For the two years 1677 and 1678, for instance, there are almost 4000 manuscript pages in Reeve's hand in seventeen manuscripts still extant, and there would probably have been more if some treatises had not been torn up to be used as cartridge cases during the French Revolution. Wood had been shown Cressy's manuscript abridgement of the Middle English mystical work *The Cloud of Unknowing* by Reeve who, in 1689, would also abridge Cressy's life of Augustine Baker for inclusion in Wood's book, *Athenae Oxonienses*.

Reeve seems to have remained in France until the accession to the English throne of the Catholic King James II in 1685. Teaching in the Benedictine schools at Douai and La Celle-en-Brie, near Meaux, he was well away from the disturbance caused by the Popish Plot, in which he had been mentioned as a conspirator. At La Celle, he was visited by Bossuet, who held him in high regard. At the beginning of 1688, Reeve turned down the possibility of returning to his beloved Oxford and Magdalen College School, where James II had promoted him to a mastership as part of his policy to introduce more Catholics into Oxford. Reeve felt the university was in too disturbed a state over the introduction of Catholics into senior university positions. He went, instead, to the Blue Coat School at Gloucester, but was imprisoned for some months during the 1688–9 Revolution. After being set at liberty in the summer of 1689, he went to reside with Sir Charles Browne, one of his old pupils, at Kiddington, and visited Oxford from there. Wood, busy with his book on Oxford worthies at this time, continued to bombard Reeve with questions, but there is no evidence that they personally met each other again, despite the malicious rumour that

they played card-games with each other on Sunday after-
noons. Wood, in any case, might have felt mysticism and the
monastic life had turned Reeve's head, as it had Cressy's, for
he wrote of the latter:

> While he [Cressy] continued in Oxon he was accounted a
> quick and accurant Disputant, a Man of a good Nature,
> Manners and natural Parts, and when in Orders, no inconsid-
> erable Preacher. But after he had spent divers Years in a
> Religious Order, and was returned into England, his former
> Acquaintance found great alterations in him as to Parts and
> Vivacity, and he seemed to some to be possest with strange
> Notions, and to others, a reserved Person, and little better
> than a Melancholic.[9]

Happily, Reeve had avoided the persecution of English
Catholics provoked by the Popish Plot at the end of the
1670s, which was particularly vicious in Oxford. In 1678
the Pope was burned in effigy and the net of suspicion cast
wide to draw in those who had even the slightest dealings
with Catholicism. The clamour focused on the Jesuits and
their sympathisers in particular, but friends and acquaintances of monks were among those who also suffered. Thus,
Anthony Wood's papers were searched for incriminating
material, eliciting his sardonic retort that 'A man that is
studious and reserved is popishly affected.' Wood tarried
some time at Weston with the Sheldons, until the storm had
passed. Ralph Sheldon himself was clapped in Warwick gaol
on account of the Plot. During 1679, the returns of popish
suspects by the Heads of Houses to the Vice-Chancellor kept
the temperature up in the university, and Wood busied
himself collecting Popish Plot pamphlets, including a copy
of a letter about the Plot by the Benedictine, Peter Caryll,
to Dame Catherine Maura Hall, recently retired Abbess of
Cambrai. Into this collection also came an account of the
martyrdom of Oliver Plunkett in July 1681, written by Plunkett's fellow prisoner, the monk Maurus Corker, and
transcribed by Ralph Sheldon, as well as other of Corker's
published works on the Plot which were given to Wood by
Sheldon.

James II, following his accession in 1685, was determined

to encourage Oxford to be more tolerant to his own faith and exploited every means at his disposal to effect this. His principal ally here was the Society of Jesus, for the Jesuits understood how vital it was to capture the major seats of learning for the Faith and to infiltrate them with Catholic doctrine so that Oxford and other universities might take their places alongside the great continental Catholic universities. The Society had also an international reputation for converting intellectuals to Catholicism. It was necessary, then, to expand the number of Catholic academics and allow freedom of Catholic worship in Oxford. The Benedictines, despite being ardent supporters of James and being favoured by the King in many respects, were tangential in this enterprise. Oxford Catholicism during the earlier part of the King's reign was centred on the chapels established by the leading converts Obadiah Walker, Master of University College, known as 'Obadiah Ave-Maria' to his tormentors, and John Massey, who became Dean of Christ Church in 1686. Both these maintained secular priests and Jesuits as chaplains. A member of Walker's 'club' of converts was, incidentally, a Greenwood from Brize Norton, from a family which employed Benedictine chaplains throughout much of the eighteenth century. Benedictine efforts during this time were centred on the establishment of a small monastery at St James's Palace in the capital, and news of this and of the sermons of the Benedictine Court preacher, Philip Ellis, reached Oxford through the news sheets. From January 1688, information about Benedictines in London would also reach Oxford through Dom Wilfrid Reeve who returned to the capital in that month. In the face of mounting anti-popery among members of the university and townsfolk, James II touched for the Evil, a miraculous cure for scrofula traditionally associated with the monarchy, in September 1687 and then prayed in Walker's and Massey's chapels.

The culmination of the King's policy to educate Oxford in tolerance towards Catholicism was to be seen in his attempts throughout 1688 to introduce Catholics into Magdalen College, especially among the Fellowship. The story of the university's resistance to the King's plan is well known. Suffice it to say that many of the new Catholic fellows were reputable scholars in their own right, and were headed by a Catholic President, Bonaventure Giffard, Vicar Apostolic and 'Sorbonist'. The clamour against Catholics at Magdalen was so deafening and the King's own preoccupations for the safety of his throne so absorbing that his policy was in tatters by the end of the year. In November too, heightened political and religious tension inflamed the riotous mob to deface and close the popish chapels in Oxford. By this time, many of those who comprised 'the flower of English Catholic scholarship' were on their way back to Flanders, prevented from contributing 'to those seats of learning an added lustre so long denied them through exile'.[10] There was, in this wretched affair, only a trace of Benedictine involvement, which, although slight, demonstrates a degree of continuity with Oxford's recent preoccupation concerning Benedictine monasticism. In February 1688, the King had sought to intrude the monk Augustine Constable as one of the Catholic fellows at Magdalen.

Constable was an apt choice for Oxford, and his credentials were known to James. He came from a distinguished Yorkshire recusant family and had been professed at Douai in 1649. In 1688, he was a member of the new Benedictine community at St James's Palace, and since he was recommended for the Magdalen Fellowship in February of that year, it is quite likely that Wilfrid Reeve, late of Magdalen and back in London at this juncture, had a hand in his appointment. As a donnish Benedictine and a representative of the English Catholicism which the King felt might appeal to university circles, scholarly, tolerant and devout, Constable was an ideal choice. He was a king's chaplain. He had been educated in the University of Douai and whilst at St James's, he had made ample use of the royal library. He was the owner of the Guisborough Psalter, one of the group of fourteenth-century manuscripts belonging to the Tickhill Psalter family. He was actively interested in offering and expanding educational facilities, being a notable benefactor to the Benedictine college in Douai. Beyond all this, Constable would have been the latest in a line of Benedictines known to Oxford who demonstrated a deep interest in spiritual matters and in Benedictine mystical teaching. His sister,

Barbara, a Cambrai nun and disciple of Augustine Baker, had written out in 1645 the 450 pages of Baker's *Directions for Contemplation* for her brother, even before he was clothed as a monk, and his extant sermons are full of allusions to 'spiritual internal prayer' and 'affective prayer'. His Latin copy of the 'Paradise of Prayers' is today at Ampleforth, whilst his catechetical treatises are to be found in manuscript at Downside.

A royal warrant, issued on 24 February 1688, demanded that Constable be admitted as a Fellow of Magdalen. He was formally admitted on 16 March, but only a few months later, on 25 October, he was removed by the college Visitor, at the same time as other Catholic fellows. Magdalen's Batells or Buttery Book does not record any payments incurred by Constable, which implies that he did not take up residence in the college. For this absence, no reasons are known, but perhaps he was reluctant to come to Oxford, knowing that the tide was turning against James and his pro-Catholic policies, and he might have foreseen that by the end of 1688 all the Oxford Catholic chapels would have been closed and the Catholic Fellows of Magdalen dispersed. Constable, however, survived in England throughout the Revolution and between 1693 and 1697 was superior of all the Benedictines in the south of England, a measure of the respect in which he was held by the monks.

If the links between Oxford and the monks in the seventeenth century had been tenuous, during the eighteenth century they were to be almost non-existent, and survived only through the mediation of Oxford-educated tourists visiting the continental Benedictine monasteries, and through the continuing diligent research by Oxford antiquarians into the monasticism of a previous age. For their part, some monks bridged the gulf by seeking the patronage of distinguished Oxford alumni, but the commonest way by which the university had any impact on the English Benedictines was through books published by the University Press. From the late seventeenth century the libraries of Oxford colleges had begun to purchase the great series of Church Fathers edited by the Benedictines of the Congregation of Saint-Maur, and in his *Treatise on Monastic Studies*, published in

1691, the Maurist scholar, Jean Mabillon, had acknowledged the value of Thomas Hyde's 1674 catalogue of printed books in the Bodleian Library as a research tool. Throughout the last decades of the century, Mabillon was corresponding with Oxford scholars such as Dr Edward Bernard and seeking their help with the Maurist patristic editions. Certain English Benedictines consciously imitated Maurist pretensions and pursuits, fostering friendships with their French counterparts and concentrating on their own library collections. The earliest complete English Benedictine library catalogue, that of St Edmund's, Paris, begun in 1702, shows that the monks were anxious to read contemporary works rolling from the Oxford University Press. The majority of the twenty-three Oxford books listed were, for safety's sake, demoted to the section in the library devoted to 'Heretical and Heterodox Books', and to the 'Hell' cabinet, but their very presence, nevertheless, demonstrates some sympathy with the works of Laudian authors and with writers who appealed to the non-jurors, such as Peter Heylyn (1600–62), Richard Allestree (1619–81) and Luke de Beaulieu (died 1723). This English Benedictine catalogue also reveals that the monks were abreast of contemporary oriental scholarship at Oxford; Thomas Hyde's *History of the Ancient Persians*, and the *Epistles* of the Cottonian librarian, Thomas Smith (1638–1710), on the manners of the Turks and his survey of the oriental churches, would have been on the shelves in the monks' library when it was used by the Chevalier Andrew Michael Ramsay, composing his immensely popular novel, *The Travels of Cyrus*, in the 1720s.

This Benedictine disfranchisement of eighteenth-century Oxford shifts our attention towards the alternative continental universities which monks attended as students and professors, such as those at Douai, Pont-à-Mousson (1572–1762) and the Sorbonne in Paris. Oxford had strong similarities with these European sisters. All were bastions of conservatism and upholders of the Gallican or Anglican Churches. Oxford's bachelor clerical dons were comparable to the celibate members of the religious orders who filled the teaching posts in these continental universities. The income of both was supplemented by the holding of benefices, a valuable prerequisite, incidentally, for those English Benedictines who graduated from the Sorbonne. Regular attendance at religious services was obligatory for students and teachers at Oxford and its European counterparts. In both, examinations were based on oral disputations, and Latin was the lingua franca. In Oxford and in the French universities, theology belonged to the faculty of higher studies, being a preparation for ordination. So ubiquitous was the influence of established Christianity in Oxford, that its colleges were often called seminaries, as colleges were in Catholic Europe, and John Aubrey voiced the criticism of Oxford that 'instead of giving to young Gentlemen the Accomplishments according to Juvenal, they returne home with the learning [if any at all] of a Benedictine Monke; with some Scholarly Canting. Thus in lieu of giving him the Breeding of a Gentleman, he is sent home with that of a Deacon.'[11] A further identity of interest between eighteenth-century Oxford and English Catholics at continental universities would have been a common attachment to Jacobitism which provided, as we shall see, the basis of a friendship between Oxford's non-juring dons and monks.

There were, on the other hand, enough differences between Oxford and the French centres of learning to make Oxford somewhat alien and foreign to English monks attached to continental universities. Douai, 'the Athens of the North', and Pont-à-Mousson were creations of the Counter-Reformation and designed to counter the Protestant threat. They were also smaller: whilst Oxford had some eighteen colleges and seven halls in 1688, the University of Douai comprised six colleges and eighteen seminaries. Oxford's tradition of anti-popery survived in the effusions of the *Terrae-Filius*, the licensed university jester, and in its defensive Anglican apologetics. Socially, Douai's students tended to be of modest means and to come from the provinces, and most of the Benedictines staffing the Vedastine College, among whom were numbered the English monks, were from a similar background. By contrast, while Oxford had its poor scholars or 'servitors', it tended to recruit from the establishment upper classes those gentlemen-commoners who made it something of an aristocratic finishing school. These contrasts were presumably in part the reason for the difference in tone between Oxford and the French institutions, for Oxford gained some notoriety in the eighteenth century for the complacency of its tutors and the dissipation of its undergraduates. Such shortcomings, for instance, drove Edward Gibbon in 1752 to Catholicism and persuaded many other able youths to seek a more stimulating education on the Grand Tour, the route preferred, of course, by the sons of English Catholic aristocrats who were debarred from Oxford and who often hired a monk to accompany them as tutor, as Lord Palmerston was to do. Although monks attending the Sorbonne were ordered to wear the habit and not turn aside to linger in the Parisian cabarets, French university life was generally more cloistered than that of Oxford. The preponderance of religious orders induced a high level of sobriety at Douai, and helped to make religious confraternities and sodalities the principal forum of a student's social life. For their part, the English Benedictines encouraged their students and friends to join their own confraternities. The Wesleys' Holy Club, founded in the 1720s, and the progenitor of Methodism, was perhaps the closest Oxford came to having a confraternity of this type.

The earnestness of Catholic university education on the continent owed much to Jesuit ideas of holistic formation of the young. The typical Oxford product 'represented as monkish, narrow, devoid of social grace and lacking in civility' might thus be contrasted with the purposeful and charming diplomat ideally produced by following the advice of the English Jesuit William Darrell's *The Gentleman Instructed in the Conduct of a Virtuous and Happy Life*, which had reached its tenth edition by 1732 and was standard reading in Catholic households and Benedictine colleges. The Jesuits had also been responsible for creating the *internat*, a sharply defined curriculum in which an introduction to philosophy, theology and the humanities was given in colleges before students went up to university. The Benedictines ran many of the more prestigious colleges which followed this system. Although English public schools provided a curriculum which prepared their youth for Oxford, it seems not to have been as rigorous, lengthy or prescriptive as that of the Jesuits. In regard to university studies, the French universities patronised by the English monks argu- ably stole a march on Oxford as the century progressed. Oxford was slow, it seems, in recognising the value of New- tonianism and 'natural philosophy', and left its promotion to individual enthusiasts. In contrast to this, there is the example of the academic career of the Benedictine New- tonian astronomer and mathematician, Charles Walmesley, Fellow of the Royal Society and eventually Bishop of the Western District, who was one of only a pair of monks who completed the ten-year course which led to a Sorbonne DD. In 1764, the year when Edward Bentham, the Regius Pro- fessor of Divinity at Oxford, instituted lectures designed to prove that 'theology might rejoice' in scientists like Newton, Boyle and James Bradley, Walmesley had drawn up a course of studies for student monks which pointed them in the direction of the new physical sciences and which merely formalised the tuition he had been giving for some time.

During the eighteenth century, particular interest in Ben- edictine monasticism survived at Oxford largely through the endeavours of a new generation of antiquarian scholars. Whilst the attraction to Benedictine mystical works fell away, the fascination for monastic history continued unabated in scholars like Thomas Hearne, who inherited in many dif- ferent ways the mantle of Anthony Wood. Both were retailers of Oxford gossip as well as non-juring Jacobites whose anti- quarian research brought them the friendship of English monks. Hearne's political beliefs caused him to live on the margins of university life. He had been appointed librarian janitor at the Bodleian in 1702, but on refusing to take the oaths to the Hanoverians in 1715, had been dismissed. From that time, he made the Ashmolean Library his base and was fortunate to secure the continued willingness of the mag- nanimous University Press to publish his editions of medieval texts. Over forty of his volumes were thus pub- lished, financed, in turn, by a complex machinery of subscription and distribution. Being deprived of access to most of the Oxford library collections, Hearne was forced to depend on private collections outside Oxford. Wood's

Catholic literary patron had been Ralph Sheldon; Hearne's was principally Charles Eyston of East Hendred, although he was also acquainted with Sir Robert Throckmorton, an old student and generous patron of the English Benedictines, who lived at Buckland, just west of Oxford. It was Sir Robert who had made the classic statement about 'antiquaries' like Eyston and Hearne that 'They are Men that love to make remarks, and they prefer walking to riding upon that account.'[12]

There was an expanding market for Hearne's meticulously edited texts among the educated gentry, and there was the first faint impression in such circles that medievalism, monasticism and Oxonianism were of a piece. In 1717, at the height of Hearne's editing, Alexander Pope, himself a Catholic, wrote: 'I . . . lay in one of the most ancient, dusky parts of the University, and was dead to the world as any Hermite of the desart', and some decades later, Horace Walpole echoed such sentiments, noting: 'the moon rose as I was wandering among the colleges, and gave me a charming venerable Gothic scene, which was not lessened by the monkish appearance of the old fellows stealing to their pleasures.'[13]

Hearne's editions of the Tudor antiquary, John Leland, had been published between 1709 and 1715, before his departure from the Bodleian, and contained vital documents copied from the monastic libraries on the eve of the dissolution. A set of Hearne's 1715 edition of Leland's *Collections* in six volumes survives, inscribed as gift from Charles Eyston, Knight, of Hendred, Berkshire, in 1725 to the monastery of the English Benedictine community of St Laurence at Dieulouard, and bearing the monastic library's pressmark. This may have been the very set which the Eyston chaplain, the Franciscan, Cuthbert Parkinson, mentions that he made use of in his edition of the *Historical Collections of the English Franciscans* which appeared in 1726, and which bore a congratulatory letter of Hearne as its preface. Thus, the Eystons were responsible, it seems, for introducing Hearne's study of medieval monastic sources to the eighteenth-century successors of the medieval monks. 'Charles Eyston, Knight' was the son and heir of Hearne's great friend,

Charles Eyston, known as 'the Antiquary'. Hearne frequently walked to Hendred House from Oxford between 1711 and Eyston's death in 1721, and would make ample use of rare books found in the Hendred library, whilst Eyston would come over to Oxford and dine with Hearne at the Mitre. Their friendly collaboration bore fruit in 1722 when Hearne published Eyston's *Little Monument to the once famous Abbey and Borough of Glastonbury* (1716) in his *History and Antiquities of Glastonbury.* Eyston, meanwhile, enjoyed cordial relations with the monks. His second son Basil was professed as a monk at Douai in 1733, and he always boasted that ex-monastic land only prospered when it was in the hands of Catholics, like his own family. The threat of the 'abbey lands' being returned to their original owners had been a subject of hot debate in Oxford and elsewhere during James II's reign, and had caused the non-juror, Nathaniel Johnston, who had been involved in the Magdalen College stirs, and his Benedictine brother, Henry Joseph Johnston, to publish a disavowal in *The Assurance of Abby and other Church-lands to the possessors* (London, 1687). The monk Johnston was a close friend of his fellow Benedictine, Basil Eyston.

It was Charles Eyston the antiquary who informed Hearne that Thomas Southcott (called 'Wadsworth' by Eyston), a Benedictine, whom Hearne had met in Oxford in the summer of 1719, was to become President of the English Benedictines (1721–41), that he was 'a man of great sense and Prudence, and . . . hath an excellent secular Head'. It was Southcott, according to Eyston, who had directed King James II 'in the true Method of Passports'. This is our only evidence of Southcott, a notorious Jacobite agent and paymaster and a close friend of Alexander Pope, passing through Oxford. His Jacobitism must have endeared him both to Eyston and Hearne, and presumably to the Oxford Jacobite and non-juring underworld.

The best example, however, of the informal relations conducted by a Benedictine and an Oxford scholar in the eighteenth century appears to be the extant correspondence of the 1720s between Dom Gilbert Knowles and Thomas Hearne. Knowles[14] was a poet and botanist who had been introduced to Hearne at Oxford in 1718 by the great phys-

ician and collector of antiquities, Dr Richard Mead, who had
cured Knowles of blindness. Books soon began to circulate
among the three, including Knowles' own botanical work,
published in 1723 and dedicated to Mead, on behalf of
which the monk pressed Hearne to become a patron.
Hearne willingly used his own experience of publishing to
advise the monk about printing and collecting subscribers.
Knowles numbered another Oxford botanist, Dr Richard
Dyer of Oriel, among his friends. Dyer was described by
Hearne, a close friend, as 'a very healthfull man and a great
walker'. The monk Knowles yearned to be accepted in university circles and was therefore inclined to conceal his
monastic vocation from his Oxford correspondents. A conversion to Anglicanism and residence in Oxford became
particularly attractive when he persuaded himself that his
Benedictine brethren had ill-used him, and William Wake,
Archbishop of Canterbury, attempted to persuade Bishop
John Potter of Oxford to find a position for Knowles within
the university 'where he will be entirely separated from his
former friends, and his Conversation may be much better
known than in London.' However, 'a violent flux' forced
Knowles back to his monastery at Douai in 1725. Here, he
did his best to collect books from Flemish monasteries on
behalf of Anglican scholars like Wake. Knowles' career illustrates the strength of Oxford's appeal to scholarly
Benedictines, who might find themselves living, like him, in
the wilds of West Riding and believing themselves deprived
of academic sustenance. His offer to collect books on the
continent for English academics was made at the same time
as the Bodleian was concentrating on improving its own
continental holdings through dealers like George Clarke
who were scouring France for desirable items.

It seems that Oxford's pursuit of Benedictine monasticism
through the researches of its most distinguished antiquarian
scholars persisted through the eighteenth century. Hearne
was succeeded by Richard Rawlinson, a fellow non-juror,
whose voluminous collections were deposited in the Bodleian in 1756. They included a correspondence of 1655
between monks and nuns which dealt with the teachings of
the mystic, Augustine Baker, although Rawlinson appears to

have had less direct interest in this school of spirituality than had his seventeenth-century antiquarian forebears. Rawlinson had engaged in friendly controversy on the subject of scriptural interpretation with the English Benedictine Procurator when he had visited Rome in 1723 and had visited at least one of the monasteries on the continent belonging to the English monks, where he had made notes on its historical artefacts.

But the most celebrated Oxonian to visit an English monastery during this century was undoubtedly Dr Samuel Johnson. In 1775, the university had conferred on the doctor an honorary DCL, and in October of that year, he visited St Edmund's, Paris, and in November, the Benedictine nuns at Cambrai. At St Edmund's, he was 'very kindly used by the English Benedictine friars', dined with the prior and librarian, though he found the dinner 'tasteless' and 'meagre', and was very satisfied to be given a free run of the library, whose valuable books he listed. He stayed 'till it was time for the Fryars to go to bed'. The librarian who brought out 'books of the greatest rarity and assisted him in his researches' was Dom James Compton, who later absconded after reading issue 10 of Johnson's *The Rambler*, on Repentance, and became an Anglican clergyman. Although it is hard to believe Compton's assertion that he had dissuaded Johnson from retiring to St Edmund's to end his days, Johnson, nevertheless, maintained him when he found refuge in London. Johnson had ambivalent views, it seems, about the monastic life, criticising monasteries as 'only retreats for persons unable to serve the public'. He had put aside any intention of settling in Oxford, which he compared to a monastery when he insisted that 'he that lives well in the world is better than he that lives well in a monastery.' Nevertheless, he proudly told Boswell that he had had a cell appropriated to him in the Paris priory. At St Edmund's, Johnson also conversed with the prior and with 'Friar' Cuthbert Wilks, and then 'parted very tenderly' from them. Wilks was a bright and recent graduate of the Sorbonne, and a close friend and contemporary of the Benedictine, Bede Brewer, the holder of the second eighteenth-century English Benedictine Sorbonne doctorate. Brewer's earliest biblical thesis on prophecy, published in Paris in 1766, shows his familiarity with the innovative work of the famous Oxford Hebraicist, Robert Lowth (1710–87).

Cuthbert Wilks' radical Cisalpine views had earned him the sobriquet 'No. 45' amongst his brethren, but Dr Johnson was charmed by him, and took him under his wing. He believed that a familiarity with Oxford circles would benefit Wilks enormously, and so, in May 1776, gave him a letter of introduction to Dr Adams, the Master of Pembroke, Johnson's old college. Johnson's description of Wilks here as 'a learned Benedictine' suggests that respect for monastic scholarship had persisted in the university. Wilks thus took Oxford in his way, and impressed Adams by his learning. Wilks, whose stormy ecclesiastical career was still ahead of him, kept his friendship with Johnson warm; in his collection of books at his death in 1829 was Johnson's *Life of Richard Savage*, the 'criminal biography', first published in 1744, which revealed Johnson's knowledge of the London underground and poor.[15]

The occasion of a monk turning up at the door of the Master of Pembroke in 1777 and introducing himself as such, is an indication of growing tolerance within the eighteenth-century university to those who dissented from the Anglican establishment, even though an attempt to repeal subscription to the Thirty-Nine Articles had been unsuccessful in 1772. The French Revolution, however, forced the university to look more kindly on Catholicism and to take pity on the numerous French clergy seeking refuge in England. A measure of its sympathy was its willingness to allow the University Press to print a copy of the Vulgate in 1797 for the use of the emigrés. Between 1794 and 1795, most of the communities of English Benedictines also found their way back to England and re-established themselves. The monks, however, were still barred from entry into the university; the 1791 Catholic Relief Act provided that no Catholic fill any office or place at Oxford, and that no Catholic keep a school there. The religious tests, taken on matriculation at Oxford, remained in force until 1871.

FURTHER READING

L. W. B. Brockliss, *French Higher Education in the Seventeenth and Eighteenth Centuries* (Clarendon Press, Oxford, 1987).

A. Clark (ed.), *The Life and Times of Anthony Wood, Antiquary, of Oxford, 1632–1695, Described by Himself,* OHS (o.s.) 19f (1891–1900), 5 vols.

G. Scott, *Gothic Rage Undone: English Monks in the Age of Enlightenment* (Bath, 1992).

L. S. Sutherland and L. G. Mitchell (eds.), *The History of the University of Oxford: Volume V: The Eighteenth Century* (Oxford, 1986).

PART III

Saint Benet's Hall

15

The Foundation of St Benet's Hall

ANSELM CRAMER osb[1]

Saint Benet's Hall was not known by that name until 1918. The origin of the institution of Halls is medieval: any Master of Arts was permitted by the university to maintain a private Hall, from which he could present candidates for degrees. Such Halls lay at the very origin of the University of Oxford. There was a multiplicity of Halls, students sitting at the feet of a Master, and only gradually did the colleges emerge out of this haphazard system. Even at the end of the nineteenth century, the structure of the university remained fluid, and the concept of the Hall remained enshrined in St Edmund Hall. Only later were they amalgamated into the larger colleges which we know today. This modern Benedictine Hall owes its foundation mainly to the vision and energy of Fr Anselm Burge, Prior of Ampleforth 1885–97. In considering its foundation, however, we need to look further back than the Oxford or the Benedictines of the 1890s.

From Queen Elizabeth to Queen Victoria the English Catholics laboured under the burden of penal law, which eased only gradually, towards the end of this period. As late as 1780 the petition organised through the Protestant Association under Lord George Gordon sparked the massive riots in London against Catholics that led to 285 deaths and a wave of 'no-popery' agitation throughout the country. When 'Emancipation' came it was in reality a gradual process, extending from 1778 (the Catholic Relief Act) through 1829 (when legal emancipation was granted) to the repeal of the Ecclesiastical Titles Act by Gladstone in 1871.

One of the effects of the penal laws had been to cut off Catholics from the university. Until the mid-nineteenth century Catholics, in common with other 'Dissenters', were barred from the university by the need to subscribe at matriculation to the Thirty-Nine Articles. This condition was removed by Oxford in 1854 and Cambridge in 1856. From this time, however, for some forty years it was the Catholics who were unwilling to take advantage of this relaxation. Two factors pulled in opposite directions: the need for some form of higher education had long been felt in the Catholic body, but in the mid-nineteenth century there existed a certain mistrust of the universities.

The revolutionary upheaval which moved all the English (and Scottish and Irish) religious houses and colleges out of France, and from other sites in Europe, in fact released a good deal of energy which expressed itself in the rapid foundation of new colleges or the transplantation of old ones, notably St Edmund's (Ware), Stonyhurst, Ushaw, Ampleforth and Downside between 1794 and 1814. Of these Stonyhurst and Ushaw probably remained the strongest until late in the century. It was in these places that a desire for higher education of some kind developed. Lingard, the notable church historian, was working at Ushaw; similar growth was occurring within the Jesuit sphere at Stonyhurst, and Ampleforth was teaching Hebrew at the time of Waterloo. No doubt similar processes were at work in the colleges remaining in other European countries; for example, the Scots monastery at Ratisbon escaped secularisation in 1803 (the only monastery in Germany to do so) because of the value of its school in the eyes of the local prince. The general desire for Catholic higher education may help to explain some of the intensity of the arguments in mid-century about the universities, Manning's simultaneous prevention of university access and encouragement of a new Catholic foundation, as well as the problems which gathered about Newman's head in Dublin.

As early as the 1820s Bishop Augustine Baines, of the Western District, conceived an ambitious, indeed grandiose, scheme to establish a diocesan seminary and school on the magnificent site of Prior Park, just outside Bath. But it was so far ahead of its time that it became a sort of Bristol Channel Bubble. Even Bishop Baines' somewhat dubious machinations did not suffice to lure to his foundation an adequate staff from either Downside or Ampleforth, and the project in practice never stood a chance of real success. No doubt he derived the idea from his own school-days with the English monks at Lamspringe in Germany. The idea may well have been a norm there; it was certainly in the air in the very early 1800s, at a time when in his pre-episcopal days he was thinking and writing about education as (effectively) headmaster of Ampleforth. The idea of a Catholic university or college, which had thrived so fruitfully in the Jesuit colleges which sprang up all over Europe in the mid-sixteenth century, was the concept which had underlain St Omer's. It was now transferred to England, and underlay the title *College,* applied to Stonyhurst, to Ampleforth at least as early as 1822, and Downside around 1834, not to mention others such as Cotton, Ratcliffe and Mount St Mary's. It formed part of the colleges at Ushaw, Oscott and Ware, which only later narrowed their purpose to the seminary education of the diocesan clergy. The term was not merely a pretentious name for a boys' school, but expressed the concept of a general religious and educational college which could extend from the age of about seven through to what we would call postgraduate studies, passing fluently from humanities to philosophy and theology in a way directly descended from the medieval *trivium* and *quadrivium.* Certainly, some sort of tertiary education, though not of too serious a kind, is implied by Chichester's remarks in his 1882 account of schools, about Stonyhurst pupils:

> the class of parlour boarders, miscalled Philosophers, allowed to keep horses, to ride about the country, to fish and to shoot, just as if they were Oxford undergraduates, although some of these young men are 22 years of age, and many of them are foreigners, who come merely to pick up the language.[2]

Not all colleges covered all the ground. Ampleforth did not, but they saw themselves in that light and so used the term which to them, coming from the continent, was the most natural. This was the ideal which Manning and others

pursued at Kensington as late as 1873, perhaps encouraged
by Bishop Clifford's success in 1867 in reviving Prior Park on
the lines originally laid down by Bishop Baines. The college
in Kensington was, however, short-lived. There were various
reasons why it failed. The first rector seems to have enjoyed
little grasp of accounts, the seminaries and religious orders
felt their own establishments threatened, and there was at
this time a growing tension between the regulars and the
bishops. Finally, the lay leaders of the Catholic community,
the aristocracy and the Catholic landed gentry, had their
eyes too firmly set on the social and career advantages of
Oxford and Cambridge. In an era of widespread church-
building – to which the current rash of centenaries bears
witness – their financial muscle was a factor not to be over-
looked.

Despite this thirst for higher education, there was prevalent in Catholic ecclesiastical circles a certain mistrust of
the universities. Both Newman and Manning voiced these
hesitations. Manning, already a power as Provost of the
Westminster Chapter in 1857, was anxious not to expose
young Catholic men to the dangers of the university market-
place of ideas. In this he was encouraged by the advice of
many of the Tractarian converts, who in their new zeal vigorously repudiated their old pastures, feeling that Oxford was
passing through a period of agnosticism, perhaps in part a
reaction to the Tractarians themselves. Manning and his
friends may have been right in their view that the Catholic
plant was yet too delicate to be exposed to these cold winds,
that irreparable damage might have been done. Perhaps the
young Catholic men were simply not sufficiently educated
in the Catholic schools, as yet very few. At any rate, at the
persuasion of the bishops, a willing and anxious Rome
issued a decree forbidding Catholics to attend the universities. This did not, of course, include London, newly
established in 1825, and by now long used as a support by
Catholic colleges, led by Downside in 1838, who used
London for what we would now call external degree courses.
By 1842 Downside had been joined in this by Ushaw, Stonyhurst, Ware, Prior Park and Oscott.

Towards 1880 pressure on the bishops was mounting to

allow individual Catholics to go to Oxford or Cambridge. One man, mentioned by von Hügel,[3] even got permission from the Pope (to the annoyance of the Bishop of Northampton), but it is suggested that the Pope misunderstood his Italian. Others just went, sometimes with the permission of their bishops. There were, of course, Catholics and clergy with university degrees, who had become Catholics after their time at university, and it was now becoming generally felt that exclusion was no longer in the Catholic interest. An Oxford convert, Hartwell Grissell,[4] was energetic in arousing interest. He was supported by Lord Braye and viewed with sympathy by Bishops Clifford and Hedley, at Clifton and Newport respectively. It should be remembered that as yet Baines' territory, the old Western District, in which their dioceses lay, had no higher education of its own. London had Ware, the Northern District had Ushaw and Stonyhurst, the Midlands had Oscott and the Oratory School. The Western had only Prior Park, which was not then thriving.

Bishop Hedley was among the strongest advocates of the admission of Catholics to the universities. It is somewhat of an anomaly that, although the leading figures in the thrust towards the universities, Baines and Hedley, were monks of Ampleforth, Ampleforth itself played almost no part in the process until the very end. It therefore becomes a question why Hedley was so percipient; he had never been near a university himself. He once wrote, 'I would have given anything to be permitted to go to Oxford.'[5] When a request was sent to Rome in 1883, Cardinal Simeoni countered by asking all the bishops for their views, with instructions not to consult each other first. Some were for retaining the current arrangement, among them Ullathorne, but Hedley and Clifford urged that a tacit permission should be given to reside at the universities, and that a strong Catholic mission be established there.

In his initial submission to Rome on the university question, in 1883, Hedley categorised Catholic young men of about eighteen years of age into three possible groups. First there were those who intended to proceed to the priesthood or some form of religious life; for them there were the seminaries or the colleges abroad. Then there were those who intended to go into one of the professions or trades; for these, except perhaps for medicine or law, the universities of the time were no special help. And there were the nobility, gentry and the rich or leisured class. About these he was specific:

> I calculate that there would be about two hundred ... But they are important because the Catholic status in the nation is dependent on them, and they are the source of our wealth and resources.[6]

An ideal solution would be a Catholic university, but recent experience at Kensington had shown that this idea was unworkable. Thus the young men were left with the possibility of the army or the navy, or they would 'in great measure lose their time'. Warming to his theme, Hedley maintained that at Oxford and Cambridge the 'best youth of England' were to be found:

> Here they meet celebrated scholars, are fired with enthusiasm for culture. Here they meet with one another. Here the whole genius of the place, the professors, the students, the libraries, the examiners, the recreations, unites to give to the English gentleman that tone or character which his class easily recognise. It is easy therefore to understand why many English Catholics consider it almost necessary to send their sons to Oxford or Cambridge.
>
> That such institutions are dangerous to Catholic faith or morals cannot be denied. I would prefer, with all my heart, a Catholic university. But I advocate the permission for Catholics to reside there as an alternative that is less dangerous than the allowing of the young men to be idle or to find themselves outside their own class in society.
>
> It is notorious that at this moment young English Catholics of the highest classes are the most ignorant, the most frivolous and the least serious of their class.[7]

We may ask why Hedley was so insistent. He was born in 1836 in Morpeth, the county town of Northumberland, and went to school at Ampleforth in May 1848, having received a lift there in the coal-cart. He did well in the school, which was reviving in the 1850s. He became a monk in 1854, straight from school, having apparently acquired some skill as a musician, which he later turned to good account: when back on the school staff it was he who helped to teach the future liturgical composer Egbert Turner. In 1862 Hedley was called to teach at the Benedictine study-house at Belmont, Hereford, which suggests ability, and was quite soon helping the bishop. After some time as his coadjutor he succeeded to the see of Newport and Menevia in 1881, a post he retained until his death in November 1915. Throughout his time as a bishop he remained a faithful friend of his own community: he often visited (he hardly missed an annual prize-giving day), and was the virtual founder, indeed the policy director, of the *Ampleforth Journal* (1895). As editor for a time of the *Dublin Review,* and author of many sermons and of many spiritual books, some of them still occasionally used, he made good use of his opportunities. His approach to Rome in 1883 on the university question was therefore quite prompt.

Hedley himself was in a finely balanced position. He was in no way in favour of a simple reversal of policy, and in fact expressed considerable hesitation and caution,[8] for he did not underrate the risks, as risks there are in the early stages of any introduction of new ideas. He saw clearly the need, and the opportunity, of a Mission. This is the origin of the Oxford and Cambridge chaplaincies, which to this day come under the hierarchy, rather than (as in other universities) the local bishop. At all events Hedley's persistence and determination to turn the Church round on the issue of universities made him the obvious choice to be President of the Catholic Universities Board when it was set up in 1896.

In January 1885 Rome turned the idea down. It looked like an end: in fact it was a beginning. Cardinal Manning died in January 1892, and Herbert Vaughan succeeded. It was said that Hedley would have succeeded, had he not been lame. It is certainly the case that he was the most prominent among the bishops, Ullathorne being dead. Vaughan had originally followed Manning's line, for it is difficult to divert the old from their cherished ideas, but Vaughan did not hold his view so strongly that he could not change it. So within three years of Manning's death the archbishop and bishops had drawn up (January 1895) *Resolutions* for submission to Rome, with a view to allowing Catholics to attend the two universities and proposing safeguards.

With surprising alacrity, on 2 April 1895 a decree was issued by Pope Leo XIII relaxing the ban, but with conditions, of which the chief were that the permission was a concession for exceptional cases, that there were to be Catholic lecturers to the new undergraduates, and that their conferences were to be frequent, or at least sufficient. The Jesuits moved swiftly, closely followed by the Benedictines.

'OUR OXFORD HOUSE'

Scholarship of a kind had not been lacking in the northern community of St Laurence at Ampleforth. Perhaps the intellectual thread may be traced from the initiative of Prior Cockshoot (1838–46), who was responsible for the founding of a common novitiate and house of studies for the English Benedictines at Belmont, and for sending two monks to Parma in Italy to study theology. One of these, Laurence Shepherd (chaplain to the Benedictine nuns of Stanbrook 1863–85), a disciple of Guéranger, founder of Solesmes, revived the study of Augustine Baker and the English mystics, as well as initiating the proper study of plainchant. To him we owe the volume of *Paléographie Musicale* in which the Worcester Antiphonal is studied. He also preached the retreat at Downside which sowed the seed of the English monastic reforms at the turn of the century. The other, Austin Bury made a collection of 700 theological books. In the 1860s and 1870s men like Stephen Kearney were collecting, rebinding and cataloguing an impressive collection of scriptural and patristic works. His original catalogue is dated 1866. It was in his time or thereabouts that the library acquired the whole of Migne's Patrology. It is clear that Ampleforth was not then the intellectual desert that people have sometimes supposed, even though the community was limited in resources, did not believe in display and had a deep commitment to the working classes, particularly the near-destitute exiles from Ireland in industrial missions like

Merthyr Tydfil and Liverpool. There was a strong sense of family life about the school, which was only about eighty strong.

It was from this background that the monks of Ampleforth, under Prior Burge and influenced strongly by Bishop Hedley, produced at this time two institutions which are still thriving in essentially the same form a century later, namely St Benet's Hall and *The Ampleforth Journal.* It is not surprising that Prior Burge should have conceived this idea which was so much in line with Hedley's way of thinking. Quite apart from the Bishop's regular visits to Ampleforth, the younger man had been closely associated with Hedley during most of his monastic life. Born in London in 1846, he became a monk in 1865, doing his studies as English monks then did at the cathedral priory of Belmont at a time when Hedley was playing a large part on the teaching and pastoral staff there. He spent some years teaching at Ampleforth, being in charge of studies from 1874 to 1877 before being sent as chaplain to Mgr Petre's school at Woburn Park, Weybridge. This school was another attempt to meet the growing demand on the part of the laity for better quality Catholic education. Here he had the valuable experience of other ideas in schooling, particularly of giving the older boys responsibility. In 1881 Hedley asked for him as bishop's secretary, a position from which he was moved only when he was selected as Prior of Ampleforth in 1885.

Anselm Burge was a man of ability, of energy, and also a musician, being described by a contemporary concert review as 'a great vocaliser', and appearing in programmes as a performer of Mozart piano concertos. He galvanised the Ampleforth community into building an entirely new monastery, in which they still live; he would have built more if funds had been equal to his plans. He played a great part in the debates then in progress on the reform of the Constitutions of the English Benedictines, and in the more practical problems of the distribution of the numerous Benedictine missions (later to be called parishes) among the three houses of the Congregation. There is no doubt about his ability or indeed his vision, but some about his ability to ride storms. There was much opposition to almost each of his plans, and he seems to have had some sort of breakdown, resigning as prior in December 1897, only four months after he had set up what was to become St Benet's Hall. He moved to a Liverpool parish, Grassendale, and there lived in respected authority until his death in July 1929.

Prior Burge later described the idea of an Oxford House as having come to him suddenly. In a letter written in 1926 to Fr Justin McCann, then Master of the Hall, he writes,

> Many thanks for the copy of your article[9] on our Oxford House, to me of course every detail is interesting. I have only one little criticism to make & that is with regard to Fr Clarke sj. I did not find him so warm as you represent him, nor did he ever urge us to make our foundation. I found him polite, but cool. The one who gave me most welcome encouragement was Card. Vaughan. I wrote to him and then sent F. Crow to interview him. He was all kindness.
>
> I think that I alone was responsible for the move. It was 'borne in upon me' and I held back for some time, as I found no one in my entourage to support me. In fact I think it was a special light from above which made me persevere. I was very ill at the time and very depressed and the opposition was very strong. How I held on to the idea I can never explain.
>
> It does not enter into the scope of your article to deal with the opposition to the enterprise, but the opposition was very widespread, both at home and abroad. One good Missioner at a public dinner prophesied that in 10 years after Oxford the Community at Ampleforth would be a mere handful. Douai was especially opposed, and Granville Ward went about his friends denouncing the scheme with the usual 'Ward' exaggeration. Perhaps it is hardly advisable to publish such things far & wide, but they ought to be preserved *mémoire pour servir.* The photos are very good & most welcome to us who have never seen the place; the facade is most imposing.[10]

This is confirmed by the minutes of the Prior's Council for 22 July 1897. There is unfortunately no record of the debate, merely the laconic note (but you are laconic when you have to write minutes in Latin),

> Since the Holy See had removed its prohibition against Catholics residing in the universities, it was agreed that a House be established at Oxford, to which juniors and postulants could

be sent to study. Fr Edmund Matthews was appointed Superior.

There was in fact quite a lot of discussion about whom to send to Oxford in the first instance. Fr Clarke was insistent in his advice that you could not send novices or newly professed to Oxford, let alone young postulants; but Prior Burge felt that to send anyone else would weaken the school staff, and was certain that no one would be released from Belmont. As it was, Elphege Hind was recalled to Ampleforth to teach after only two years of his course; despite returning in 1903 as monastic superior for four years, he never completed his degree. If Burge did not send his two postulants, he might never get started.

Thus Fr Edmund Matthews, Br Elphege Hind, William Byrne and Stanislaus Parker (who were merely postulants, just out of the school) arrived in early October 1897 at 103 Woodstock Road, being preceded by a housekeeper, Mrs Doherty, on loan from the monastery. Matthews became the first monk to take a degree since the Reformation, and Parker would later become Master. The house is still in existence, opposite St Philip and James church, and is now a guest-house. The Hall lived here till 1904, when it moved to the former Grindle's Hall in Beaumont Street, on the Playhouse site, from which it removed in 1922 to the present building in St Giles.

It was all very well for the Prior's Council at Ampleforth to agree to establish a House at Oxford. They do not, however, seem to have considered how this could be fitted into the existing scheme of things according to the university regulations. A Master of Arts could obtain a licence to open a Private Hall 'for the reception of students who shall be matriculated and admitted to all the privileges of the university without being required to be a member of any existing College or Hall, or of the Non-Collegiate body'.[11] For the Jesuits Fr Richard Clarke sj ma, a convert, obtained such a licence and set up Clarke's Hall in 1896 (later successively Pope's Hall, Plater's Hall and from 1918 permanently as Campion Hall). He was a pioneer with Oxford experience, having been a Fellow of St John's and a rowing Blue. But

Ampleforth had no Oxford graduate among its members. None of the monks was an MA. From the university's point of view, none of them was other than a mere student. It cut no ice in their system that the 26-year-old Fr Edmund was an ordained priest and monastic superior: he was not a Master. Thus all that could be done, if the monks were to stay together and form a community as monks should, was to rent a house and apply for admission to the non-Collegiate body (later St Catherine's).

A further difficulty was that the building was not an approved Lodging-House, and any Licensed Lodging-House for undergraduates had to be approved by the university and conform minutely to conditions about light, air and sanitation. To complicate the issue, the Controller of Lodgings took the view that he could not negotiate directly with a student. However, the Delegacy of Lodgings gave provisional sanction, 'pending further consideration', initially for the October Term only. In the following spring the Delegacy of Lodgings wrote to say it could not extend the temporary permission beyond the end of the academic year:

> It will therefore be necessary for the authorities of Ampleforth College to make other arrangements for the residence of their students within the University, and I shall be glad to lay before the Delegates any proposal which you may have to make in this direction.[12]

There seemed to be no future in the venture of establishing an Oxford house, into which Ampleforth had entered so blithely. Later, Burge did not remember that the experienced Fr Clarke, the Superior of the Jesuits, had been particularly helpful; he was 'polite but cool' to this little group of outsiders, who seemed to have lost their way. The coolness, if coolness there was, may be due to the fact that Fr Clarke no doubt remembered that they had neglected his advice about whom to send to the new foundation. Catholics became worried, and Matthews wrote to Ampleforth,

> There is considerable alarm among the leading Catholics at the mere prospect of our departure, and they are determined to do all they can to prevent it.[13]

It was Shadwell, the careful but not unsympathetic Controller of Lodging Houses, who seems first to have spotted the possible solution, for he wrote in March 1898 to Fr Oswald Swarbreck, assistant Procurator at Ampleforth (Fr Crow being away):

> I have no instructions from my Delegates to suggest the course which should now be taken; but I observe that at Cambridge arrangements have been made to open a public hostel connected with the St Edmund's College, Ware: and speaking only for myself I think that a similar proposal, or one on the smaller scale of a Private Hall, such as that of Father Clarke at Oxford, would be the best way of providing for your students. It would be the essential part of any such arrangement that the resident head should be a member of Convocation. In the case of St Edmund's Hostel at Cambridge the Master is to be a Member of the Senate, the corresponding body there.[14]

Where could Ampleforth find a Master of Arts? Fortunately the community of Fort Augustus Abbey, although not at that time part of the English Benedictine Congregation, but perhaps remembering with gratitude the part played by Laurentian monks in their foundation, provided a willing volunteer in Fr Oswald Hunter-Blair, MA of Magdalen, who offered his services to Ampleforth. He was an Etonian convert, a contemporary and friend of Oscar Wilde's at Magdalen, a baronet who moved with unusual ease between the normally distinct worlds of the Catholic and Protestant aristocracies. He had become a Catholic at Oxford, having served as a stretcher-bearer in the papal army (which, in fact, had no stretchers) in the siege of Rome in 1870, and later heard both Manning and Newman preach in the new Catholic church of St Aloysius in the Woodstock Road. In his mid-twenties he became a monk in the new monastery of Fort Augustus on the shores of Loch Ness. When he went to take over the new Benedictine house, he was in his mid-forties and formed a considerable contrast with the young monks studying there. He had a fine presence, a tremendous repertoire of funny stories which he collected in notebooks that would be regularly consulted before social engagements, and an obvious gift for friendship. After an operation in

1908, he spent a year as assistant chaplain to the Catholics in the university, then some time in Brazil helping with a Benedictine foundation, before becoming Prior and then Abbot of Fort Augustus from 1913 to 1918. He died in 1939.

Even though Hunter-Blair had the qualification of MA necessary to apply for a licence to open a Private Hall, he lacked the requirement of a short period of previous residence. He was, however, accepted as a person fit to preside over the Lodging House, and after one year was able to set up as Master in October 1899. We may thus say that St Benet's was, strictly speaking, a monastic body before it was a university establishment. From the first, the monastic Office was recited publicly in choir, though initially only from Lauds. Ever since then it has retained some duality, for the Master is the monastic superior (though he has never had the title of prior) and subject to the Abbot of Ampleforth, while at the same time being Master of a constituent body of the university.

Under Hunter-Blair Edmund Matthews continued to have the general management of the Hall, and from 1901, when he received his BA, he acted also as tutor to the students. But in 1903 he was recalled to Ampleforth as headmaster. He was succeeded by Fr Elphege Hind (to 1907) and Fr Aelred Dawson (to 1908). The following year Hunter-Blair left Oxford to undergo a serious operation, and Fr Anselm Parker, one of the four original students, was sent from Ampleforth to serve as Deputy Master and superior, becoming Master in his own right in November 1909. The Hall thus became Parker's Hall. Fr Anselm combined both functions, superior and Master, for one year: 'I was for a term Deputy Master for Fr H.B., then Temporary Master for a year...'[15] But from 1909 to 1914 Fr Cuthbert Almond, historian and first editor of *The Ampleforth Journal*, became monastic superior. Perhaps Fr Anselm was at first considered too junior, having been ordained priest only in July 1907. In any case, in 1914 he again took on the function of superior, which he held till he resigned 'through ill health' in 1920. The ill health did not prevent him being for a time headmaster of Fort Augustus Abbey School – a nice compensation for the loan of Hunter-Blair – and living to the age of eighty-two.

The instinct to become established in a suitable freehold building was very strong, and developed into a desire to build: between 1903 and 1905 eleven small houses were bought in Beef Lane and Pembroke Street. This is an indication that, despite the initial opposition described by Prior Burge, the Oxford venture, once launched, won more support. These houses, however, did not prove a good investment, as the area was regarded as a slum, and the block of houses was at the wrong end of Pembroke Street. The project of building here was never pursued. When the present pair of houses in St Giles was purchased in 1922, the Beef Lane property was put on the market, but the bidding failed to reach the reserve price of £5000, and the university declined even a special offer price of £4500. In the end they were sold in October 1927 to Pembroke College, who have now so developed the site that Beef Lane has practically disappeared.

It was also in the time of Fr Hind that other orders began to make use of the Hall. Monks of Douai had featured since 1901, including the redoubtable Ignatius Rice, who was to be headmaster of Douai for the impressive span of years from 1915 to 1952. In 1904 came the Dominican Bede Jarrett, who achieved the top History First in his year, and in 1932 went on to found the Oxford Blackfriars. There were also two Rosminians.[16]

A Central Catholic Hall

Not long after this a grander project began to take shape, to set up a single Catholic hall for all the religious orders and seculars, perhaps stimulated by the development in the university administration which would eventually lead to the concept of the Permanent Private Hall. The old idea of a special Catholic university or college was still alive. At Ampleforth this was first discussed by the Abbot's Council in October 1917. They regarded the project as 'a great one and full of important possibilities', but agreed that 'it was as yet in too inchoate a state' for any position to be taken. The following year brought more detail:

> Fr Abbot consulted the Council with respect to the proposed amalgamation of the various small halls conducted at Oxford by the religious orders and seculars into one central hall on the Norfolk property [now the St Cross site]. The trustees had sent a memorial proposing two plans, one that the central hall should absorb the private halls, the other that the private halls should remain as hostels, but a central hall be founded which the students of the private hall should frequent regularly for lectures, etc. The trustees asked that a representative should be sent to a meeting which should consider the matter in all its bearings. The opinion of Council generally was that the scheme was Utopian and hardly practicable.[17]

Nevertheless Frs Edmund Matthews and Anselm Parker were sent to the meeting, and on 11 April the Council again discussed the matter. Again the project was considered too vague for a definite attitude to be taken, though 'Fr Abbot was going to London to meet the Cardinal etc, to discuss the matter.' On 4 June 'Fr Abbot gave an account of his meeting with the Cardinal, the Abbots of Downside and Douai and Messrs Hope and Urquhart etc, to discuss the Oxford project. All the proposed schemes had been rejected, and the meeting had been abortive.' Four months later Fr Abbot informed the Council that the sending of clerics, not priests, to the university had been forbidden to the secular clergy. The university was still considered a dangerous place for Catholic clerics. Indeed the Bishop of Northampton had made such difficulties over Catholic institutions at the University of Cambridge that St Edmund's House and Benet House remained considerably more restricted than the Oxford religious houses of study. The Council minutes show that the possibility of sending non-priests remained open to the orders:

> The authorities at Rome showed a disposition to grant it to us, but we were asked to state the safeguards that we would employ. Fr Abbot was in correspondence with the President in the matter.[18]

On 15 January 1919 the Council noted that 'Rome allowed

us to go on as at present for ten years', but no more was heard of the grandiose plan for a central Catholic Hall. After the First World War Catholics were pressing forward into every institution which would forward their growth into the normal ways of national life.

A PERMANENT PRIVATE HALL

In fact, at the same time as these negotiations, and seemingly quite independently of them, other arrangements had been quietly progressing to completion in Oxford. The status of Private Hall had the inconvenience that the license for the Hall was issued personally to the Master. Thus on the death or removal of the Master the Private Hall lapsed. This had caused difficulties to both Jesuit and Benedictine houses, overcome by a helpful expedient on the part of the university: a temporary Master was allowed, while he qualified for the Mastership by a year of residence. This was not a satisfactory nor a stable solution, and in 1915 Fr Anselm Parker approached the Hebdomadal Council to enquire about the possibility of making the two Private Halls into permanent institutions. He was seconded by the Master of the Jesuit Hall, Fr Plater. The university listened sympathetically, and in early 1918 the Statute was passed, allowing for the establishment of a Permanent Private Hall, 'on condition that provision has been made for the government of the Hall on a permanent footing, and that the Hall is not established for the purpose of profit'.[19] The consent of Convocation was granted on 14 May 1918, in the case of 'the Permanent Private Hall to be known as St Benet's Hall', the licence being granted to the Abbot of Ampleforth. In his annual speech at the opening of the Michaelmas Term 1918, the Vice-Chancellor wished the two new Halls success. 'In Catholic quarters,' notes McCann, 'the event was welcomed as a sign of reconciliation between Oxford and the Religious Orders.'[20]

SAINT GILES

Soon afterwards the Ursuline nuns, wishing to return to France, offered their former school and chapel at Nos. 38 and 39 St Giles, St Benet's present building. This pair of houses was built about 1838 by one Samuel Collingwood on the site of some stables. At first Collingwood lived in the northern house and leased the other to Dr Bliss, a lawyer. On Dr Bliss' death it was bought for £1,870 by Revd Richard Michell. In September 1890 his widow leased the property for seven years to Marguerite de Léopardy and five other nuns (two of them had English names, three French). At the end of the lease Michell's son, a Shropshire vicar, sold the house outright to the nuns for £3,500. They financed this by mortgages from Charles Eyston and later from a French lady named Alix Liebert de Nitray, who came to live in the convent. Here they ran a small school for girls and young boys.

In 1909 Mme Liebert took for the nuns a lease of the more southerly of the two houses, which had just been vacated by Professor Charles Oman of New College (1860–1946). His daughter Carola remembered her childhood there.[21] They built the top-floor mansard (in two stages), and in 1911 the chapel. The architect was a priest, Canon Scholes (1844–1920), himself a product of Prior Park, and designer of many churches and convents. This replaced the iron shed which stood at the bottom of the garden of the northern house, and to which led the covered walkway which still exists. It is of some interest that both the alterations made by the nuns and their buyer's survey were signed by George Keogh, who had been at school with Prior Burge, and advised him on the rebuilding of the monastery at Ampleforth.[22]

However, it is a reasonable inference that the combined building constituted by the two still separate houses was too small for a successful school, and did not generate enough income to offset the capital debt. For whatever reason, in 1922 the nuns decided to return to France. They sold the northern house to the monks for £6200, and Carola Oman sold the southern one for £6700. In 1926 McCann tried to buy one of the next-door houses, but £7000 was considered too much for No. 40, and the Council declined even to consider No. 39A. Yet six months later the university paid £17,000 for Nos. 40 and 41, and £2000 for No. 39A. McCann was perhaps not for nothing of a trading family. On the other hand, Bede Turner's financially miraculous building programme at Ampleforth was at that time in full swing, and cash would have been short.

The move to the present building and the unification of the two houses were supervised by Fr Justin McCann, who had become Master and was academically the most distinguished of the holders of that post. Born in Manchester in 1882, he became a monk in 1900 and a priest in 1909. Appointed Master in 1920, he remained in that post till 1947. During that time his reputation as a scholar grew steadily as he published translations from Latin, German and French, and assembled in easily accessible form much previously obscure knowledge of monastic and spiritual history. On his retirement to an industrial parish in Warrington, he did not cease from his researches. If he was out of range of the Bodleian, he was but a short distance from the John Rylands Library in Manchester. He died in Warrington in 1959.

On Fr Justin McCann's retirement, Fr Gerard Sitwell was appointed Master (1947–64). Most of his academic work concerned the English mystics, on whom he lectured and published extensively. However, these post-war years were strange: no novices had been accepted in the monasteries between 1941 and 1946, and the post-war novices were not yet ready for university studies (or, in some cases, further university studies). Consequently between 1945 and 1949 there were only nine matriculations, only one of which was of an English Benedictine (Fr Gregory Freeman of Douai, later Abbot of Douai for twenty years till his early death in 1989). The rooms in the northern house were let to Trinity College. These years were marked in the memories of those who experienced them as years of austerity both of food and of atmosphere.

In strong contrast was the expansive leadership of Fr James Forbes, Master from 1964 till he returned to the abbey to die of cancer in 1979. His special interest was in porcelain, of which he had an impressively wide knowledge. His extensive alterations and improvements to the buildings still betray his faultless taste. He was no dry academic, but a warm and generous person, whose countless small acts of kindness continue to come to light. Perhaps his greatest gift was for friendship, and it was said that the University Church was more thronged for his memorial service than for any other in a quarter of a century.

The Present

Eight Masters have ruled the Hall in a century. Frs Oswald Hunter-Blair (1898), Anselm Parker (1909) and Justin McCann (1920) were followed by Frs Gerard Sitwell (1947), James Forbes (1964), Philip Holdsworth (1979), Fabian Cowper (1989) and the present Master, Fr Henry Wansbrough (1990). Of the past Masters, only Fr Philip is still living. In the first half-century there were something over 100 undergraduates, three-quarters from the Ampleforth community. Since then the proportion of Amplefordians has fallen, but a more significant change lies in the at first cautious introduction of lay members, initially living out, and limited by the university to five in number at any one time, and then, as the vocations to the monastic life fell off around 1970, in larger numbers, and living in, till at one time it looked as though only the Master would be a cleric. But in the eighties an attempt was made, with growing success, to increase the monastic element and to establish a balance. In 1996–7 there were seventeen.

It is obvious that any educational establishment needs pupils as a source of income, whether paid privately or by the nation, and St Benet's is no exception. But there is a more significant difference. The Hall was begun because it was realised that the university had much to offer young monks, and that the school would never grow strong without graduates among the monastic staff: this was realised by other houses too, especially by Douai Abbey once they were established back in England. And with few exceptions the monks read for secular degrees: no one could conceive in those days of Catholics sharing theology with Protestants. If there were theologians at the Hall, and in the thirties and forties there were, the most widely known names being perhaps Aelred Graham and Hugh Aveling, they studied with the Dominicans at Blackfriars.

Since the seventies, new monks have tended to come not straight from school as they had done in the past (in 1897 Byrne and Parker were seventeen, whereas Hind was twenty-three and Matthews twenty-six), but after studies at university. In consequence, for monks, St Benet's is predominantly a theological *studium*. This is really quite a radical difference, but if it is remembered that from the very beginning it has been seen as a monastic community, with choral office at least recited, and a common recreational life and monastic customs of abstention and poverty, the change can easily be represented as a development (in Newman's sense) and not a corruption. The combination of Catholic or sympathetic lay students with the young monks is a benefit for both. Indeed, the situation is in effect almost exactly that which Baines, Newman, Manning, Hedley and all the other nineteenth-century Catholic leaders who considered the question were in reality seeking as they felt their way forward.

16

Abbot Justin McCann

ANTHONY MARETT-CROSBY OSB

In 1920, there came to St Benet's Hall a new Master, fresh from a year on the mission at Liverpool. It proved a moment of transition, the end of the first chapter and the beginning of the consolidation and confirmation of the Hall. It was a process that worked in two directions, strengthening the Hall's position within the life of Ampleforth and the English Congregation and equally ensuring its place within a growing university. Such a task could not be completed over-night, and it was to prove of great benefit to St Benet's that the young Master of 1920 was to remain in office until 1947. That longevity of tenure is remarkable in itself, but in those years he also established himself as a monastic scholar of high quality, the most eminent scholar of Ampleforth before Hugh Aveling and a noted contributor to the wider world of Benedictine studies in the early twentieth century.

Justin McCann was clothed in the Benedictine habit in 1900, the year in which the community finally elected its first abbot. He entered the community directly from school at Ampleforth, though not without attempts by his parents to divert his interest to other ways of life. His family was of Irish extraction, though he was born and brought up in Manchester, and he remained throughout his life both con-scious and unashamed of his Irish background. In the Ampleforth of its day, this was perhaps something of a rarity; it was a close-knit community, drawn largely from the Lanca-shire parishes served by the community, and with a strongly English air.[1] He spent his first two years in the common congregational noviciate at Belmont, and from there he was sent to Oxford, where he lived at St Benet's under Fr Oswald Hunter-Blair. The convergence in one house of two more different characters is hard to imagine, and later in his life McCann certainly expressed considerable reservations when it was suggested that Hunter-Blair might spend his retirement at the Hall. Nevertheless, McCann must have been one of the star pupils of his day, for his double first in Greats was a remarkable achievement, considering the nature of the Ampleforth education at that time. It was an academic triumph comparable to the earlier success of Fr Edmund Matthews, and with it behind him McCann returned to Ampleforth, to teach in the school that Matthews was slowly building up.

For the next twelve years, Ampleforth was to be McCann's home, though he spent less time in the school than might have been expected. He did teach, but he did not find it an easy task and there were many other jobs to which he was called. He served as monastery librarian, as monk responsible for the welfare of junior monks in the monastery and as priest in charge of Helmsley. Few of his sermons and teaching notes survive from this period, but what remains demonstrates clearly that he had already appropriated to himself a spiritual language that he was to retain throughout his life. His earliest homilies at Helmsley are punctuated with references to the value of renunciation, and it was at this time that he wrote his highly influential Catholic Truth Society pamphlet entitled *Self-Discipline*. This pamphlet opens with the portrait of the young man provided by Plato in *The Republic*, a young man pursuing in total freedom the desires of his will. Plato's young man is dismissed by McCann as 'one who scorns discipline', and it is the desire to recover the positive value of discipline within Christianity that shapes the work. It is to be acquired through effort, and most especially through habit. He writes that 'the secret of the success of the cricketer, of the musician, of the scholar, is habit', and while McCann knew little of the needs of cricket or music, he was to prove in his own life the value of habit in academic endeavour.[2]

In 1916, McCann received an appointment that was to

change the direction of his life. At the age of thirty-four, he was made prior of the Ampleforth community, and found himself in a position of authority under Abbot Fr Oswald Smith. It would never have been an easy task, and it is significant that in his later letters he makes not a single reference to his three years in this office.

One reason for this was Ireland. It was unfortunate that at the height of the crisis over Irish independence a community with so English an outlook as Ampleforth should have had as prior someone of clear Irish extraction. McCann's Irishness was never political, but equally it was never suppressed, and at a time of national ferment, which could not but be reflected in the monastic community, he would have found himself an isolated figure. This may in part be the explanation for his term as prior ending in 1919, and he was sent instead to be a curate at St Anne's, Liverpool.

Once at Liverpool, McCann had entered the other world of English monasticism, that of the mission. The serving of parishes was at this date the main work of the Ampleforth community, and throughout his life McCann kept in close touch with the missionary work of the community. He spent many of the long vacations in the busy city parishes of Cardiff and Liverpool, and he spent the last years of his life in an active semi-retirement at St Mary's, Warrington. It is quite conceivable that in 1919 he could have made his home on the missions forever, but after only a year he was summoned to Oxford, to take on the post of Master of St Benet's to replace Fr Anselm Parker. Parker's departure from St Benet's was made necessary by illness, and it seems that McCann felt that his appointment always had a temporary feel to it. His continued link with the parishes suggests that he and his superiors continued to regard this ministry as a likely part of his monastic life, and it was only with some effort that later abbots were to persuade him to take holidays away from Ampleforth parishes.

If his appointment as Master had a temporary feel, then the St Benet's to which he came had little of permanence about it. Much had changed since Anselm Parker became Master in 1908, especially the establishment of St Benet's as a Permanent Private Hall in 1918, but Parker had had little time to consolidate the position of the Hall within the university. This was to be McCann's first task.

The first essential step in that process was the purchasing of the St Giles' site. The 1922 move from Beaumont Street gave St Benet's a permanent home, and one already provided with the basic needs of a monastic house, notably a chapel. Indeed, throughout his time as Master McCann remained interested in the possibility of extending the St Benet's site especially to the south by the purchase of 39a St Giles. In 1926, this house was being used as a hotel, and writing to Abbot Matthews McCann reflected that its purchase would have the appealing consequence of reducing the noise. The reason for McCann's enthusiasm was easy to see, but equally the reasons that led the Abbot and the Abbot's Council to reject his ideas were sound. In the 1920s and 1930s, money was not readily available at Ampleforth, and St Benet's was a considerable expense. In 1928 Abbot Matthews wrote that 'Oxford is a big expense on our revenues, and if it were not that the school is flourishing we could not meet it'. That situation had not changed dramatically by 1936, when the Abbot reflected that the accumulated expense of running the Hall would have paid for the building of the new church.

The lack of funds may also have been one reason why the internal furnishings of the Hall were hardly changed during McCann's years as Master. Improvements were made to the dining room and the chapel, but the decor was spartan and dominated by brown linoleum. Few of those who attended the Hall in these years remember it as a place of comfort, though in 1926 Abbot Matthews described the rooms of the junior monks as palatial, and feared that a similar standard of accommodation would not be available for them from Ampleforth in the vacation. Finding somewhere for the brethren to live outside term was a consistent difficulty and things reached such a head in 1933 that the Abbot mused that 'we can always fall back on the disused buildings in the farmyard'.[3]

Lack of money was only one reason for the spartan feel of the Hall, for this undoubtedly conformed to McCann's own preferences. He himself was slow to acquire creature comforts, though a major step forward was taken in 1935 when he purchased both a radio and a wristwatch, the former for the use of the whole community. So unlikely was the idea of McCann wearing a wristwatch that Abbot Matthews felt obliged to comment on it, writing that 'it is not easy to picture you wearing such a thing'.

McCann had very little doubt that the purpose of St Benet's was work. In this, he himself set the pace, and the archives at Ampleforth are an enduring witness of the practical application of his understanding of hard work. A vast series of his notebooks survives, containing his collected academic endeavours. There are pages of medieval and early modern monastic texts, copied in a uniformly neat hand from manuscripts in the Bodleian and other libraries. McCann worked with an unflagging zeal, and he expected those under his care to do the same. He expressed his theology of work in many of his conferences, reaching its clearest form in a conference on 'the Problem of Occupation in the Monastic Life' given in the last years of his Mastership.[4] There he declared that one of the most persistent causes of monastic decline was 'the lack of serious and genuine work', and he regarded the lack of sufficient work as a much greater problem than its super-abundance. Giving people too much to do was in his view 'very healthy', and he supported this with an interpretation of St Benedict's precept on living by the work of one's hands. Above all, he insisted that work should be done well, and he castigated those Catholics who 'expected piety to cover ... work of a very inferior quality'. In a beginning of term conference given some time before the Second World War he compared the zeal for labour that should be shown by a monk with that of Henry Ford, thereby demonstrating that spiritual labours should match those of the greatest businessmen.[5]

In consequence, McCann was disinclined to be lenient with those who wished to abandon their studies for other activities. He was especially averse to the time taken by sport, an activity he saw as purposeless. Equally, he was violent in his verbal assaults upon the reading of novels and newspapers, a view he advanced in *Self-Discipline* and which he continued to preach throughout his life. He took as his example St Ignatius of Loyola, writing that 'there is a sense in which the Jesuit Order and all its splendid record was the outcome of that religious reading which the young Ignatius undertook in his convalescence'.[6] Idle reading was the ultimate crime, not merely because it wasted time but because it filled the mind with irrelevant and passing things. It is said that one of McCann's most persistent fears was that the young monks at the Hall would spend too long reading the paper.

The application of this understanding of work was not limited to his own private notes. McCann published widely and influentially, especially in the early years of his time as Master. His particular study in this early period was the theologian Karl Adam, whose writings he translated into English with great success. In 1931 Abbot Matthews wrote to McCann that 'your name will be associated with Karl Adam forever', an unfortunate prediction since less than two months afterwards Adam came under suspicion in Rome as his *imprimatur* was removed.

One might have expected such a reversal to have rebounded upon McCann himself. There is however a sense in which, although he was deeply committed to the work of translating Karl Adam, McCann was temperamentally unsuited to be at the cutting edge of theology, and he seems to have found it easy to leave Karl Adam behind. He turned instead to the Rule of St Benedict, and immersed himself in the growing controversy among European Benedictine scholars over the Dialogues of St Gregory and the relationship between the Rule of St Benedict and the Rule of the Master. In making this shift, McCann was doing what so many scholars did in the middle years of the twentieth century, turning away from the dangerous areas of theology and choosing instead something that could be nothing other than safe. For monastic scholars, the Rule was evidently the safest of topics, and McCann made a considerable contribution to scholarship in this field, especially through his Life of St Benedict and his celebrated translation of the Rule itself. On the academic issues of his day, McCann tended towards the more conservative side, always defending the priority of St Benedict over the Rule of the Master. He was the leading English monk involved in these Benedictine academic controversies after Cuthbert Butler, and his writings remain an outstanding example of patient and detailed scholarship in a field where such care has not always been uniform.

It was such scholarship that he also brought to bear on another area of monastic study, long of interest to English Benedictines. The survival of the late medieval spiritual tradition in the post-Reformation English Benedictines is a remarkable example of the continuity over the Reformation, expressed most clearly in the writings of Augustine Baker. This spiritual inheritance had never been forgotten, but it had perhaps lacked a coherent academic underlay. It was this that McCann provided, recovering the teaching of Baker from his scattered manuscripts and providing a remarkably lucid account of the mass of unsorted material that was dotted around the monastic houses of England. In 1952 he wrote of the Baker manuscripts that 'on a rough estimate the total number of words is well over a million. The present writer ventures to mention as a curious circumstance that he is the only person on our planet who has traversed this vast expanse of words'.[7] As he read, he copied, and as he copied he published. As early as 1922 he published Baker's *Confessions*, and the Baker material collected for Volume 33 of the Catholic Records Society is his own work. More widely, he produced a version of *The Cloud of Unknowing* which has remained the standard text, and at the end of his life he translated *The Imitation of Christ*, always his favourite spiritual work.

Yet a survey of the academic achievements of McCann does not do justice to his industry over this period. He was also deeply involved in researching questions of contemporary interest to the English Congregation, both researching and publishing on its post-Reformation history. When the General Chapter of the English Congregation rejected the account of its history compiled by Fr Basil Whelan, it was to McCann that they turned to find an alternative. McCann himself regretted the manner in which the Congregation had suppressed Whelan, but he nevertheless provided an alternative, which he himself admitted was considerably dependent upon the suppressed work. During the war, he focused his research upon a narrower topic, the endurance within the Congregation of the medieval titles of abbeys and cathedral priories. With the Downside scholar Fr Hugh Connolly he presented a report of the question to the General Chapter of 1942, in which all the characteristics of McCann's scholarship are evident. It is a carefully argued, fully annotated study, providing for the chapter fathers not merely an interpretation but editions of the relevant documents. It is the work of two painstaking scholars, and was surely a most remarkable diversion in the dark days of the Second World War.

But for all his academic success, McCann remained clear in his own mind that the monastic vocation was prior to any scholarly work. For him, the work of God was a genuine labour, and could not be replaced by study. Thus he wrote that 'the monk who lives in libraries, hurries over his prayers and gives all his time to manuscripts is a savant but not a monk',[8] and it is surely fair to see in this description a portrait of temptation that was not so far from his heart. His conferences to the monks at Oxford consistently emphasise the value of regular monastic discipline, something to be observed with even greater fidelity at St Benet's, where the full conventual life was impossible. Typical is an expression with which he concludes a beginning of term conference in 1934: 'I exhort you at the beginning of a new term to do your best in your religious life, both in its prayer and in its work.'[9]

In such a view of the monastic life, recreation took only a small place. In one of his periodic conferences on renunciation, McCann expressed his fear that recreation was taking up too much time, and he saw self-denial as especially important at Oxford, where the distractions were all the greater.

The importance of such a message was underlined for McCann by a contrast which he increasingly drew between the St Benet's of his own day and the years of its foundation. Speaking to his juniors, he declared: 'You know little of the hard life that was led by those who started the Oxford house, a life of sheer hard study and with very little distraction.[10] McCann was in no doubt both that this pioneering spirit had existed and that it had been subsequently lost, a loss which he for one regretted with increasing bitterness. His own message of hard work and renunciation was preached time and again, though increasingly it referred back to a golden age now long gone.

Amidst this unremitting labour of the religious life, McCann suffered from consistently poor health. Both Abbot Matthews and later Abbot Herbert Byrne were concerned time and again to ensure that he gained proper rest and recuperation in the vacations, and his annual holiday with Prior Laurence Buggins at Swanage was his principal relaxation. On one occasion, Abbot Matthews persuaded McCann to take a holiday in Rome, though a later attempt to persuade him to go on a cruise was a complete failure. He was not one to whom holidays came easy, and he clearly regarded the vacations at Oxford as a time when much work could be achieved. But it was achieved only by living a solitary life out of term, described by Abbot Byrne as eremitical. At such times, however congenial it was to McCann personally, there was always the danger that he would lose a sense of the value of his own work, and in 1943, when McCann was spending Christmas alone in Oxford, Byrne wrote, 'You are doing an important, a necessary job, and doing it well. Far from being useless, you are filling a whole man's place in the scheme of things.'[11]

No work is ever for life in a monastery, McCann knew this well, and the fact he spent twenty-seven years as Master of St Benet's could not possibly have been predicted. In 1940, he came close to being appointed procurator or cellarer of the Ampleforth community, and his name was frequently mentioned in connection with earlier parish appointments. But as years went by, McCann became increasingly synonymous with St Benet's, and once war had started it was clear that no one else could manage the Hall with his dedication.

Yet the end of his tenure as Master had to come, and in 1947 he was moved to St Mary's, Warrington, where he served as a curate and used his spare time in furthering his academic interests at the John Rylands library in Manchester. Despite his ill health, he was to serve at Warrington for a further twelve years, and before his death in 1959 he was honoured with the title of Abbot of Westminster, one of those medieval dignities which he had worked so hard to protect. They were years when he continued to write and publish, and with Fr Columba Cary Elwes he edited in 1952 the volume of articles celebrating the 150th anniversary of his community's coming to Ampleforth, entitled *Ampleforth and its Origins*.

It has frequently been noted that the history of many religious foundations seems to need there to be two founders. The first provides the inspiration, the initial vision of the institution, while the second provides for its consolidation and its firm placing in the life of the Church. In a small way, the history of St Benet's echoes this pattern, for if the initial inspiration came through Prior Anselm Burge, it was McCann who ensured that the vision of an English monastic house of studies in Oxford survived. It is characteristic perhaps of such a second founder that he should look back to the early days with admiration and longing, but equally that he should have created an institution that was capable of enduring. His was not the fiery zeal of a Francis, but it may have been the patient work of a Bonaventure.

17

TWO TWENTIETH-CENTURY MASTERS

PATRICK BARRY OSB

FR GERARD SITWELL

Fr Gerard Sitwell was appointed Master of St Benet's Hall in 1947. He himself regarded the appointment with quizzical surprise. It took him from the tranquil concerns of the farm in the Ampleforth valley to the comparative turbulence of academic endeavour. There were aspects of the appointment to St Benet's to which he took quite naturally; others he tolerated with an inner serenity he had learned in his early monastic life. In taking up this appointment he moved effortlessly from the broad interests of a northern countryman to the world of undergraduates struggling for a degree and the delights of donnish scholarship that could easily have been his own main interest in life, if things had fallen out differently. He simply took it all as it came. There was nothing of careerism about him.

The Mastership of St Benet's was the summit of his achievement, but it was not the fulfilment of cherished ambition. In true Benedictine fashion he was by 1947 inured to accepting whatever came his way – whatever his abbot required of him. When he was a young priest, after a period of teaching English, German and Religious Studies in the school he had been sent into the procurator's office to help with the school bills. Helping with the school bills meant in those days transcribing by hand the details for each boy from a ledger onto a standard form to be sent to parents. He was joined in this tedious task, fit only for a clerk of modest accomplishments, by Br Thomas Loughlin. After gaining a first in Chemistry at Liverpool and a doctorate and rejecting the urgent request of the university that he should stay and continue his research, Br Thomas had completed his novitiate and was sent into the office to transcribe school bills. Thus they sat together on high stools and applied their highly qualified minds to this simple task. After a while it struck them so forcefully that this was a bizarre use of high academic qualifications that they disturbed the peace of the office with peals of uncontrollable laughter. After that they just got on with the work. Their willing acceptance of this strange situation would have pleased St Benedict greatly, but some careful explanation of the connection between their laughter and humility would have been needed to elicit his approval of the laughter.

The clerk's work did not last too long and in 1940 Fr Gerard was given charge of the farm at Ampleforth. That had a deep appeal to him, so that for seven years he almost reverted to the ethos of his Northumbrian family. He strode with a farmer's gait about the valley and on the hills behind, but always tenaciously clung to his clerical status by the distinguishing mark of a shapeless black hat. Fr Gerard had been an impressive long-distance runner in his youth and also a great rider of horses. He agreed to look after a thoroughbred horse for one of his contemporaries in the difficult war years. The horse had to be exercised and looked after. He was therefore to be seen from time to time in the Gilling Woods patrolling on this beautiful creature. It was a time of contentment, when he seemed to fit his work and his work him, while the prayer and regularity of monastic life was the matrix of his life with a stronger hold on him than any work in which he was engaged.

From that world of north-country farming he came to be Master of St Benet's Hall. It is true that in the monastery he had done a stint as master of studies with the responsibility of managing the studies of junior monks. He had also been sub-prior. Neither of these experiences, however, can be counted as a fitting preparation for the responsibilities of the Master of the Hall. Yet new potential was opened up in a distinguished chapter of Fr Gerard's life which was concerned with academic study, lecturing and writing.

As a young monk Fr Gerard had read English at St Benet's Hall. In the course of these English studies he was attracted to the English mystic writers. After taking his degree he had stayed on at St Benet's for a further three years to study for the theological degree of STL at Blackfriars, but he did not stay on to take the degree. In those early studies before his ordination the foundation was laid on which his scholarship and writing flowered when he returned to Oxford as Master of St Benet's Hall. He began to lecture in the English School and to engage again in serious work on the English texts which had first attracted his attention as an undergraduate. Soon he began to produce scholarly work which was far removed from his former preoccupations with harvests and farm economics.

In 1953 Orchard Books published his translation into modern English (with notes and introduction) of Walter Hilton's *Scale of Perfection*. This was followed by two other Orchard Book editions of *The Ancrene Riwle* in 1955 and *Holy Wisdom* by Augustine Baker in 1972. There were two other small volumes published while he was Master of St Benet's: a translation of the *Life of St Odo of Cluny* and a short work on *Medieval Spiritual Writers*. In addition Fr Gerard wrote a substantial number of articles and talks at Oxford on spiritual and historical subjects. These publications are the evidence of an awakening in Fr Gerard of gifts and interests which had lain dormant in the years of teaching in the school and managing cows.

There was a real sense in which he entered into his own at Oxford and found a congenial milieu in which he felt at home. Where others had to adjust to the world of scholars and dons, Fr Gerard took to it quite naturally and thought the world of Oxford a very normal world indeed. A conversation he once had with some of the younger monks in the Hall was often recalled. Fr Gerard seems to have referred to the opinions of 'the ordinary man in the street'. He was challenged about his meaning and replied that by 'ordinary man in the street' he had meant someone like the average Oxford don.

All this study and writing brought to the Master of St Benet's respect on the high tables of the university and a reputation for just the sort of scholarship which seemed especially appropriate in those days to a Benedictine. It was a reputation without glitter, for Fr Gerard was no witty conversationalist. He was at home with scholarly friends to whom he was drawn by their learning. He was eager to be helpful and pastoral in the help he gave individuals when he recognised their need. As for the young in his charge, he did not have an easy rapport with them. He was shy and somewhat remote, unless the magic of his sudden smile broke out. Then he was transformed. His smile banished all hint of severity and asceticism and opened up a hidden warmth. He gave a strong monastic example but he never quite entered into the world of the young undergraduates. This was not surprising as the world moved into the ethos of the sixties and everything began to change. The world of the scholarly was being invaded by interests that were alien to Fr Gerard.

By 1964 it was understandably time for him to move on from St Benet's to a different work. He had sustained the ideals of scholarship at St Benet's in his time as Master. He had given the academic support and guidance that was needed by the undergraduates in his charge. But a different age was advancing in which society and the university itself were changing rapidly and nothing would ever be quite the same again. Father Gerard passed on to his successor a Hall which still held together on the old patterns but was now in need of new approaches. It was ready for the new panache and energy of another Master, Fr James Forbes.

Fr James Forbes

Fr James came to be Master of St Benet's just at the right time. It was the right time for him and it was the right time for the Hall. Vatican II had come to an end and the Church was learning to come to terms with it and adapt to hitherto unheard-of changes. It was the time of the Beatles, of

Carnaby Street, of the beginnings of student protest. Fr James was resilient and equal to all these things. No one would ever have thought of him as an icon of the sixties or an incarnation of Vatican II. His strength was that of calm consistency and fidelity to his commitment. His Anglican mother, to whom he was devoted, once pointed to an immaculately dressed archdeacon in the streets of Oxford and said, 'Louis, why cannot you be a *real* clergyman like that?' He laughed, and could often tell the story later because he was untouched by the temptation. He was similarly untouched by the burning questions of the time. There was a real sense in which he always went deeper than that. He lived by a strong and simple dedication to Catholicism and to his brethren in his monastic community whom he always sought to serve. The key to Fr James' character was a profound uncomplicated faith in which he never wavered and a truly wonderful openness and delight in other people, for whom he always had a welcome and ready hospitality.

There were other more obvious aspects of the new Master – his knowledge of porcelain (on which he was soon lecturing in the university) and of pictures, his taste for elegance in the decoration of the house and his weakness for the aristocracy. He had been a greatly valued guestmaster of the school. During the war he had saved the affairs of the headmaster from chaos by acting as his secretary on top of his teaching. After the war he had for three years gained invaluable experience when he was put in charge of all the catering and household at Ampleforth with the title, chosen by himself, of Steward. After that he was the driving force in the building of the abbey church at Ampleforth between 1957 and 1961. He had personally and heroically made a unique and lasting contribution to the community and its life by pioneering the very concept of a fund-raising appeal. In the fifties, when he started, the very idea of an appeal was generally regarded as a distasteful intrusion from America. Fr James almost single-handed got advice from America, set up the procedure and attracted the countless donations which had made the completion of the church possible and paid for it. These in outline were the battle honours to his credit when he came to St Benet's.

Changes were quickly seen. At the time St Benet's was a drain on the deficit side of the abbey budget. Fr James began to turn the tide by making headway in creating revenue. He realised that current legislation had made it possible for monk-students to get grants. He successfully applied for these grants, organised the accounts and began to produce a surplus. To maintain the Hall for a small and fluctuating community was uneconomic. He went out to attract lay undergraduates, bringing admission policy into line with practice of the other colleges. Thus the foundation was laid for making St Benet's for the first time a financially viable enterprise and one that contributed more to the mainstream of university life. In the ten years from 1968 to 1978 the yearly figures showed a turn-round from deficit to a substantial positive outcome.

Fr James was tireless and a fast worker. Since he was the only senior official of the Hall, he was inevitably the resident Pooh Bah and suffered from no shyness about it. In fact he gloried in his multi-faceted life. He was to be seen at solemn meetings of Heads of Houses, in the learned meetings of Senior Tutors, in the anxious meetings of Deans, at pragmatic meetings of Bursars; he was even invited to the knowing meetings of Head Porters. For the Hall and its community he carried in himself the burdens of all these officials. As time went on there was probably no one in the university who was so well informed about the varying shades that mingled in the kaleidoscope of university and college life. At the end of his time the comment of one don was that there was no one in Oxford who was so widely known and so well loved. He was accepted everywhere. He fell asleep in one ceremonial meeting of Heads of Houses and woke with such a start that he accidentally flung his mortar-board into the middle of the room. That didn't dent his reputation; it only added to the legend.

As to the undergraduates in St Benet's, both monastic and lay, all his contacts and influence were put at their service in getting tutors to teach them and arranging courses to suit them, in giving them the support and encouragement they so often needed and in developing interests in a wide range of university activities, including sport. St Benet's even started to compete in rowing. The doors were open in hospitality wider than they had ever been before, and Fr James' guest-nights changed from his predecessors' rather modest and infrequent dinners fortified by very ordinary port wine. Fr James was criticised by his community for the lavishness of his more frequent guest-nights, but he was used to criticism and always met it with an impervious grin or resilient laughter. It was not the feasting that mattered to him; it was the hospitality, the meeting and talking with people and his desire, often for pastoral reasons, to draw them into St Benet's. All the time he was promoting understanding between St Benet's and the university. He thought it right to attract them. Among many in Oxford an invitation to a guest-night in the Hall came to be highly prized.

It was fine to fill St Benet's, to cover the outgoings with steady revenue, to encourage a sound spirit among his men and to get a more formal Junior Common Room going. However, as the number of monks decreased and the laymen predominated, the ideal of a Benedictine community based on common prayer receded. Fr James was himself a model of fidelity to regular life but, in spite of his example and encouragement, the chapel receded in importance. There were sometimes tensions between laity and monks which arose not from the fault of either but from confusion about the nature of the institution and its role. Was it radically a monastic house with a limited number of laymen who partially conformed to its monastic ethos? Or was it an ordinary Hall of the university with a number of monks in residence? It was very much the thing in the sixties and seventies to have an identity crisis. That is what befell St Benet's in those years. It was by his own strong personality and beneficence that Fr James held it together without ever finding a real solution. That had to await calmer times and new initiatives in another generation. Once admissions policy had changed through economic pressures the problem was inescapable.

Fr James pioneered the hiring of the Hall to vacation groups. Somehow he got onto good terms with the University of North Carolina, and they became his most faithful clientèle. He managed it himself and gave them the warm welcome of an experienced guestmaster. The Americans loved him and cherished the connection. Inevitably he was invited over to lecture on porcelain.

As school guestmaster Fr James had been greatly loved by Old Amplefordians, for whom he always had a warm welcome. They came readily to him at Oxford so that St Benet's became quite a centre for them and for other undergraduates as well. It is a pity that insufficient note was often taken of the diversity of his clientèle. Undoubtedly St Benet's became familiar to various members of the English and continental aristocracy, but at no time was Fr James without those devoid of such pretensions who relied devotedly on him for help, support and advice. He did once write to me on behalf of a foreign duke and began his letter: 'Dukes, to judge by the attitudes prevalent today, are definitely among the deprived.' He knew that I knew that the deprived didn't have to be dukes to arouse his interest and help.

At the end of his time as Master, Fr James presided over a Hall which had developed in ways beyond our dreams before he took over. It was full to capacity and lay students lived out in the second and third year. St Benet's had positive revenue to meet not only running costs but also repairs and improvements. It was better known than it ever had been before, and the Master himself seemed to be known to everyone and to know everyone. He had a real interest and position in the university as well as in the Catholic community of Oxford. It seemed quite natural that he was asked at short notice to preach in the University Church, when the Cardinal Archbishop of Westminmster was unable to fulfil an engagement there. There were new problems on the horizon and new challenges to meet, as is always the way. But Fr James' achievement was impressive in itself and had laid the foundation for very positive future developments. It was fitting that he died in office from an illness that came quickly, and on a note of fulfilment and achievement.

Epilogue

Since the formative times described in the final chapters, St Benet's has developed in various directions. The House was formed to give Benedictines, primarily Ampleforth monks, the opportunity of studying for university degrees. Its influence has not, however, remained confined by this purpose. Two developments may, perhaps, be highlighted, the inclusion of laymen and the extension to theology.

From early days the abbey of Douai has sent monks to study at St Benet's, and other orders also made use of the Hall. The Rosminians early sent a number of students to the Hall. A large number of other abbeys, both British and foreign, particularly in the United States, have regularly provided students. In the academic year 1995/6 ten abbeys were represented, including two in France, two in the United States and one in Germany. In the first half-century no laymen were admitted, apart from one postulant who intended to enter the novitiate at Ampleforth after his degree. It was only after the Second World War, initially under pressure of the vacuum of monks, that the important step was taken of opening also to laymen the possibility of studying at Oxford from within the Benedictine tradition. This began gradually. In 1948 Paul Rhodes, a Stonyhurst Old Boy returning from war service with the RAF, was accepted to 'migrate' from Wadham College to finish his degree. The following year three lay undergraduates, two of them educated at Ampleforth, were matriculated for St Benet's. Thereafter a thin trickle of laymen continued to join the monks, seldom more than one or two a year until the late 1960s. By that time the stream of young monks suitable to read for degrees was drying up: young men tended to enter the monasteries later, and many already had degrees on entry; it was also a period when there seemed to be overall fewer vocations to the monastic life. The balance swung so far that in the three years 1977–9 only one monk was matriculated, compared with thirty-five laymen. Consequently it was felt by some that St Benet's was becoming partly a back-door entry into a university for whose places competition was becoming increasingly fierce, and in the late 1980s there were a couple of years when no laymen at all were matriculated. It was clearly important to achieve a correct balance between monks and laymen, so that the essentially monastic atmosphere of St Benet's was maintained.

Another development has been the part played by St Benet's in theological education. At the time of its foundation it would hardly have been conceivable that monks should study theology at a university where the influence of the Established Church was overpowering. However, since the foundation of Blackfriars in 1932 a regular stream of monks had studied theology at this *studium* of the English Province of the Dominicans just down the road. Thus the dual role of St Benet's, monastic and university, continued. In the wake of the Second Vatican Council, the ecumenical climate and developments on both sides made the theology taught in the university less threatening to Catholics, so that a BA in theology became an acceptable and useful formation for Catholics. Many of the young monks, who already had degrees in a variety of subjects, now began to be sent to St Benet's to study for a second degree in theology.

Futhermore, also in the wake of the Council, the number of Catholic lay men and women reading theology continued to rise. Theology was no longer considered a subject fit for study only by priests and religious. It was now a far cry from the immortal comment of Mgr Talbot in a letter to Cardinal Manning (1859), scorning the need for a theologically educated Catholic laity, 'What is the province of the laity? To hunt, to shoot, to entertain. These matters they understand, but to meddle with ecclesiastical affairs they have no right at all.'

At the same time the number of colleges willing to admit undergraduates to read theology fell. The part played by the Permanent Private Halls (the three Catholic Halls, Campion, St Benet's and Greyfriars, had by now been joined by other nonconformist bodies, Mansfield, Manchester and Regents Park Colleges) therefore became more and more significant in the theology faculty, with regard both to students and to lecturers and tutors. For the year 1995/6, of the thirty-nine matriculated students at St Benet's, no less than fifteen were reading for degrees in theology, of whom nine were laymen.

In conclusion one may say that the story of St Benet's has a dual significance. The establishment of a Benedictine house of studies in Oxford was in direct continuity with the moves many centuries earlier by great abbeys, some even further away than Ampleforth, to maintain their own levels of training and scholarship by making use of – and contributing to – the facilities of the University of Oxford. How important to monastic life this was always considered to be is shown by the decree of Benedict XII in 1336 that every abbey should send one in twenty monks to study at the university. How important this was in the development of the university itself must be clear both from the ancient foundations still flourishing in Oxford and from the accounts in previous chapters of this book.

The significance is, however, wider than this. It is symbolic of the integration of the Catholic community into the normal life of the nation. From being a hunted and persecuted minority, the Catholic community in England has striven over the last two centuries to take its place and play its part alongside others in the institutions of the country. Education is by no means the least of these. At the beginning of the century university education among English Catholics was a rarity, restricted almost entirely to converts, and to those few who had received the somewhat suspect benefits of a university education at Rome or elsewhere on the continent. This was one of the principal factors in the suspicion and sometimes contempt with which Catholics were regarded, setting them apart from the mainstream of national life in England. The great old Catholic families, who had kept the faith throughout the penal times, had tended to withdraw more and more into their own society, united by marital ties as well as by a common faith and practice. The steadfast provincial Catholics, like those of

Lancashire, were content to remain within their own spheres, neither interfering in nor interfered with by more national outlooks. The newer immigrant Catholics, brought in especially as labourers during the expansion of the railways in the 1840s and in increasing numbers after the disastrous Irish potato-famines, for some decades lacked the resources which made real integration a possibility. Real integration into the full life of the nation, which would enable Catholics to take a confident part in all aspects of national life, required equality of status in education, and so in the last analysis at the universities.

The Oxford venture has been of crucial importance in the formation not only of Benedictine communities in England but also in the formation which these have passed on by their schools and other educational means. More important, it is symbolic of the general confidence of the Catholic population, which has made possible the removal of inhibiting barriers. More particularly it has made possible a renewal of that rich tradition of a Benedictine presence at the universities which has been documented in this volume. Perhaps it would not be entirely fanciful to see a small sign of both these elements in the appointment of the Master of St Benet's in 1995 to a lectureship in theology at the erstwhile Gloucester College.

Henry Wansbrough OSB

Notes

Introduction

1. *Dialogues*, Book 2, prologue.
2. Ibid., Book 2, ch. 35.

1: St Frideswide of Oxford

1. Birch (ed.), *Liber Vitae of Hyde Abbey* (Hampshire Record Society, 1892), p. 94.
2. Charter of Aethelstan in D. Whitelock, *English Historical Documents* vol. 1 (London, 1979), pp. 590–3. For discussion of the Anglo-Saxon background see F. Stenton, 'St Frideswide and Her Times', in *Preparatory to Saxon England* (Oxford, 1970), pp. 224–33.
3. J. Morris (ed. and trans.), *The Domesday Book: Oxfordshire* (Chichester, 1978), p. 157.
4. William of Malmesbury, *Gesta Pontificum Anglorum*, ed. Hamilton, *Rolls Series* (London, 1870), p. 315.
5. J. Blair, 'St Frideswide Reconsidered', in *Oxoniensia* 52 (1987), pp. 71–127.
6. Cf. H. Mayr-Harting, 'Functions of a Twelfth Century Shrine: The Miracles of St Frideswide', in H. Mayr-Harting and R. I. Moore (eds.), *Studies in Medieval History Presented to R. H. C. Davies* (London, 1985), pp. 193–207.
7. Oxford, Bodleian Library, MS Digby 177, 1vff, printed in *AASS* Oct. VIII, pp. 568–89. For further discussions of the miracles see B. Ward, *Miracles and the Medieval Mind* (London, 1981).
8. J. Calfhill, trans. J. Blair in *St Frideswide, Patron of Oxford* (Oxford, 1994), p. 22.

2: The Role of Benedictine Abbeys in the
Development of Oxford as a Centre of
Legal Learning

1. *The Early Rolls of Merton College, Oxford,* ed. J. R. L. Highfield
(*OHS* (n.s.) 18, 1964), esp. pp. 66–8; and Henry Mayr-Harting,
'The foundation of Peterhouse, Cambridge (1284), and the
Rule of St Benedict', *EHR* 103 (1988), 318–20.

2. Alan E. Coates, *The Origin, Growth and Dispersal of the Book
Collections of Reading Abbey* (Unpublished Oxford D. Phil., 1991,
forthcoming in the Oxford Historical Monographs Series),
esp. chs. 4 and 5.

3. E. Stone, 'Profit-and-loss accountancy at Norwich Cathedral
Priory', *TRHS* 5th Series 12 (1962), 25–48.

4. A. B. Emden, *An Oxford Hall in Medieval Times* (Oxford, 1927),
chs. 2–3; W. A. Pantin, 'The halls and schools of medieval
Oxford', *Oxford Studies presented to Daniel Callus* (*OHS* (n.s.) 16,
1964), esp. pp. 36–7; J. R. L. Highfield, 'The early colleges', in
HUO i, pp. 225–9.

5. *Cartularium Prioratus de Gyseburne,* ed. W. Brown, *Surtees Society*
89 (1891), ii, 81–3.

6. The argument was first put forward in R. W. Southern, 'Master
Vacarius and the beginning of an English academic tradition',
in *Medieval Learning and Literature: Essays presented to R. W.
Hunt,* ed. J. J. G. Alexander and Margaret Gibson (Oxford,
1976), esp. pp. 266–73.

7. R. W. Southern, 'From Schools to University' in *HUO*, i, pp.
10–17.

8. 'Miracles of St Frideswide', ch. 51, in *AASS* October viii,
568–89, p. 579 E–F.

9. See also Eleanor Rathbone, 'John of Cornwall' in *Recherches de
Théologie Ancienne et Médiévale* 17 (1950), 46–60.

10. Stephan Kuttner and Eleanor Rathbone, 'Anglo-Norman Canonists of the Twelfth Century', *Traditio* 7 (1949–51), esp.
317–27.

11. E.g. Abbot Samson of Bury St Edmund (elected 1182); see
Diana Greenway and Jane Sayers, *Jocelin of Brakelond: Chronicle
of the Abbey of Bury St Edmunds* (Oxford, 1989), pp. 31, 132.

12. A famous instance, though not involving a monastery, can
be seen in Patricia Barnes, 'The Anstey Case', in *A Medieval
Miscellany for Doris Mary Stenton, Pipe Roll Society* 36 (1962), pp.
1–24.

13. For the Chichester records of the time, see *The Acta of the*

Bishops of Chichester 1075–1207, ed. H. Mayr-Harting (*Canterbury and York Society* 130 (1965)).

14. My observation on the 1170s is to some extent controversial, since there are many scholars who would see some of Henry II's most important legal 'reforms', especially *novel disseisin,* taking effect in the 1160s. But there can be no doubt that the first comprehensive eyre (1176), the embryonic King's Bench (1178), *mort d'ancestor* (1176), and the Grand Assize (1179) all belong to the 1170s.

15. E.g. W. L. Warren, *Henry II* (1973), pp. 393, 473, 604, 629.

16. The Eynsham, Oseney and St Frideswide's Cartularies have all been published in the Oxford Historical Society series, as more recently (1990–1) has the Abingdon Cartulary. The Godstow Cartulary is PRO, Exch. K.R. Misc. Books.i.20.

17. After the list of names, the copy of the text merely says *et aliis,* i.e. 'and with others' (as witnesses).

18. See *Chichester Acta,* op. cit., pp. 18–19, for the evidence.

19. *Early Rolls of Merton College,* op. cit., pp. 8–10.

20. PRO, Chartae Antiquae, E315, vol. 34, no. 86; vol. 36, no. 131; vol. 41, no. 83; vol. 41, no. 147; vol. 48, no. 111. In all of these he is first witness. Then he also appears in vol. 44, no. 44; vol. 46, no. 124; vol. 54, no. 43.

21. Beryl Smalley, *The Becket Conflict and the Schools* (Oxford, 1973), pp. 167–86; and C. N. L. Brooke in *The Letters of John of Salisbury,* ed. W. J. Millor and H. E. Butler, vol. i (1955), pp. xxxv–vi.

22. Mary G. Cheney, *Roger, Bishop of Worcester, 1164–79* (Oxford, 1980), esp. chs. 1, 4; Adrian Morey, *Bartholomew of Exeter* (Cambridge, 1937), esp. chs. 1, 4, 6 and Part II.

23. *Jocelin of Brakelond,* op. cit., p. 111.

24. *The Chronicle of Battle Abbey,* ed. and trans. Eleanor Searle (Oxford Medieval Texts, 1980), pp. 322–5.

3: THE BENEDICTINES AT OXFORD, 1283–1539

1. This article first appeared in the *Downside Review,* no. 170, vol. 57 (April, 1939). The text has been edited and Latin quotations translated. The endnotes have been revised extensively to cover modern references and to include biographical details.

2. H. E. Salter, *Map of Mediaeval Oxford* (Oxford, 1934). Also *HUO* i, maps and *HUO* ii, maps.

3. For the physical impact of religious life on Oxford, see J. K.

McConica, 'Friars Entry and Vanished Oxford', *The Allen Review* 12 (Trinity, 1995).

4. W. A. Pantin, *Chapters.*

5. This prevented the passing of land to monastic and other religious houses without royal permission. See F. M. Powicke, *The Thirteenth Century: 1216–1307* (Oxford, 1953).

6. Matthew Paris tells us this was the reason the Cistercians began sending monks to Paris. Similar fears probably encouraged the Black Monks in the same direction – see *HUO* i, pp. 213–14.

7. D. Wilkins, *Concilia Magnae Britanniae et Hiberniae*, vol. 2 (London, 1737), pp. 594–9. Cf. L. Cherubini (ed.), *Bullarium Romanum*, vol. 1 (Luxembourg, 1727), p. 218.

8. Godfrey Giffard was Bishop of Worcester from 1268 to 1302. He devoted himself almost entirely to his diocese, giving to it a strong administration. His episcopacy was only marred by a quarrel in the 1480s with Archbishop Peckham – *DHGE* XX, pp. 1275–9.

9. Register of the Bishops of Worcester: Godfrey Giffard (1268–1302), Worcester County Library MS. BA26 48/1(i), folio 205 (ccvi). Also see J. W. Bund (ed.), 'The Episcopal Register of Godfrey Giffard' in *Worcestershire Historical Society* (1899–1902, 2 vols.), esp. vol. II, p. 230.

10. John Giffard (1232–99) was Baron of Brimpsfield in Gloucestershire, with large possessions in the Cotswolds, and a predilection for the Abbey of Gloucester. He was a cousin of the Bishop of Worcester, Godfrey Giffard. After supporting de Montfort in the Civil War, he switched to the side of Gilbert de Clare, whom he persuaded to support the king – *DNB* VII, p. 1174 and also J. W. Bund, op. cit., vol. I, pp. xxiii–lvii.

11. W. H. Hart (ed.), *Historia et Cartularium monasterii S. Petri Gloucestriae*, Rolls Series 33 (1863–67), vol. 1, p. 32. W. Dugdale, *Monasticon Anglicanum* (London, 1846), vol. II, p. 533. See also R. B. Dobson, 'The Foundation of Gloucester College in 1283', *Worcester College Record* (1985).

12. For Gloucester College, see W. A. Pantin, 'Gloucester College', *Oxoniensia* 11–12 (1946–7).

13. W. R. Luard (ed.), *Annales Monastici*, Rolls Series 36 (1864–9), vol. 4, p. 488.

14. C. Reyner, *Apostolatus Benedictinorum in Anglia* (Douai, 1626), pp. 54–7. Pantin, *Chapters* i, pp. 129ff.

15. Gilbert de Clare (1243–95), 9th Earl of Clare, 7th Earl of Hertford and 8th Earl of Gloucester – *DNB* IV, p. 378.

16. A. Clark (ed.), ' "Survey of Antiquities of the City of Oxford"

composed in 1661–66 by Anthony Wood', *OHS* (o.s.) 17 (1890), vol. II, pp. 248–9.

17. C. H. O. Daniel, 'Gloucester College', *Transactions Bristol and Gloucester Archaeological Society* 16 (1891–92), p. 109.

18. A. Clark (ed.), op. cit., cf. Campbell in this book.

19. C. H. O. Daniel, op. cit., p. 108. For further descriptions of the layout, see *VCH* (Oxon), vol. III, pp. 301–7 with plan on p. 303; *HUO* ii, plans.

20. V. H. Galbraith (ed.), 'New Documents about Gloucester College' in H. E. Salter (ed.), 'Snappe's Formulary and Other Records', *OHS* (o.s.) 80 (1924), pp. 338–86.

21. Following the 4th Lateran Council in 1215 the English monks were the first to set up General Chapters. At first each province had its own General Chapter, but in 1336 the General Chapters of the northern and southern provinces were united into one chapter – W. A. Pantin, 'The General and Provincial Chapters of the English Black Monks, 1215–1540', *TRHS* 4th series, 10 (1927), esp. pp. 195–6.

22. *Historia et Cartularium monasterii S. Petri Gloucestriae*, vol. 1, p. 34.

23. Thomas de la Mare, born in early 1309, was the son of Sir John de la Mare. He had three brothers and one sister, all of whom adopted the religious life at his suggestion. After entering St Albans he rose quickly, probably due to the Black Death, eventually becoming Prior of Tynemouth and then from 1349 until his death in 1396, abbot. He was a conscientious ruler, balancing monastic duties with his secular ones – *DNB* XII, pp. 1014–15 and D. H. Farmer (ed.), *Benedict's Disciples*, 2nd edn (1995), pp. 212–16.

24. Pantin, *Chapters* ii, pp. 74–8.

25. Pantin, *Chapters* ii, p. 63. *BRUO* 1, pp. 2073–4, tells us that this dispute led to Dom Henry migrating to Christ Church Canterbury. In 1365 he became first Warden of Canterbury College.

26. Pantin, *Chapters* ii, pp. 55–8.

27. J. Greatrex, 'Norwich Monks at Oxford and Cambridge c. 1300–1530', *EHR*, vol. 106, no. 420 (1991), pp. 555–83.

28. Pantin, *Chapters* ii, p. 152.

29. The letters of Walter de Monington, Abbot of Glastonbury, do this too – Knowles, *RO* ii, pp. 22ff.

30. A. F. Leach (ed.), 'Early Education in Worcester', *Worcestershire Historical Society* (1913), pp. xli–xliii.

31. The Magnificat Antiphons at Vespers in the week before

Christmas are known as the O Antiphons, since they all begin
'O Sapientia', 'O Adonai', etc. The party which followed
Vespers on each day was paid for by the monastic obedient-
iaries in turn. The cellarer's O was naturally 'O Clavis' (20
December), as he held the keys.

32. Dudley and Fordham were both monks of Worcester. John
Dudley was a scholar at Oxford in August 1388 and was still
there in 1392–3. After this he had a varied career as an obedi-
enitary in his monastery, while outside he was also active. In
1392 he acted as assessor to the Bishop of Hereford at the trial
of a Lollard and in 1407–8 he went with John Fordham
(scholar at Gloucester College *c.* 1392) to visit Henry IV and
Archbishop Arundel to discuss the problem of heresy in
Oxford. Fordham, after a spell at the Curia (1395–6), also
became an obedientiary, first as almoner and then from 1401
as prior until his death. He attended the Council of Constance
as Henry V's ambassador, was one of the proctors of the EBC
and was also President of the General Chapter. He died in
1438 – *BRUO* 1, pp. 598, 705.

33. A. F. Leach (ed.), op. cit, pp. 26–9, 46–56.
34. H. T. Riley (ed.), *Gesta Abbatum monasterii S. Albani,* Rolls Series
28, vol. III, pp. 391, 410.
35. C. H. O. Daniel, op. cit., p. 110.
36. *HUO* ii, p. 546. Also R. B. Dobson, op. cit., pp. 13–14.
37. *Gesta Abbatum monasterii S. Albani,* vol. III, p. 280.
38. Such variety of attendance may be seen with other monasteries. Those who had their courses interrupted did not
necessarily return, while some may indeed have come with the
sole purpose of learning to preach. See M. R. Foster, 'Thomas
Westoe: a monastic book-buyer at Oxford about 1300', *Viator*
23 (1992), pp. 189–99.
39. Thomas Millyng was a monk of Westminster. He studied at
Gloucester College 1456–66. He became Abbot of Westminster
in 1469 and Bishop of Hereford in 1474. He died in 1492 –
BRUO 1, pp. 128–3.
40. E. H. Pearce (ed.), *Register of the Monks of Westminster*
(Cambridge, 1916), pp. 26–8.
41. This indicates that many students, as well as studying, would
have been compelled to say obits.
42. For Durham College, see 'Some Durham College Rolls', in H.
E. D. Blakiston (ed.), 'Collectanea', *OHS* (o.s.) 32 (1896);
HUO i, index, plans and plates.
43. Richard Hoton or de Houghton was probably born at

Houghton Spring. In 1289 he became Prior of Durham. He died in Rome, while appealing against his bishop, Anthony Bek (1284–1311) on 9 January 1307 – *DHGE* XXV, p. 1259.

44. Wilkins, *Concilia*, vol. II, pp. 614–17.

45. Other colleges did have some seculars, though. Gloucester College between 1419 and the end of the century had seven secular students out of the total of 77 (see T. H. Aston, 'Oxford's Medieval Alumni', *P&P* 74 (1977), pp. 3–40). Durham had monastic students paying rent for rooms from other northern monastic houses, such as York or Whitby.

46. 'The Rites of Durham', *Surtees Society* 15 (1842), p. 81.

47. For Canterbury College, see Pantin, *Canterbury*, i–iv.

48. J. B. Sheppard (ed.), *Literae Cantuariensies, Rolls Series* 85, vol. 1, pp. 358, 392. Pantin, *Canterbury* iv, p. 211 (doc. 4) and also pp. 2–8.

49. Simon Islip was in 1307 a fellow of Merton; he then became a prominent ecclesiastical lawyer. He entered royal service, becoming chaplain, secretary, councillor and keeper of the privy seal to Edward III. In 1349 he was elected after the successive death of three archbishops, one of which had been due to the Black Death. He died on 26 April 1366 – *DNB* X, pp. 511–14.

50. These buildings were demolished in 1783 – Pantin, *Canterbury* iv, pp. 131–53, and *HUO* ii, plan.

51. This was probably Wycliffe the Reformer – see Knowles, *RO* ii, p. 21; Pantin, *Canterbury* iv, pp. 17ff (for a general history of the struggles), and also *DNB* X, p. 514, 'Islip'.

52. Simon Langham was a monk of Westminster in *c.* 1335 and in 1349 became first prior and then abbot. In 1366 he became Archbishop of Canterbury and in 1368 was made a cardinal priest. This angered Edward III, and Langham was forced to resign his see. He regained royal favour, but despite much complicated manoeuvring never recovered Canterbury – *DNB* XI, pp. 540–1.

53. *Literae Cantuariensis*, vol. II, pp. xxviiff.

54. Pantin, *Canterbury* iii, p. 159.

55. For this confusing early history, see Pantin, *Canterbury* iv, pp. 9–46.

56. William de Islip was the nephew of the Archbishop – Pantin, *Canterbury* iv, pp. 14–15.

57. Pantin, *Canterbury* iii, p. 7.

58. Peter Langley was born in *c.* 1508. He became a professed member of Christ Church, Canterbury in 1527. He was at

Canterbury College at its dissolution in 1538 and at Christ Church at its dissolution on 4 April two years later – *BRUO* 2, p. 340; Pantin, *Canterbury* iv, p. 224.

59. Translated from Pantin, *Canterbury*, iii, pp. 149–50. Nicholas Bennett was a monk of Christ Church, Canterbury, professed in 1524, still there in 1534. He was a fellow of Canterbury College in 1528 or 1529, vacating it between 1535 and 1538 – *BRUO* 2, p. 42; Pantin, *Canterbury* iv, p. 218.

60. Pantin, *Canterbury* iii, pp. 126–7. Pantin presumes this to be canon law. See also Aston, op. cit., p. 19 and *HUO* ii, p. 571.

61. Strickland and Gibson (eds.), *Statuta Antiqua Universitatis Oxoniensis* (Oxford, 1931), p. cxvi.

62. *HUO* ii, p. 576.

63. M. Burrows (ed.), 'Collectanea', *OHS* (o.s.) 32 (1896), pp. 41–55. Some did, however, have grander rooms – *HUO* ii, p. 562 mentions the provisions made for the Warden of Durham College, among others.

64. G. Chaucer, *The Canterbury Tales*, ed. W. W. Skeat (Oxford, 1900), Prologue, p. 9, lines 293–6.

65. For a more modern view of the statistics, see T. H. Aston, op. cit., pp. 18–19.

66. F. A. Gasquet, *The Eve of the Reformation* (London, 1919), p. 42.

67. Gloucester College, while not free of heresy (Pantin, 'Gloucester College', op. cit., p. 72), produced the essentially conservative Robert Joseph (cf. Marett-Crosby in this book) and John Feckenham, last Abbot of Westminster (see *AJ* 42.3, 43.1 (1937) and *DHGE* XVI, pp. 803–9).

68. *CLP* Henry VIII 4.3962.

69. Thomas Coventry was a monk of Evesham and a student at Gloucester College from ?1530 to 1539. His letter to Cromwell is preserved in *CLP* Henry VIII 14/2.437.

70. T. Wright (ed.), 'Letters relating to the Suppression of the Monasteries', *Camden Society* 26 (1843), p. 70.

4: GLOUCESTER COLLEGE

1. This article has been reprinted with alterations from *Worcester College Record* (1983) with the kind permission of the author.

5: FROM CATHEDRAL CLOISTER TO GLOUCESTER COLLEGE

1. Both manuscript and printed references relating to the monks who are mentioned in this chapter will be found in my *Biographical Register of English Cathedral Priories of the Province of Canterbury* (Oxford, 1997) under their names.
2. Benedictine monks in the Middle Ages were generally known by their toponymic, that is, their village or town of origin, in place of a family name; hence the frequent use of 'de', at least until part way through the fifteenth century.
3. Woolstone was the priory manor closest to Oxford, some 20 miles south-west.
4. In the 1390s there were once again three Winchester monks at Oxford.
5. There was at least one other Worcester precedent for an early departure for Oxford: John de Preston, acolyte, who was at Oxford in 1336/7 after admission only a year or two before. One explanation for these shortened periods of claustral study may possibly be that the monk in question had received his early education in the almonry school and therefore had had previous experience of monastic life as a resident within the enclosure.
6. During these years he was no doubt also engaged in lecturing in the cloister.
7. A few included in these totals did some or all of their studies at Cambridge.
8. He had probably begun working on his doctorate before being recalled.
9. The manuscripts referred to at Worcester are identified as Q.13, F.139, Q.46 and F.118; the Bodleian manuscript is Bodley 692.
10. There is an extant list of some 30 volumes taken to Oxford for the use of John Lawerne and his fellow Worcester monk-students.
11. Printed in *The Letter Book of Robert Joseph*, ed. J. C. H. Aveling and W. A. Pantin, *OHS* (n.s.) 19, p. 265.
12. This complaint, which was made during an episcopal visitation, has been frequently quoted and its importance exaggerated.

6: THE BLACK MONKS OF DURHAM AND CANTERBURY COLLEGES: COMPARISONS AND CONTRASTS

1. H. Rashdall, *The Universities of Europe in the Middle Ages,* new edn by F. M. Powicke and A. B. Emden, 3 vols. (Oxford, 1936), vol. iii, pp. 190–1.

2. R. B. Dobson, 'The Religious Orders 1370–1540', in *HUO* ii, pp. 540–1; *VCH* (Oxon) iv, pp. 22–35, 364–8; T. G. Hassall *et al.,* 'Excavations at Oxford' in *Oxoniensia* 35 (1970), pp. 10–15; 36 (1971), pp. 6–8; 38 (1973), pp. 286–94; *Rewley Abbey: an Archaeological Assessment* (Oxford Archaeological Unit, 1986).

3. *An Inventory of the Historical Monuments in the City of Oxford* (Royal Commission on Historical Monuments, England, 1939), pp. 35–47, 124–5.

4. Ibid., p. 48; Pantin, *Canterbury* iv, pp. 49–50.

5. M. Maclagan, *Trinity College, 1555–1955* (Oxford, 1955), pp. 3–5, 10–11.

6. Pantin, *Canterbury, passim;* H. E. D. Blakiston, 'Some Durham College Rolls', *Collectanea* III, ed. M. Burrows, *OHS* (o.s.) 32 (1896), pp. 1–76.

7. 85 Durham monks participated in the election of Bishop Antony Bek in July 1285: *Records of Antony Bek, bishop and patriarch, 1283–1311,* ed. C. M. Fraser, *Surtees Society* 162 (1953), p. 182. Cf. R. B. Dobson, 'The Monks of Canterbury in the Later Middle Ages, 1220–1540', in *A History of Canterbury Cathedral,* ed. P. Collinson, N. Ramsay and M. Sparks (Oxford, 1995), pp. 116–17; *idem.,* 'English Monastic Cathedrals in the Fifteenth Century', *TRHS,* 6th ser., 1 (1991), pp. 156–7.

8. R. B. Dobson, 'The Foundation of Gloucester College in 1283', *Worcester College Record* (1985), pp. 12–24; cf. 'New Documents about Gloucester College', ed. V. H. Galbraith, in *Snappe's Formulary and Other Records,* ed. H. E. Salter, *OHS* (o.s.) 80 (1924), pp. 342–56.

9. Blakiston, op. cit., pp. 27–35; Dean and Chapter of Canterbury [DCC] Register G, fo. 217; Pantin, *Canterbury* iii, pp. 34–46.

10. *Gesta Abbatum S. Albani,* ed. H. T. Riley, 3 vols., *Rolls Series* (1867–69), i, p. 217; Rashdall, op. cit., vol. iii, p. 32; D. Knowles, *The Monastic Order in England, 940–1216,* 2nd edn (Cambridge, 1963), pp. 333–5.

11. Pantin, *Canterbury* iv, pp. 3–4, 9–10.

12. Ibid., pp. 3–4; Dobson, 'Monks of Canterbury', op. cit., pp. 99–102.

13. *Extracts from the Account Rolls of the Abbey of Durham,* ed. J. T.

Fowler, 3 vols., *Surtees Society* 99–100, 103 (1898–1901), vol. ii, pp. 486, 492; *Historiae Dunelmensis Scriptores Tres*, ed. J. Raine, *Surtees Society* 9 (1839), p. 73.

14. Dean and Chapter of Durham [DCD], 1.5. Ebor., no. 9; J. Scammell, 'Some Aspects of Medieval English Monastic Government: The Case of Geoffrey Burdon, Prior of Durham (1313–1321)', *Revue Bénédictine* 68 (1958), p. 228; *Registrum Palatinum Dunelmense*, ed. T. D. Hardy, 4 vols., *Rolls Series* (1873–8), i, pp. 45–6.

15. Rashdall, op. cit., vol. i, pp. 506–7, 536–9; Dobson, 'Gloucester College', op. cit., p. 17.

16. On Uthred of Boldon see references in D. H. Farmer, *New Light on Uthred of Boldon*, in this volume.

17. *Durham Account Rolls*, op. cit., vol. iii, pp. 591–3; R. B. Dobson, *Durham Priory: 1400–1450* (Cambridge, 1973), pp. 345–7.

18. Pantin, *Canterbury* iv, pp. 9–18; Dobson, 'Monks of Canterbury', op. cit., pp. 100–102.

19. The extraordinarily long (1366–84) and tortuous course of the litigation which preceded the formal establishment of Canterbury College is described in detail in Pantin, *Canterbury* iv, pp. 18–46.

20. DCD, Register II, fo. 184; 4. 6. Ebor., no. 2; Dobson, 'Durham Priory', op. cit., pp. 348–51.

21. Pantin, *Canterbury* iv, pp. 100–104, 122–9; Dobson, 'Monks of Canterbury', op. cit., pp. 103–5.

22. Pantin, *Canterbury* iii, pp. 81, 115–16; iv, pp. 143–7. There seems no reason to doubt the Canterbury monks' own statement that, except for the hall and two *camere*, all the buildings of their Oxford college (including its chapel) were built during the priorate of Thomas Chillenden (1391–1411): see *Literae Cantuarienses*, ed. J. B. Sheppard, 3 vols., *Rolls Series* (1887–9), vol. iii, p. 116.

23. DCD, Durham College Accounts, 1398–9, 1414–15, 1415–16; Dobson, 'Durham Priory', op. cit., pp. 349–50; Blakiston, op. cit., pp. 71–3 (a summary account of expenses on the building of the chapel in 1406–8); '*Inventory of Historical Monuments in the City of Oxford*', op. cit., pp. 112–13.

24. Pantin, *Canterbury* iv, pp. 145–66; Blakiston, op. cit., pp. 36–41; J. Newman, 'Oxford Libraries before 1800', *Archaeological Journal* 135 (1978), pp. 248–65.

25. Pantin, *Canterbury* iv, pp. 147–9. For repairs to the warden's chamber at Durham College, see, e.g., DCD, Durham College Account Rolls, 1408–9, 1432–3; and for its furnishings in 1428

and 1456 (including a 'good bed' decorated with a star and the names of Jesus Christ) see Blakiston, op. cit., pp. 46, 54.

26. DCD, Durham College Accounts, 1540–1, 1541–2; Pantin, *Canterbury* iii, pp. 120–1.

27. *BRUO* 2, p. 1093; Pantin, *Canterbury* iv, p. 224; Dobson, 'Durham Priory', pp. 354–5.

28. A. B. Emden, *BRUO*, 1501–1540, pp. 564–5, 624–5.

29. Ibid., pp. 281, 564–5; Dobson, op. cit., p. 355; Pantin, *Canterbury* iv, pp. 229–30.

30. DCD, Cawston MS (Lit.D12). fo. 20v; *BRUO* 1, pp. 399–400, 589.

31. See the relevant entries in *BRUO* for the careers of Priors William Ebchester (1446–56), John Burnby (1456–64), Richard Bell (1464–78), Robert Ebchester (1478–84), John Aukland (1484–94), Thomas Castell (1494–1519) and Hugh Whitehede (1519–39). All these priors were Oxford doctors of theology except for Richard Bell, later Bishop of Carlisle, who never proceeded beyond the bachelor's degree.

32. Pantin, *Canterbury* iii, pp. 151–4; iv, pp. 48–9; Dobson, 'Religious Orders, 1370–1540', op. cit., p. 550; *idem.*, 'Monks of Canterbury', op. cit., pp. 103–4.

33. *CLP* Henry VIII, 16, 712; DCD, Durham College Accounts, 1540–1, 1541–2; Dobson, 'Religious Orders', op. cit., p. 550.

34. I owe these statistics to the detailed researches (and generosity) of Mr Alan Piper.

35. Knowles, *RO* iii, pp. 3–7, 195–8; A. G. Dickens, *Late Monasticism and the Reformation* (London, 1994), pp. 17–23.

36. *The Rites of Durham*, ed. J. T. Fowler, *Surtees Society* 107 (1903), p. 97.

7: BENEDICTINE MONKS AND THEIR BOOKS IN OXFORD

1. *Bullarium Romanium*, iv (Turin, 1859), pp. 357–60.

2. See A. Coates, 'The Library of Durham College, Oxford', *Library History* 8/5 (1990), p. 126: the *c.* 1400 and 1409 lists of books sent to Oxford are printed in H. E. D. Blakiston, 'Some Durham College Rolls', *Collectanea* iii, ed. M. Burrows, *OHS* (o.s.) 32 (1896), pp. 38–9 and 40–41 respectively; the 1404 list is noted in H. D. Hughes, *A History of Durham Cathedral Library* (Durham, 1925).

3. The 1315 *Status Collegii* is printed in Blakiston, op. cit., pp. 35–7.

4. The book list of *c.* 1390–1400 is in W. A. Pantin, 'Catalogue of the Books of Durham College, Oxford, ca. 1390–1400', *Formularies which Bear on the History of Oxford ca. 1204–1420*, ed. H. E. Salter, *OHS* (n.s.) 1 (1942), pp. 240–5.

5. A. J. Piper, 'The Libraries of the Monks of Durham', *Medieval Scribes, Manuscripts and Libraries: Essays Presented to N. R. Ker*, ed. M. B. Parkes and A. G. Watson (London, 1978), p. 247; for the 1418, 1419 and 1434–5 lists, see Blakiston, op. cit., p. 41 note 3.

6. Pantin, *Canterbury*, iv, p. 155, with the statute printed in ibid., iii, p. 181.

7. Ibid., iv, p. 155.

8. M. B. Parkes, 'The Provision of Books', *HUO* ii, p. 450.

9. Ibid., p. 450.

10. Ibid., pp. 452–3, with references and details of the manuscripts where they survive.

11. Ibid., p. 453, with reference to Lund; on Westoe and Graystanes, see pp. 448–9; on Westoe see also M. R. Foster, 'Thomas of Westoe: a Monastic Book-buyer at Oxford about 1300', *Viator* 23 (1992), pp. 189–99; R. B. Dobson, *Durham Priory 1400–1450* (Cambridge, 1973), p. 375, with further examples of acquisitions on pp. 375–6.

12. Parkes, op. cit., p. 453, with references.

13. Ibid., p. 450, with references.

14. N. R. Ker, *Medieval Libraries of Great Britain: A List of Surviving Books*, 2nd edn (Royal Historical Society Guides and Handbooks 3) (London, 1964), pp. 15–16, 232; [D. M. Rogers], *The Benedictines and the Book: an exhibition* [at the Bodleian Library] *to commemorate the 15th centenary of the Birth of St Benedict AD 480–1980* (Oxford, 1980), no. 74.

15. Parkes, op. cit., p. 451; A. E. Coates, 'The Origin, Growth and Dispersal of the Book Collections of Reading Abbey' (unpublished D.Phil. thesis, University of Oxford, 1992), p. 147, except that Richard of Reading cannot now be identified with Richard Bannister, and the inscription is probably to be dated to the fourteenth, rather than to the thirteenth, century. The present author is currently revising the thesis for publication in the Oxford Historical Monographs series.

16. Parkes, op. cit., p. 451.

17. Ibid., p. 454; N. Orme, 'Glastonbury Abbey and Education', *The Archaeology and History of Glastonbury Abbey: Essays in Honour*

of the 90th Birthday of C. A. Ralegh Radford, ed. L. Abrams and J. P. Carley (Woodbridge, 1991), p. 290.

18. Parkes, op. cit., p. 454, with references.
19. Ibid., pp. 454–5, with John Lawrence corrected to John Lawerne by Dr Greatrex.
20. Ibid., p. 452.
21. A. Coates and K. Jensen, 'The Bodleian Library's Acquisition of Incunabula with English and Scottish Medieval Monastic Provenances', *Essays Presented to Andrew Watson*, ed. J. P. Carley and C. G. C. Tite (forthcoming, London, 1996), no. 6.
22. Parkes, op. cit., p. 447. The correction of the identification of Philip comes from Dr Greatrex.
23. Ibid.
24. Pantin, *Canterbury* iii, p. 181. On university chests, see T. H. Aston and R. Faith, 'The Endowments of the University and Colleges to *circa* 1348', *HUO* i, pp. 247–87.
25. Coates, 'Reading Abbey', op. cit., pp. 153–4, with transcriptions of the three pledge notes, and a discussion of the provenance details showing that the book had a Reading provenance from its copying until the dissolution. For other examples, see Parkes, op. cit., p. 452.
26. Parkes, op. cit.
27. Ibid., pp. 451–2.
28. These inventories have been edited in Pantin, *Canterbury* i, and discussed in *Canterbury* iv, pp. 157–65.
29. Pantin, *Canterbury* i, pp. 80–92, 107–11, and *Canterbury* iv, pp. 155–6.
30. *Canterbury* iv, p. 156.
31. Ibid., p. 165.
32. N. R. Ker, 'The Provision of Books', *HUO* iii, pp. 464–5.
33. For the Durham College book lists see above 'Provision', notes 2–4.
34. For Hatfield's statutes see R. B. Dobson, 'The Religious Orders 1370–1540', *HUO* ii, p. 571 and note 109.
35. Ibid., p. 563.
36. Blakiston, op. cit., pp. 43 (1428 inventory) and 51 (1456 inventory).
37. Ker, op. cit., pp. 146, 291 and *Supplement*, ed. A. G. Watson, p. 54, the latter updating the number of surviving manuscripts given by Dobson, op. cit., p. 563.
38. Pantin, *Canterbury* iv, p. 160, with the library discussed generally on pp. 155–60; *Canterbury* i, pp. 3–6, 97–100.
39. *Canterbury* iv, p. 160; i, pp. 11–15, 100–1.

40. *Canterbury* iv, p. 161; ii, p. 173.
41. *Canterbury* ii, p. 176.
42. *Canterbury* ii, p. 179; iv, p. 161.
43. *Canterbury* iii, p. 111; iv, pp. 161–2.
44. *Canterbury* iv, pp. 161–2; for a plan, see *HUO* ii, college plans, pl. 3; on Reading see Coates, 'Reading Abbey', op. cit., p. 136, with references, and Pantin, *Canterbury* ii, pp. 223–40.
45. *Canterbury* iv, p. 162; ii, pp. 181, 209, 223.
46. *Canterbury* iv, p. 162; ii, pp. 209, 220.
47. *Canterbury* iv, p. 162.
48. Ibid.
49. Ibid. On chained libraries in general see B. H. Streeter, *The Chained Library* (London, 1931).
50. Pantin, *Canterbury* iv, pp. 155–6.
51. This account draws heavily upon Coates, 'Durham College', op. cit., pp. 125–31.
52. Ibid., p. 128, and note 20.
53. Ibid., pp. 128–9, and note 24.
54. Ibid., p. 129, and notes 25–6; Piper, op. cit., p. 247; B. H. Streeter, op. cit., pp. 219–25.
55. Coates, 'Durham College', op. cit., p. 129, and notes 27–8.
56. Piper, op. cit., p. 247, with an example of the numbers on the books illustrated in pl. 80.
57. On the library's subsequent history, see A. Coates, 'The Old Library of Trinity College, Oxford', *The Bodleian Library Record* 13/6 (1991), pp. 466–78.
58. Coates, 'Durham College', op. cit., p. 128, and note 21.
59. J. Newman, 'Oxford Libraries before 1800', *Archaeological Journal* 135 (1978), p. 249.
60. Coates, 'Durham College', op. cit., pp. 128–9.
61. Ibid., p. 129, and notes 22–3. For the medieval stained glass currently in the Old Library, see R. Gameson, 'The Medieval Glass', *The Old Library, Trinity College, Oxford*, ed. R. Gameson and A. Coates (Oxford, 1988), pp. 15–34.
62. Coates, 'Trinity College', op. cit., p. 467.
63. Newman, op. cit., p. 249; V. H. Galbraith, 'New Documents about Gloucester College', *Snappe's Formulary and Other Records*, ed. H. E. Salter, *OHS* (o.s.) 80 (1924), p. 353.
64. Ker, 'Provision of Books', op. cit., p. 463; A. J. Piper, 'Durham: Benedictine Cathedral Priory of St Cuthbert' and 'Oxford: Durham College . . .', *Supplement*, op. cit., pp. 16–34 and 54, replacing the relevant sections in *Medieval Libraries . . .* as

quoted by Ker. The one printed book is listed by Piper on p. 54.

65. The lists are published in Pantin, *Canterbury* i, inventories B–H; Ker, 'Provision of Books', op. cit., pp. 463–4, with individual references to Pantin.

66. Pantin, *Canterbury* i, inventories C and E, with references given in Ker as above, note 65.

67. Ker, op. cit., p. 464; Dobson, 'Religious Orders', op. cit., p. 563.

68. Ker, 'Provision of Books', op. cit., p. 464.

69. A. I. Doyle, *The Printed Books of the Last Monks of Durham* (Durham Cathedral Lecture, 1974), revised as 'The Printed Books of the Last Monks of Durham' (Graham Pollar Memorial Lecture, 1987), published in *The Library*, 6th ser., 10/3 (1988), pp. 6–14, with other examples given.

70. Ibid., p. 6.

71. Ibid., p. 7.

72. Ibid., pp. 11, 13.

73. Ibid., pp. 13–14.

74. Coates and Jensen, op. cit., no. 5.

75. Ibid., no. 12.

76. Ibid., no. 4.

77. *The Benedictines and the Book*, op. cit., no. 64.

8: BENEDICTINE WOMEN AT OXFORD: THE NUNS OF GODSTOW

1. General accounts of Godstow are few and dated. Most available antiquarian information can be gleaned from A. Clark (ed.), *The Life and Times of Anthony Wood*, vol. 1, OHS (o.s.) 19 (1891), pp. 339–46; C. E. Doble (ed.), 'Remarks and Collections of Thomas Hearne', vol. 2, OHS (o.s.) 7 (1886), pp. 392–5; *Monasticon*, vol. 4, pp. 357–77 (with Godstow seal showing Ediva); D. Ganz, 'The Buildings of Godstow Nunnery', *Oxoniensia* 37 (1972), pp. 150–7; R. Gough, *British Topography* (London, 1780), vol. 2, p. 85 (with refs, to other topographical material); VCH (Oxon), vol. 2, pp. 71–5.

2. See Clark, op. cit., vol. 2, pp. 67–97.

3. Clark, op. cit., vol. 1, pp. 339–46. The accounts in Wood's books are in Oxford, Bodleian Library, MS Wood D. 11, fols. 23^v–36^r and MS Wood E. 1, fols. 72^r–74^v, and 75^r.

4. The plan is the same size as his notebook from the 1660

Godstow visit (now Oxford, Bodleian Library, MS Wood E. 1),
where he tells us in a marginal note that it is now to be found
in notebook AV (= Oxford, Bodleian Library, MS Wood D. 11).
Today the plan is in neither book; but the pages of MS Wood
E. 1 at this point have been at some time rebound out of order,
exactly as they might be had a bifolium been removed, leaving
the remaining pages loose.

5. Oxford, Bodleian Library, MS Wood D. 11, fol. 30^r. The other
   surviving MSS are an imperfect Latin version of the register,
   slightly earlier than the Rawlinson MS, now PRO, Exch. K.R.
   (Misc. Bks. i.20 [1404]), and a fifteenth-century psalter and
   liturgical book, Manchester, Chetham's Library, MS 6717
   (Mun. A.6.74).

6. A. Clark (ed.), 'The English Register of Godstow Nunnery,
   near Oxford, written about 1450', EETS nos. 129, 130, 142
   (London, 1905, 1906, 1911).

7. Wood says that Godstow means 'the place of God' or 'the place
   where God is daylie worshipped', Clark, *Life*, op. cit., vol. 1, p.
   341.

8. The others were Elstow and Malling. Before the Conquest, all
   nunneries were abbacies rather than priories. See L. Eckenstein, *Woman under Monasticism* (Cambridge, 1896), p. 204.
   All Cistercian nunneries in England were priories.

9. J. des Longrais, 'Le Statut de la femme en Angleterre dans le
   droit commun médiévale' in *La Femme*, vol. 2 (*Recueils de la
   Société Jean Bodin pour l'histoire comparative des institutions* 12,
   Brussels, 1962), pp. 135–241.

10. S. Thompson, *Women Religious: the Founding of English Nunneries
    After the Norman Conquest* (Oxford, 1991), p. 182, notes that it is
    possible that it was only under Henry II's patronage that
    Godstow became an abbey. No conclusive evidence survives
    one way or the other.

11. M. Biddle (ed.), *Winchester in the Early Middle Ages* (Winchester
    Studies 1, Oxford, 1976), p. 257.

12. Biddle, op. cit., 1110 survey, entry no. 57.

13. Ibid., 1110 survey, entry no. 237.

14. Ibid., 1148 survey, entry no. 71.

15. Ibid., 1148 survey, entry no. 705.

16. Thompson, op. cit., p. 172, lists the nine nunneries which
    were abbacies in the entire period from the Conquest to the
    dissolution. Five of these were established by noble widows,
    one (Malling) by Gundulf of Rochester, two by earls, and one
    only became an abbey long after its foundation.

17. See generally works cited for further reading. Also C. Fell, *Women in Anglo-Saxon England* (London, 1984) and P. Stafford, *Queens, Concubines and Dowagers* (London, 1983).

18. See, for an interesting, but sometimes equally biased counter-view, R. Gilchrist, *Gender and Material Culture* (London, NY, 1993).

19. At the dissolution, five religious houses had incomes of more than £2000 p.a. Of these, four were Benedictine. Sixteen other Benedictine houses (including the nuns of Shaftesbury) had incomes between £1000–2000 p.a. See generally, D. Knowles and R. N. Hadcock, *Medieval Religious Houses, England and Wales* (London, 1971).

20. Of these, about two-thirds date from post-1400, and more than a half are liturgical books or Bibles. Of the remainder, 23% are in Latin, 10% in French, and 67% in English. It is difficult to make such figures accurate, however, since there is still rather a tendency to assume that an unattributable book has come from a men's house rather than a women's house. But we know that Benedictine women used books as their male counterparts did, and some nuns' book-lending habits, for example, were exactly like those of Benedictine men, as laid down in the Rule: see T. R. Gambier-Parry, 'Lending Books in a Medieval Nunnery', *Bodleian Quarterly Record* 5 (1927), 188–90, on the customary of Barking Abbey.

21. D. N. Bell, *What Nuns Read: Books and Libraries in Medieval English Nunneries* (Kalamazoo, Mich., 1995), p. 33. N. R. Ker, *Medieval Libraries of Great Britain: A List of Surviving Books* (2nd edn; London, 1964) agrees that, 'survival has usually been a matter of chance' (p. xi).

22. For the statistics for nuns' books and remarks on literacy, see Bell, op. cit., *passim.*

23. Eckenstein, op. cit., pp. 207–13.

24. 'The wyseman tawht hys chyld gladly to rede bokys, and hem well undurstonde; for, in defaute of undyrstondyng, is offtymes causyd neclygence, hurte, harme, and hynderaunce, as expery-ence prevyth in many a place. And for as muche as women of relygyone in redynge bokys of latyn, byn excusyd of grete undurstandyng, where it is not her modyr tonge . . . Wher-fore, a poore brodur and welwyller . . . to the goode Abbas of Godstowe, Dame Alice henley, and to all her couent, the whych byn for the more party in Englyssh bokys well y-lernyd . . .' Quoted from A. Clark, *English Register*, op. cit., p. 25.

25. Eckenstein, op. cit., pp. 356–8.
26. See generally, *HUO* i and G. Leff, *Paris and Oxford Universities in the Thirteenth and Fourteenth Centuries: an Intellectual and Institutional History* (New York, 1968).
27. *HUO* i, p. 227.
28. Quoted in full in *Monasticon*, vol. 4, pp. 366–7; the 1284 text is in C. Trice Martin (ed.), 'Registrum epistolarum fratris Johannis Peckham archiepiscopi Cantuarensis', 3 vols., *Rolls Series* (London, 1882–5), vol. 3, pp. 845–51 (Latin) and 851–2 (French).
29. *Monasticon*, p. 366.
30. '*Oveke ceo nous defendons de part Deu ke nule nonein ne parle a escoler de Oxeneford, se il nest sun parent prechein, e ovekes ceo saunz le conge la abbesse especial.*' *Registrum epistolarum*, op. cit., p. 851.
31. A. Hamilton Thompson (ed.), *Visitations of Religious Houses in the Diocese of Lincoln* (Horncastle, 1914–29), vol. 2 (Bishop Alnwick, 1436–49), p. 218.
32. Lincoln Episcopal Registers: Register of Visitations, Bishop Alnwick, fol. 26d, quoted in Power, *Medieval English Nunneries* (Cambridge, 1922), p. 398.
33. Hamilton Thompson, op. cit., p. 114. Interestingly, and perhaps not surprisingly, at the same visitation that the abbess made this report, many of the nuns reported to the bishop that all was well! One, Dame Agnes Wylde, considered the pigs that were rooting about in and fouling the church grounds the most serious issue!
34. Hamilton Thompson, op. cit., vol. 1 (Bishop Gray), p. 67.
35. Lincoln Episcopal Registers: Register of Memoranda, Bishop Gynewell, fol. 100d, quoted in Power, op. cit., p. 401.
36. MS Wood E. 1, fol. 75^r.
37. See, for example, the engraving reproduced with notes by Gough in *The Gentleman's Magazine* (Nov. 1791), p. 985. All the engravings of the plan are based on the same original, and thus copy the mistake.
38. Quoted in *VCH* (*Oxon*), vol. 2, p. 74.
39. Quoted in *Monasticon*, vol. 4, p. 359.
40. E. Wilson, 'A "Damned F . . . in Abbot" in 1528: The earliest English example of a four-letter word', *Notes and Queries* (March 1993), pp. 29–34.

9: THE CISTERCIANS IN OXFORD, 1280–1539

1. On Cistercians at Paris see P. Glorieux, *Repertoire des maîtres en théologie de Paris au xiiie siècle* (Paris, 1933–4), vol. ii, pp. 249–73; on Peter Ceffons see Damasus Trapp, 'Peter Ceffons of Clairvaux', *Récherches de théologie ancienne et médiévale* 24 (1957), 101–54. In general on the Cistercians at Oxford see *VCH (Oxon)* ii, pp. 81–3 (Rewley); A. G. Little, 'Cistercian students at Oxford in the thirteenth century', *EHR* 8 (1893), 83–5; R. C. Fowler, 'Cistercian scholars at Oxford', *EHR* 23 (1908); *Formularies which bear on the History of Oxford*, eds. H. E. Salter, W. A. Pantin and H. G. Richardson, *OHS* (n.s.) 4–5 (1942), ii, pp. 281–327; *Letters from the English Abbots to the Chapter at Cîteaux, 1442–1521*, ed. C. H. Talbot (Royal Historical Society, Camden 4th series iv, 1967); *The Early History of St John's College Oxford*, eds. W. H. Stevenson and H. E. Salter, *OHS* (n.s.) 1 (1939), pp. 1–110.

2. *Statuta Capitulorum Generalium Ordinis Cisterciensis 1116–1786*, ed. J. M. Canivez (Louvain, 1933–41), vol. ii, pp. 200, 209, 213, 217.

3. Ed. Little, *EHR* 8, p. 84; see *St John's College*, op. cit., pp. 6–7.

4. *CCR* 1381–5, 17; Oxford Archaeological Unit, *Oxford Station (Rewley Abbey) Archaeological Field Evaluation* (Oxford, 1994), and accompanying plan.

5. *The Register of John de Grandisson, Bishop of Exeter*, ed. F. C. Hingeston-Randolph (London, 1894–9), vol. ii, pp. 1132–3.

6. British Library, MS Add. 10374, fols. 86–7, printed *St John's College*, op. cit., pp. 60–1; Worcester Cathedral, MS Q.99, fols. 73r–82v, calendared by A. G. Little and F. Pelster, *Oxford Theology and Theologians, 1282–1302*, pp. 224–5, 313–17. On Kirkeby see also C. G. Talbot, 'English Cistercians', *Studia Monastica* iv (1962), pp. 204–5, though British Library, MS Royal 8.A.xviii is too late to be in his collection.

7. *BRUO* 1, pp. 263, 1532, 1617, 1711–12, 1760, 1795; Talbot, op. cit., pp. 205–6.

8. *Two Wycliffite Texts*, ed. Anne Hudson, *EETS* 301 (1993), p. 41.

9. *BRUO* 1, pp. 524–5; Talbot, op. cit., p. 207, though his attributions of texts to Crumpe seem dubious. On Crumpe see also J. McNulty, 'William of Rymington, Prior of Salley', *YAJ* 30 (1930–1), pp. 321–47 and 31 (1931–2), pp. 62; and Hudson, *The Premature Reformation* (Oxford, 1988), pp. 45–6.

10. *CCR* 1381–5, pp. 17, 337; *St John's College*, op. cit., pp. 11–12, 62–6.

11. W. A. Pantin, 'The halls and schools of medieval Oxford' in *Oxford Studies presented to Daniel Callus, OHS* (n.s.) xvi (1964), pp. 74–5; *Stat. Cap. Ord. Cist.*, op. cit., vol. iv, p. 386; *St John's College*, op. cit., p. 13.
12. Henry Chichele's licence to acquire a site for St Bernard's College, ibid., p. 67; and see also p. 14.
13. W. J. Blair *et al.*, 'Frewin Hall, Oxford, a Norman mansion and a monastic college', *Oxoniensia* 43 (1978), pp. 64–6; *St John's College*, op. cit., p. 13.
14. Ibid., pp. 14–19; H. M. Colvin, 'The building of St Bernard's College', *Oxoniensia* 24 (1959), pp. 37–48.
15. *St John's College*, op. cit., pp. 15–16, 69–73.
16. *Letters to Cîteaux*, op. cit., pp. 86–9, 120–2.
17. *Letters to Cîteaux*, op. cit., pp. 63–6, 114–16, 120–2, 148–9, 181–3; Colvin, op. cit., pp. 40–1, 43.
18. *BRUO 1*, p. 43; *Letters to Cîteaux*, op. cit., pp. 44–6, 55–6, 63–8, 70–1.
19. *BRUO 1*, pp. 966–7, 1072, 1496, 1620–21; *BRUO 2*, p. 179.
20. Ibid., p. 18; VCH (Oxon) ii, 83.
21. *St John's College*, op. cit., pp. 30–3.
22. Ibid., pp. 36–8.
23. Ibid., p. 39.

10: New Light on Uthred of Boldon

1. The chronology of Uthred's life is in *BRUO* 1, pp. 212–13. I am especially indebted to Dr Alan Piper of Durham University, who put his own research on Uthred at my disposal and to Mr Roger Norris for help in a recent visit to the Dean and Chapter Library of Durham Cathedral, made possible by the generous sponsorship of St Benet's Hall.
2. For this important episode see M. D. Knowles, 'The Censured Opinions of Uthred of Boldon', *Proceedings of the British Academy* 37 (1952), 305–42. Uthred's views in a modified form have been revived by P. Glorieux in *Nouvelle Revue Théologique* 59 (1932), 865–92 and *Mélanges de Science Religieuse* 6 (1949), 185–216 and P. Gumpel, *Downside Review* 72 (1954), 346–63.
3. *Historiae Dunelmensis Scriptores Tres*, (Surtees Society, 1839), appendix p. cclxiii, emending *secularibus* to *scolaribus* with W. A. Pantin.
4. See Pantin, *Chapters* iii, pp. 248, 277ff.

5. This division is found early, e.g. the lives of both the Emperor Charlemagne and King Alfred.

6. These paragraphs depend on Pantin's analysis of the works cited in the further reading.

7. The relevant manuscripts for this study in the Durham Cathedral library are B.III.30 (miscellaneous monastic elements in part I and Lives of the Fathers etc. in part II); B.IV.41 (mainly monastic constitutions of various dates and places with a Life of St Thomas of Canterbury, the Rule of St Benedict, the regulations for Durham College, Oxford etc.); B.IV.45, with similar contents. All these date from the early fifteenth century.

8. Surtees Society, vol. 107 (1903), pp. 124–36.

9. The Latin text of these meditations was published in *Analecta Monastica* (Rome) 4 (1955), 141–245 and in English again (translated by Dame Frideswide Sandeman) in *Christ Crucified and Other Meditations* (Gracewing, 1995). An article, s.v. John of Farne, is to appear in the new edition of the *Dictionary of National Biography*.

10. For Uthred's influence at Durham see R. B. Dobson, *Durham Priory, 1400–1500* (Cambridge, 1975), especially pp. 345–6.

11. For a short comparison of these two great monks see D. H. Farmer in *Benedict's Disciples* (2nd edn, Gracewing, 1995). The *Meditacio Devota* was printed in *Analecta Monastica* (Rome) 5 (1957), 187–206.

12. The text comes from the prologue to Anselm's Prayers and Meditations in *Opera omnia* III, ed. F. S. Schmitt (Edinburgh, 1946), pp. 3–4.

13. J. Leland, *Commentarii de Scriptoribus Brittannicis* (Oxford, 1709), vol. II, p. 392; Bale, *Index Scriptorum Brittanicorum*, ed. R. L. Poole and M. Bateson (Oxford, 1902), p. 463.

14. *The Anonimalle Chronicle*, ed. V. H. Galbraith (Manchester, 1927), is the principal source for his appointment as one of four ambassadors to the Pope, his safe-conduct, capture and release. The mission lasted from July 1373 until February 1374.

11: Robert Joseph and His Letter Book

1. Thomas Hearne, 'An account of several Antiquities in and about the University of Oxford', in *The Itinerary of John Leland the Antiquary*, vol. II, ed. Hearne, pp. 92–4. Cf. also Thomas Hearne, 'Remarks and Collections', ed. C. E. Noble, vol. 1

(*OHS* (o.s.) 2, 1884), pp. 243–4, 260. In general on Edward Lhuyd see F. Emery, *Edward Lhuyd* (Cardiff, 1971). Quotation on his collection in W. O. Pughe, *The Cambrian Biography* (London, 1803), p. 1.

2. Text in National Library of Wales, MS Peniarth 119, fols. 503–742, published as *The Letter Book of Robert Joseph, Monk-Scholar of Evesham and Gloucester College, Oxford*, ed. H. Aveling and W. A. Pantin (*OHS* (n.s.) 19, 1967 for 1964), hereafter *Ep.R.J.*

3. *Ep.R.J.* 73.30–33. Terence was among Robert Joseph's favourite classical authors.

4. Ibid., 63.16–18.

5. Ibid., 110.29–30.

6. Ibid., 147.4–5 to Ralph Aynysworth, then a Master at Peterhouse and one of Robert Joseph's few connections with the university, but see note 25. Cf. also 103.13–16 and 153.5f for other difficulties with messengers.

7. Ibid., 28.13f, with *RB* 54, 'On no account shall a monk be allowed to receive letters, devout tokens, or any small gift whatsoever . . . without the abbot's permission.'

8. *Ep.R.J.* 5.5, 22.7, 23.4, 63.2, 93.4. Other words he found difficult to spell include *hilarascenter* (72.41) and *rhetorica* (10.6).

9. Ibid., 11.5–6, 49.93 ('*e dormintoriolo nostro post percatas matutinas*'), 63.1, 73.1–3.

10. For example, *Ep.R.J.* 99.1, where the 'F' of 'Feckenham' is a vain attempt at fine style (MS Peniarth 119, fol. 625).

11. *Ep.R.J.* 72.38f and 79.32.

12. Ibid., 103.13–16, see note 6 above.

13. Ibid., 113.1–4 for the warning, with 81.124–6, 82.37–8 and 137.12–13 for signs that his humour was not always appreciated.

14. Ibid., 26.7, 57.11–33.

15. Ibid., 3.13–14.

16. Ibid., 81.129–131 with 70.4f and 51.4.

17. Authorship of letters is discussed in W. A. Pantin, 'English monastic letter-books' in *Historical Essays in Honour of James Tait*, ed. J. G. Edwards and others (Manchester, 1933), pp. 201–22, esp. pp. 207–8.

18. W. A. Pantin, 'A medieval treatise on letter-writing with examples', *BJRL* 13 (1929), pp. 326–82 for what follows.

19. Ibid., pp. 353–5. On Pygot see *BRUO* 1, p. 1529 and J. H. Tillotson, *Monastery and Society in the Late Middle Ages: Selected*

Account Rolls from Selby Abbey 1398–1537 (Boydell Press, 1988), p. 53 and *passim.*

20. Text in Pantin, *Canterbury* iii, pp. 87–93.

21. J. K. McConica, *English Humanists and Reformation Politics Under Henry VIII and Edward VI* (Clarendon Press, 1965), p. 76 and *passim* pp. 76–105.

22. Ibid., p. 94. See also A. B. Cobban, *The Medieval English Universities: Oxford and Cambridge to 1500* (Scolar Press, 1988), pp. 243–57; W. A. Bruneau, 'Humanism, the University and the Monastic Life', *British Journal of Education Studies* 20 (1972), 282–301.

23. *Ep.R.J.* 24.21–27. On Lily, see *DNB* XI.1143–5 and McConica, op. cit., 49–51. See *Ep.R.J.* 47.46 for Lily in the novitiate.

24. William Hormann, *Vulgaria viri doctissimi Guil. Horman caesoriburgensis* (London, 1519).

25. *Ep.R.J.* 24.18 for the copy of the book, with 71.11 for the 'lubrications'.

26. See below, note 44.

27. Oxford, Bodleian Library, MS Bodley 692, fol. 6bf for the eulogy of Peter Lombard. See also N. D. Hurnard, *Studies in the Intellectual Life of England from the Middle of the Fifteenth Century till the Time of Colet* (Oxford D.Phil. Thesis, 1935), pp. 10–47, 311–18. I am grateful to James Clarke for this reference.

28. On Corpus Christi see J. K. McConica, 'The rise of the undergraduate college' in *HUO* iii, pp. 17–21; also J. G. Milne, *The Early History of Corpus Christi College, Oxford* (Blackwell, 1946), pp. 2–3. Text of Oxford's letter to Fox in *Epistolae Academicae 1508–96*, ed. W. T. Mitchell (*OHS* (n.s.) 26, 1990), pp. 29–30. The story of the Bishop of Exeter is preserved in Milne, op. cit., p. 3: 'shall we build houses . . . for a company of bussing monks?'

29. See C. H. Clough, 'The cult of antiquity: letters and letter collections', in *Cultural Aspects of the Italian Renaissance: Essays in Honour of P. O. Kristeller,* ed. C. H. Clough (Manchester University Press, 1976), pp. 33–67.

30. See A. Tilley, 'Greek studies in England in the early sixteenth century', in *EHR* 53 (1938), 221–39.

31. Cited in E. F. Jacob, 'Some early examples of euphemism in England', *BJRL* 17 (1933), 264–90.

32. Ten letters were written from Ombersley near Worcester and two probably from Oxford.

33. *Ep.R.J.* 25.5–6, cf. 20.22f, 46.27–8, 54.18–19, 76.118, 111.18f for the comparison with Aeneas.
34. See above, note 16, with G. May, op. cit., pp. 44–9 on Thomas de Marleberg. Pantin, *Chapters* ii.193 for the 1444 statute.
35. *Ep.R.J.* 63.20f, 167.14. On Litchfield as 'pharaoh' see 54.20f, 132.25; in contrast, E. A. B. Barnard, 'Clement Litchfield, Abbot of Evesham', *Transactions of the Worcestershire Archaeology Society* (n.s.) 5 (1928), 38–51 for a more sympathetic view.
36. *Ep.R.J.* 100.1f with editorial note, p. 150. 'Salting' was a ceremony of induction wherein a new member was forced to drink salt water.
37. Ibid., 11.10, cf. 147.17.
38. Ibid., 73.29, 90.25f, 168.4. For Glastynbury see above note 19, and for Henry of Eastry see C. E. Woodruff, 'Letters to the Prior of Christ Church Canterbury from University Students', *Archaeologia Cantiana* 39 (1927), 1–34. See also note 40 below.
39. Knowles, *RO* ii.1–7.
40. Tillotson, op. cit., pp. 54, 65, 124, 207 note 7.
41. *Ep.R.J.* 93.1–3 for the bracelet, 133.1–4 on presents, 59.33f for the scales; also C. H. Haskins, *Studies in Medieval Culture* (Clarendon Press, 1929), p. 8: 'A student's first song is a demand for money.'
42. On books in general, see A. Coates, 'Benedictine Monks and their Books in Oxford' in this volume. For Robert Joseph's desire for books, see *Ep.R.J.* 20.20, 24.18, 32.8–9, 36.9f, 73.10f. For More's *libellum*, perhaps his *Utopia*, 71.6.
43. *Ep.R.J.*, 131.2–9.
44. Ibid., 53–33, using 'Scotist' as a description for a badly written letter. Ibid., 81.100–5 for his letter to Tailer.
45. Ibid., 21.10f, an important defence.
46. Ibid., 155.4–5.
47. Ibid., 71–22f on Tracey. In general, *DNB* XIX.1067–8 with *Epistolae Academicae*, op. cit., pp. 319f and McConica, op. cit., pp. 97–8.
48. *Ep.R.J.* 104.15f.
49. Ibid., 165.5f.
50. Ibid., 165.16–17 for his 'confession' to Grexson. Requests for prayer abound, but see 12.20–3 for his most developed view of intercession and friendship and 157.12–13 for this applied to the Mass.
51. The clearest survey of his friends is in *The Letter Book*, op. cit., pp. xxii–xxvii. The two monks of Bury were Edmund

Rougham, accused in 1528 of preaching heresy, and John Salisbury, suspected of heresy in Oxford in 1540.

52. On Placet, mentioned in *Ep.R.J.* 33.32, see *CLP* Henry VIII 9.134–5. *Ep.R.J.* 51.21–2 on monastic obligations as burdens, cf. 96.1–2.

53. Ibid., 163.20f for the eulogy, and 75.16f for his advice to Feckenham on ordination. In general on priesthood, see P. Marshall, *The Catholic Priesthood and the English Reformation* (Oxford, 1994).

54. Lyttleton is mentioned six times by Robert Joseph, and in 119.12 as '*noster sale non frictus*'. On what follows see Thomas Woodhope OSB, 'Obits of Eminent Benedictines' in *CRS* 33 (1933), ed. Hugh Connolly OSB, 240–59, a printed version of Oxford, Bodleian Library, MS, Wood B6, folios 12–44. See also C. W. Clarke, 'Worcestershire and the Benedictine Succession', *Worcestershire Recusant* 14 (1969), 2–16 and D. Lunn, *The English Benedictines 1540–1688* (Burns and Oates, 1980), pp. 27–8.

55. May, op. cit., p. 118.

12: Benedictine Monks at the University of Oxford and the Dissolution of the Monasteries

1. In 1537 there were around 50 Benedictine monks at Oxford: Gloucester College housed 30 monks from 13 different monasteries, Durham College had 8 monks of Durham Cathedral Priory and perhaps several from other northern monasteries, and Canterbury College had 6 monks from Christchurch Cathedral Priory together with an unspecified number from Winchester and Reading. In the 40 years after 1500, at least 266 Benedictines attended the university. The next largest groups were the Franciscans (181) and the Dominicans (96), but it is by no means certain that all these friars were undertaking university studies during their residence at the Oxford friaries of their orders. The second largest group of monks at Oxford was the Cistercians (54), while the Austin canons had 56 in residence in the same period. For a more detailed breakdown, see *BRUO* 2, p. xxi; but it should be noted that Emden lists only 241 Black Monks, failing to identify another 25 Benedictines who are known to have been at the university during this period.

2. H. Rashdall, *The Universities of Europe in the Middle Ages*, vol. III (Oxford, 1936), p. 190. This work was originally published in two volumes in 1895.

3. David Knowles, *RO* iii, p. 459.

4. The most recent and thorough reassessment is that of Barrie Dobson, 'The Religious Orders 1370–1540', in *HUO* ii, pp. 539–42, 546–52; but perhaps the most convincing defence of the monk-scholars comes from the pages of *The Letter Book of Robert Joseph*, ed. Hugh Aveling and W. A. Pantin (Oxford, 1967); see also T. H. Aston, 'Oxford's Medieval Alumni', *P&P* 74 (1977), 18; and Joan Greatrex, 'Monk Students from Norwich Cathedral Priory at Oxford and Cambridge, c. 1300 to 1500', *EHR* 106 (1991), 576–9.

5. Joyce Youings, *The Dissolution of the Monasteries* (London, 1971), pp. 22–3; A. G. Dickens, *The English Reformation* (London, 1989), p. 77; Joan Simon, *Education and Society in Tudor England* (Cambridge, 1967), p. 11.

6. Knowles, *RO* iii, p. 73; Dobson, op. cit., p. 575; Greatrex, op. cit., p. 576.

7. Barrie Dobson, 'The Monks of Canterbury in the Later Middle Ages, 1220–1540', in *A History of Canterbury Cathedral*, ed. Patrick Collinson, Nigel Ramsay and Margaret Sparks (Oxford, 1995), p. 106.

8. Rashdall, op. cit., vol. III, p. 191; Knowles, *RO* iii, pp. 73, 100–107.

9. *BRUO* 2, p. 256.

10. E. H. Pearce, *The Monks of Westminster* (Cambridge, 1916), p. 177; Barton was probably *prior studentium* at Gloucester College at the time of this outing.

11. A. Jessop (ed.), 'Visitations of the Diocese of Norwich, AD 1492–1532', *Camden Society* (n.s.) 43 (1888), 264; Greatrex, op. cit., p. 578.

12. *BRUO* 2, p. 188; *CLP* Henry VIII, vol. 7, 519; 9, 315; 14 (i) 27.

13. On Robert Joseph, see preceding article.

14. For Corpus Christi College see Dobson, 'The Religious Orders', p. 555n; and *VCH (Oxon)* iii, p. 219.

15. For the Byconyll Exhibitions of Glastonbury see Nicholas Orme, 'Glastonbury Abbey and Education', in *The Archaeology and History of Glastonbury Abbey: Essays in Honour of the Ninetieth Birthday of C. A. Ralegh Radford*, ed. Lesley Abrams and James P. Carley (Woodbridge, 1991), pp. 298–9; and 'The Byconyll Exhibitions at Oxford 1502–1664', *Oxoniensia* 55 (1990), 115–18.

16. For the Glastonbury visitation see *Dean Cosyn and Wells Cathedral Miscellanea*, ed. Aelred Watkin, *Somerset Record Society* 56 (1941), 159–64. It should be noted that John Neot, who was criticised by his confrères as having learnt virtually nothing during his time at Oxford, had earlier in the 1530s been congratulated by Robert Joseph for writing a letter which was more polished than anything he had seen in Oxford. As a fellow student at Gloucester College at this time, Joseph was in a good position to judge Neot's academic prowess. Neot had graduated B.Th. in 1535 and was the author of a series of prayers for the feast of St Leonard. For Neot's career, see *BRUO* 2, p. 414.

17. *Ep.R.J.*, letters 111, 115, 142 and 155.

18. 'A Description or Briefe Declaration of all the Ancient Monuments, Rites, and Customs Belonginge or Beinge within the Monastical Church of Durham before the Suppression', *Surtees Society* (London, 1842), p. 81.

19. Joan Greatrex's forthcoming *Biographical Register of the English Cathedral Priories of the Province of Canterbury c. 1066–1540* (Clarendon Press, 1997) uses a number of sources which have never been fully investigated before, most notably the obedientiary rolls of the monastic cathedral priories.

20. The data used in the writing of the present essay will eventually be available in a multi-media electronic format over the WorldWideWeb as *A Monastic Database for England and Wales in the Sixteenth Century* at the following: ⟨http://www.hku.hk/history/cunichres.html⟩.

21. Most of these additional monk-scholars are listed in *BRUO* 1, but two of them are only known through the survival of a series of wardens' accounts of Canterbury College; see Pantin, *Canterbury* ii, pp. 231–61.

22. The ratio of graduates to monk-scholars for these six monasteries were Westminster, 12:28; Glastonbury, 6:15; Bury St Edmunds, 5:15; Gloucester, 10:13; Evesham, 10:13; and St Albans, 9:12.

23. For example, Nicholas Lindesey (1523), William Bothe (1507/8) and William Brent (1507/8) of Westminster, and Hamo Throwley (1505), Christopher Eastry (1507), Simon Islep (1507) and Robert Holingborne (1508) of Canterbury Cathedral Priory.

24. These probably include monks such as John Ambrose and Nicholas Bennett of Canterbury Cathedral Priory, Robert Clarke of Glastonbury, Anthony London and John Nevyll of

Rochester, Richard Pamphilion of Abingdon, Denis Daliance and Thomas Lovewell of Westminster.

25. Monk-scholars whose academic careers were probably cut short by breaches of the peace include Thomas Tokey (Hereford, 1528), James Dorset (Winchester, 1534), John Fuller (house unknown, 1535), John Foulden and John Hesset (Bury St Edmunds, 1538), and Philip Wyett (Tewkesbury, 1538). Richard Norwich and Thomas Morton of Norwich Cathedral Priory appear to have been rusticated after an episcopal visitation of 1532 found them to be *inflati spiritu alti cordis et indebitantur in universitate*, while Robert Joseph's return to Oxford appears to have been delayed by his abbot, who was infuriated over Joseph's outspokenness within the chapter house; see *Ep.R.J.*, no. 59.

26. Monks who were resident at Oxford at the dissolution but who did not continue with their studies include Thomas Freman of Abingdon, John Hadley and Robert Nedeham of Bury St Edmunds, John Derleum and Roger Grynway of Cerne, Richard Throckmorton and John Bromesgrove of Evesham, John Ambrose, Thomas Brente and John Pantaleon of Glastonbury, Richard Cirencester of Gloucester, John Alured, William Courtmyll and Richard Woodluck of Hyde, William Erith of Ramsey, Thomas Alban and William Leonard of St Albans, and John Foster of Westminster.

27. At Magdalene College in Cambridge, for example, only 5 students out of the 44 who were members of the college between 1542 and 1558 took degrees; see Peter Cunich, David Hoyle, Eamon Duffy and Ronald Hyam, *A History of Magdalene College Cambridge 1428–1988* (Cambridge, 1994), p. 49.

28. For the Cambridge graduates, see *A Biographical List of Benedictine Monks at Cambridge University from the earliest times until 1540*, ed. Peter Cunich (Cambridge, 1993).

29. These include John Ambrose, Chancellor of Canterbury Cathedral Priory in 1538, Robert Clarke, Prior of Glastonbury in 1539, Denis Daliance, Prior of Westminster (1536–40), John Halywell, Feretrar at Durham (1513–14), John Harris, Sub-Prior of Tavistock in 1538, John Morton, Master of the shrine of St Thomas at Canterbury in 1538, Richard Norwich, third Prior and Pittancer at Norwich in 1532, John Phagan, Archdeacon of Glastonbury in 1538–39, William Vertue, Warden of the Lady Chapel at Westminster (1534–36), Nicholas Welles, Precentor at Eynsham in 1536, and William Wylome, third Prior and Feretrar at Durham (1531–40).

30. The houses which sent their monk-scholars only to Buckingham College (the Cambridge *studium generale*) were
Colchester (1 monk), Crowland (3), Ely (9), St Benet of
Hulme (1), Selby (1), Spalding (1), Thorney (1) and Walden
(1), while one monk from St Benet of Hulme is found at
Gonville Hall. It is certain that there were several more monks
from Colchester, Crowland and Warden at Cambridge during
this period, but their names are not known, and it is also likely
that a number of monk-scholars from Selby were sent to study
at Durham College in Oxford during this time. The houses
which sent monks to both Oxford and Cambridge were Bury
St Edmunds (13 at Oxford and 2 at Cambridge), Durham (28
at Oxford and 2 at Cambridge), Norwich (2 at Oxford and 8 at
Gonville Hall in Cambridge), Peterborough (5 at Oxford and
1 at Cambridge), Ramsey (6 at Oxford and 4 at Cambridge),
Tavistock (2 at Oxford and 1 at Cambridge), and Westminster
(25 at Oxford and 3 at Cambridge).

31. For Canterbury College see Pantin, *Canterbury* iv; and Dobson,
'Monks of Canterbury', op. cit., pp. 99–115.

32. For Durham College see H. E. D. Blackiston, 'Some Durham
Account Rolls' in *Collectanea III*, OHS (o.s.) 32 (1896), pp.
1–76; and Barrie Dobson, *Durham Priory 1400–1450*
(Cambridge, 1973), pp. 343–59.

33. Pantin, *Canterbury* ii, pp. 231–61.

34. Dobson, 'Religious Orders 1370–1540', op. cit., p. 551. The
York St Mary's monks at Oxford were Robert Kyrkby and Adam
Thornton (1536).

35. Barbara F. Harvey, 'The Monks of Westminster and the University of Oxford', in *The Reign of Richard II: Essays in Honour of
May McKisack*, ed. F. R. H. du Boulay and Caroline M. Barron
(London, 1971), pp. 126–7. For the names of the Westminster
monk-scholars see *BRUO* 2 and E. H. Pearce, op. cit.

36. Glastonbury (15), Bury St Edmunds (13), Gloucester (13),
Evesham (12), St Albans (12), Worcester (10), St Augustine's
Canterbury (8), Tewkesbury (7), Ramsey (6), Hyde (6), Win-
chcombe (6), Abingdon (5), and Peterborough (5).

37. Athelney, Battle, Burton-on-Trent, Cerne, Coventry, Eynsham,
Great Malvern, Rochester, Sherborne, Totnes and Walden.

38. These were Pershore, which had 25 monks at the dissolution,
Bath (20) and Whitby (24). While there is no record of a monk
of Pershore attending the university during this period, it
seems unlikely that the Abbot (1526–39), John Stonywell
(Bishop of Pulati *in partibus*), who had been *prior studentium* at

Gloucester College *c.* 1502–3, would have neglected to send at least his required quota of students to Oxford. Stonywell was one of Robert Joseph's correspondents, as were John Compton and John Cadecraft of Pershore, and Joseph also mentions Richard Mathon and a Dom Gilbert in his letters. Joseph may have met these monks in his native Worcestershire, but it is also possible that he was a student with one or more of them in Oxford.

39. In 1537 at Gloucester College, there were four monks each from St Albans (out of a total of 54 monks in the convent in 1535), Bury St Edmunds (62 in 1535) and Hyde (21 in 1535); in 1522 there had been five monks from Westminster (43 in the convent in 1535), W. A. Pantin, 'Gloucester College', in *Oxoniensia* 11 and 12 (1946–7), 70; and during the 1520s at least seven monks of Evesham (Reginald Barnesley, John Feckenham, Richard Gloucester, Richard Grace, Robert Joseph, George London and John Newbolt) were studying at Oxford when there were less than 40 monks in the community. For monk-scholars in other houses see Greatrex, 'Monk Students', op. cit., p. 558.

40. Capon had graduated B.Th. (1512) and D.Th. (1515) at Cambridge, was elected Abbot of St Benet of Hulme in 1517, and later went on to be appointed Bishop of Bangor (1534) and Winchester (1539–57) under Cromwell's patronage. He was responsible for revising the Epistles to the Corinthians in 1542 for the English translation of the New Testament, and was reputed to be a talented preacher. For his other achievements see his *DNB* article.

41. Among these eleven there were five monks studying in Oxford at Gloucester College (including the *prior studentium,* George London), together with three graduates and three non-graduates residing at the abbey. The two other *priores studentium* from Evesham were Robert Joseph and John Newbolt.

42. There were approximately 1,500 Benedictine monks in England *c.* 1536. By the time the last Benedictine monastery was dissolved in 1540, there were nearly 200 monks who had studied at one or other of the universities and 122 of them held degrees. Twenty-five were doctors of theology.

43. Canterbury had 3 doctors and 7 bachelors in a convent of 58 monks, while Durham had 5 doctors and 9 bachelors in a convent of 66 monks; see Dobson, op. cit., p. 550.

44. J. K. McConica, *English Humanists and Reformation Politics under Henry VII and Edward VI* (Oxford, 1965), pp. 97–8.

45. *Ep.R.J.*, 21, 62, 135 and 137, pp. 28–9, 88, 205–6, 207–8. Joseph also advises a moderate approach to the rigours of study; see letter 112, pp. 166–8.

46. Cunich *et al.*, *Magdalene College*, op. cit., pp. 25–8.

47. The monks involved in the Garrett affair were John Langport of St Augustine's Canterbury, John Salisbury of Bury St Edmunds, and the Prior of Reading. The student who helped Thomas Garrett to escape from the chancellor's commissary was Anthony Delaber, a lay sojourner at Gloucester College. See also McConica, op. cit., p. 105. For Edmund Rougham, see *BRUO* 2, p. 493.

48. *BRUO* 2, pp. 115, 124. John Clifford and John Salisbury were the two men deprived of their livings.

49. For a discussion of this attitude see Greatrex, 'Monk Students', op. cit., pp. 578–9.

50. Joseph's Latin verse can be sampled in *Ep.R.J.* 13, 39, 40, 41, 101, 102, 106, 124, 139, 148, 175 and 176; while his interest in good letter-writing is expounded at length in letters 127 and 149.

51. Roger Bowers, 'Cathedral Music and Liturgy', in *A History of Canterbury Cathedral*, op. cit., p. 425; for Dygon, see *BRUO* 2, p. 182.

52. Letter Book, pp. 34–5, 238–9. Dobson, 'Monks of Canterbury', p. 108, asserts that oratorical ability was one of the most highly prized skills at Canterbury Cathedral Priory. Benedictine university preachers at Oxford included Robert Shouldham of Bury St Edmunds in 1514, Richard Thornden of Christ Church Canterbury in 1527, William Basing of Winchester in 1528, Humphrey Webley of Worcester in 1530, Thomas Kingswood of Gloucester in 1531, and John Feckenham of Evesham in 1540. William Sandwich of Christ Church Canterbury preached at Paul's Cross in 1537. Benedictines licensed to preach by their bishops include John Lawern and Roger Neckham of Worcester, George London of Evesham, and Thomas Seybroke of Gloucester. Edward Bocking of Christ Church Canterbury, executed for treason in 1534, was hailed as being *pro tempore suo predicator egregius* (*BRUO* 2, p. 54), while Edmund Rougham of Bury St Edmunds, who had himself been suspected of Lutheran opinions in 1528, was called upon to preach at Kirby's execution for heresy in 1545.

53. For example, Thomas Goldwell of Canterbury, John Melford of Bury St Edmunds, and John Warboys of Ramsey.

54. Cunich *et al.*, *Magdalene College*, op. cit., p. 21.

55. The number of degrees taken by Benedictine monks between 1500 and 1539 is as follows:

	B.Th.	D.Th.	B.Cn.L.	B.Mus.	Total
1500–04	1	1	–	–	2
1505–09	8	2	3	–	13
1510–14	23	2	4	1	30
1515–19	17	10	1	–	28
1520–24	26	1	4	–	31
1525–29	19	3	3	–	25
1530–34	17	2	3	–	22
1535–39	24	8	–	–	32
	135	29	18	1	183

56. The four monks taking bachelors' degrees in theology were George London (Evesham, 1540), Thomas Coventry (Evesham, 1541), John Matthew (Durham, 1542), and John Holywell (Ramsey, 1543); while the doctors were William Sandwich (Christ Church Canterbury, 1541), Richard Stevenage (St Albans, 1541), Richard Ramsey (Ramsey, by 1546), and John Feckenham (Evesham, 1550). In addition to these graduates in theology, John Hylpe of Glastonbury took his BA in 1539 and his MA in 1540. Monks who continued their studies but who did not take degrees were John Cross, Stephen Giles and Richard Marshall (Christ Church Canterbury), John Clifford (Gloucester), and Thomas Maynforth and Hugh Winter (Durham). For details see *BRUO 2*.

57. *BRUO 2*, p. 566; *PRO*, LR6/55/8–10.

58. For Marley see *BRUO 2*, p. 379. Other monk-graduates living in 1540 who might have been expected to consider taking up academic careers were John Dygon, Thomas Goldwell, William Gillingham, Edmund Rougham and Edmund Wetherden.

59. William Basing became Dean of Winchester, Hugh Whitehede was Dean of Durham, and Thomas Clarke, Dean of Chester, while John Salisbury was later appointed to Norwich after the resignation of William Castleton. Thomas Goldwell, Cathedral Prior of Canterbury, was not appointed to the deanship there, but rather to a prebend. William Edys, Abbot of Burton-on-Trent, was appointed dean of the new college there.

60. Thomas Bowser, John Cross, George Frebell, Stephen Giles, Peter Langley, Richard Marshall and Robert South of Christ Church Canterbury; John Matthew, Thomas Maynforth and Hugh Winter of Durham; while George Cliff of Durham continued as Warden of Durham College.

61. The monks of Glastonbury who received pensions of less than £6 per annum were John Hylpe (£5) and John Phagan (£4). Seven other Glastonbury monk-scholars who were pensioned in 1539 also received amounts ranging from £4 to £6 per annum, but the exact amount of their grants is not known because of the lacunae in the surviving records.

62. The number of monks receiving pensions within each of the ranges was: less than £6 p.a. (2), £6–7 p.a. (28), £8–9 p.a. (16), £10–19 p.a. (31), £20–49 p.a. (4), more than £50 p.a. (16); unknown (11); no pension (2).

63. It is difficult to arrive at an average figure because there were great differences between individual houses and geographical regions. In some instances, none of the monks from a dissolved house appear to have found preferment, but in others, up to a third of the convent were successful in securing post-dissolution employment.

64. For a recent discussion of Kitchen see Kenneth W. T. Carleton, 'English Catholic Bishops in the Early Elizabethan Era', *Recusant History* 23 (1996), 2–3.

65. The Cambridge bishops were Robert Blythe (alias Molton) of Thorney, Bishop of Down and Connor (1520–39) and Suffragan of Ely (1539–41); John Capon (alias Salcot) of Hyde, Bishop of Bangor (1534–9) and Salisbury (1539–57); John Chambers (alias Burgh) of Peterborough, Bishop of Peterborough (1540–56); Henry Holbeach (alias Rands) of Crowland and Worcester, Suffragan of Bristol (1538–42), Bishop of Rochester (1544–7) and Lincoln (1547–51); and William Rugg (alias Repps) of Hulme, Bishop of Norwich (1536–49); see Cunich *et al.*, *Magdalene College*, pp. 21–2. Four other Benedictine bishops do not appear to have had any university experience: William More of Walden, Bishop of Colchester (1536–41), John Bird of Hyde, Bishop of Penrith (1537–9) and Bangor (1539–41), John Bradley of Milton, Bishop of Shaftesbury (1539–1545), and John Holyman of Reading, Bishop of Bristol (1554–8).

66. John Hylpe of Glastonbury was chaplain to Sir Anthony Browne in 1547, while Gabriel Morton of Gloucester was a member of Sir Anthony Kingston's household.

67. Justin McCann and Columba Cary-Elwes (eds.), *Ampleforth and its Origins: Essays on a Living Tradition by Members of the Ampleforth Community* (London, 1952), pp. 56–7.

68. *BRUO* 2, pp. 124, 501, 402.

69. Ibid., pp. 484, 530, 606, 330. For Thomas Sparke see also S. L.

Greenslade, 'The Last Monks of Durham Cathedral Priory', *Durham University Journal* 41 (1948–9), 110. For Anthony Kitchin, see his entry in *DNB* and also Carleton, 'English Catholic Bishops', op. cit., pp. 2–3.

70. Edward Bocking and John Dering were executed at Tyburn on 21 April 1534 for their complicity with Elizabeth Barton, the Maid of Kent; William Jerome was burned as a Lutheran heretic at Smithfield on 30 July 1540; while the three abbots, Thomas Marshall of Colchester, Hugh Cook of Reading and Richard Whiting of Glastonbury, together with John Arthur (alias Thorne) and Roger Wilfred (alias James) of Glastonbury, were all executed towards the end of 1539. For Professor Knowles' opinions regarding these executions see *RO* iii, pp. 483–91.

71. The deprived prebendaries of Durham were Nicholas Marley (1560), John Tuting (1560), William Bennett (1567), William Todd (1567) and Stephen Marley (1572); see Greenslade, 'Last Monks of Durham', op. cit., *passim.* For Ramsey see *BRUO* 2, p. 474.

72. *BRUO* 2, pp. 564–5, 608–9, 145.

73. The 12 monks who had been scholars at Oxford were the abbot John Feckenham (Evesham), the prior William Este (St Albans), the sub-prior John Neot (Glastonbury), Andrew Alton (Hyde), Thomas Athelstan (Glastonbury), Stephen Bayley (St Albans), Thomas Coventry (Evesham), John Foster (Westminster), George Frebel or Frewell (Canterbury Cathedral Priory), John Goodluck (Westminster), John Langdon (Canterbury Cathedral Priory), Thomas Lovewell (Westminster) and John Phagan (Glastonbury). For a list of the original convent of November 1556, see Westminster Abbey Muniments 9327. Thomas Twysden (alias Bede) of Battle Abbey joined the community at a later date. I am grateful to Sybil Jack for this reference.

74. Feckenham held canonries at both Canterbury and St Paul's; Este was a canon of St George's Windsor, and Bayley held three livings in Hertfordshire, Essex and Norfolk.

75. David Lunn, *The English Benedictines, 1540–1688: From Reformation to Revolution* (London, 1980), pp. 3–4.

76. British Library, Harleian MS 3881, fol. 38v. The original text reads: 'with our labour and husbandrye, we may live there a fewe of us in our religious habits till the charitie of good people may suffice a greater number; and the country there, being so affected to our religion, we beleve we should fynde

moche helpe amongst them, towards the reparations and furniture of the same; whereby we wolde haply prevent the ruine
of muche, and repayre no little part of the whole to Gods
honor and for the better prosperitie of the King and Quenes
majesties.'

77. *BRUO* 2, pp. 339–40.
78. For John Feckenham's biography see Knowles, *RO* iii, pp.
    428–37; McCann and Cary-Elwes, op. cit., pp. 64–80; *DNB* xviii,
    p. 282.
79. For Fisher's humanist programme at Cambridge, see both
    Malcolm Underwood, 'John Fisher and the promotion of
    learning', and Christopher N. L. Brooke, 'The University
    Chancellor', in *Humanism, Reform and the Reformation: The
    Career of Bishop John Fisher,* ed. Brendan Bradshaw and Eamon
    Duffy (Cambridge, 1989), pp. 25–46 and 47–66.

13: BENEDICTINES OF THE SEVENTEENTH CENTURY WHO STUDIED AT OXFORD

1. Bede Camm, *Nine Martyr Monks* (London, 1931), p. ix.
2. Anthony Wood, *Athenae Oxoniensis* (2nd edn; Oxford, 1721),
   vol. ii, col. 905.
3. *CRS* 33 (1933), x–xi.
4. *XVI Revelations of Divine Love,* published by R. F. S. Cressy
   (1670). Reprinted London, 1843, with preface by G. H. Parker.
5. D. Rogers, 'The English Recusants: Some Medieval Literary
   Links', *EBC History Symposium* (1990).
6. Cf. P. Bruckman, Hugh Cressy's 'Apologia', *EBC History Symposium* (1990).
7. Wood, op. cit., vol. ii, col. 905.
8. *The Life of Edward, Earl of Clarendon Written by Himself* (Oxford,
   1759), vol. i, p. 91.
9. Quoted in *DNB* 13, p. 75.
10. *DNB* 61, p. 181.

14: OXFORD AND THE BENEDICTINES: FROM THE RESTORATION UNTIL CATHOLIC EMANCIPATION

1. Mrs Bryan Stapleton, *A History of the Post-Reformation Catholic
   Missions in Oxfordshire* (London, 1965), p. 330.

2. Elizabeth Cary, trans., *The reply of the most illustrious cardinall of Perron to the answere of the most excellent king of Great Britaine: The first tome* (Douay, 1630), sig. C2.
3. D. Lunn, 'Elizabeth Cary, Lady Falkland (1586/7–1639)', *Royal Stuart Papers*, vol. XI (London, 1977), p. 9.
4. J. Gillow, *A Literary and Biographical History or Bibliographical Dictionary of the English Catholics* (London, n.d.), vol. iv, p. 399, for list of Mallet's works.
5. A. Wood, *Athenae Oxonienses* (London, 1721), vol. ii, col. 905.
6. Ibid., pp. 993–4. A. Clark, *The Life and Times of Anthony Wood, antiquary . . . described by Himself* OHS (o.s.) 21 (1892), vol. ii, pp. 269, 270, 275.
7. J. R. Bloxam, *A Register of the Presidents, Fellows, Demies . . . of Saint Mary Magdalen College* (Oxford, 1863), p. 214.
8. Ibid., p. 216.
9. Wood, op. cit., col. 530.
10. A. C. F. Beales, *Education under Penalty: English Catholic Education from the Reformation to the Fall of James II* (London, 1963), p. 244.
11. HUO v, p. 371.
12. T. Hearne, *The Remains of Thomas Hearne . . . newly revised by John Buchanan-Brown* (London, 1966), p. 212.
13. Sutherland and Mitchell, op. cit., pp. 779, 780.
14. Gillow, op. cit., vol. iv, p. 78, and G. Scott, *Gothic Rage Undone, English Monks in the Age of Englishtenment* (Bath, 1992), pp. 148–50, for details of Knowles.
15. J. M. Osborn, *Dr Johnson and the Contrary Converts* (Yale University Press, 1594), pp. 6, 7. Douai Abbey Archives, VII.A. 1, Parker MSS.

15: THE FOUNDATION OF SAINT BENET'S HALL

1. Adapted by the Editors from a paper written in early 1996.
2. C. R. Chichester, 'Schools' (1882) in A. V. McClelland, *English Catholics and Higher Education* (Oxford, 1973), p. 31.
3. McClelland, op. cit., p. 379.
4. Ampleforth Abbey Archives JX24. The Grissell Papers were recovered too late to be used for this account.
5. J. A. Wilson, *The Life of Bishop Hedley* (London, 1930), p. 226.
6. Hedley's *Votum* in reply to Cardinal Simeoni, 1883 (Wilson, op. cit., p. 231).
7. Ibid. pp. 232–5.

8. J. C. Hedley OSB, 'Oxford and Cambridge' *Ampleforth Journal* 2 (1896), 1–13.
9. P. J. McCann OSB, 'St Benet's Hall, Oxford', *Ampleforth Journal* 31 (1926), 89–105.
10. Ampleforth Abbey Archives, JX23/E.
11. University Statutes, quoted in McCann, op. cit., p. 91.
12. Ampleforth Abbey Archives, EX46.
13. Ibid.
14. Ibid.
15. S. A. Parker OSB, *Memorandum*, 25 May 1917: Ampleforth Abbey Archives JX23/C.
16. Listed to 1925 in *Ampleforth Journal* 31 (1926), 102–4.
17. *Council Minute Book*, 16/1/1918: Ampleforth Abbey Archives BX40/1.
18. *Council Minute Book*, 9/10/1918.
19. Oxford University Calendar, 1918.
20. P. J. McCann, op. cit., p. 101.
21. C. Oman, *An Oxford Childhood* (London, 1976), passim.
22. Ampleforth Abbey Archives, EX41.

16: ABBOT JUSTIN MCCANN

1. The atmosphere of the community is elegantly pictured by Fr Paul Nevill in his chapter in *Ampleforth and its Origins,* ed. McCann and Cary-Elwes (London, 1952), pp. 237–8.
2. J. McCann, *Self-discipline* (London, Catholic Truth Society, nd), p. 8. and *passim.*
3. The correspondence between the abbots and McCann is preserved in Ampleforth Abbey Archives, EX42.
4. Ampleforth Abbey Archives, JX70/25.
5. Ampleforth Abbey Archives, JX70/30.
6. *Self-discipline,* op. cit, p. 13.
7. Cited in B. Green, 'Justin McCann OSB', *AJ* 95.1 (Spring, 1990), pp. 19–23.
8. See above note 4.
9. Ampleforth Abbey Archives, JX68/3.
10. Ampleforth Abbey Archives, JX68/44a.
11. See above note 3.

Index

326 *Index*